11/17

RELIGION VS. SCIENCE

RELIGION VS. SCIENCE

What Religious People Really Think

ELAINE HOWARD ECKLUND

AND

CHRISTOPHER P. SCHEITLE

UNIVERSITY PRESS

OXFORD
UNIVERSITY PRESS

Oxford University Press is a department of the University of Oxford. It furthers the University's objective of excellence in research, scholarship, and education by publishing worldwide. Oxford is a registered trade mark of Oxford University Press in the UK and certain other countries.

Published in the United States of America by Oxford University Press
198 Madison Avenue, New York, NY 10016, United States of America.

CIP data is on file at the Library of Congress
ISBN 978-0-19-065062-9

1 3 5 7 9 8 6 4 2
Printed by Sheridan Books, Inc., United States of America

For Karl and Anika

For Lisa and Avery

In honor of Clara Roberts (1993–2017)

CONTENTS

ACKNOWLEDGMENTS

We are thankful to the undergraduates, graduate students, and postdoctoral fellows who tirelessly collected data as part of the Religious Understandings of Science study. Special thanks to Paul Abraham, Peter Abraham, Gaby Barrios, Timothy Chang, Daniel Cortez, Kristian Edosomwan, Parker Eudy, Kristin Foringer, Colleen Fugate, Cara Fullerton, Kristen Gagalis, Adriana Garcia, Henry Hancock, Jacob Hernandez, Sally Huang, David Johnson, Simranjit Khalsa, Samuel Kye, Kelsey Pedersen, Clara Roberts, Adi Sirkes, Alexa Solazzo, Cleve Tinsley IV, Leah Topper, Amol Utrankar, Brandon Vaidyanathan, and Melanie Zook. Many thanks to undergraduate and graduate students who helped with data analysis. Special thanks to Kaitlin Barnes, Lauren Castiglioni, Esther Chan, Di Di, Juan Hernandez, Elizabeth Korver-Glenn, Dylan Mendelson, Anna Ng, Erin O'Brien, Emily Remirez, Emily Robinson, Katherine Sorrell, Hannah Thalenberg, Amber Tong, Abraham Younes, and Catherine Yuh. We are thankful for Virginia White's assistance with data analysis and project management, for Shelby Allen's and Hayley Hemstreet's assistance with the preparation of the manuscript, and for Heather Wax's assistance with editing, especially during the final stretch. This book was reviewed as part of Rice University's Religion and Public Life Program Books in Public Scholarship workshop. We are grateful to John Evans, Don Frohlich, Greg Han, Katharine Hayhoe, Elizabeth Long, Ronald Numbers, Jared Peifer, Katherine Sorrell, and Brandon Vaidyanathan for taking the time to carefully review this work. We would like to thank our editor, Cynthia Read, for the opportunity to publish this work.

Finally, our gratitude to the John Templeton Foundation for funding this research, Grant ID 38817, under the leadership of Drew Rick-Miller, as well as a collaborative partnership with the American Association for the Advancement of Science Dialogue on Science, Ethics, and Religion Program (AAAS-DoSER), which used the survey data for outreach in the scientific community. Special thanks to Jennifer Wiseman, Se Kim, and Christine A. Scheller. Although the book is a separate effort, we learned a great deal from the AAAS-DoSER program. Smaller grants were received from the Society for the Scientific Study of Religion, the Shell Center for Sustainability at Rice University, and the Rice Alumni Fund. Our deepest personal thanks to our spouses (Karl and Lisa) and to our children (Anika and Avery). They make efforts toward more informed dialogue about important public issues seem worth fighting for.

RELIGION VS. SCIENCE

CHAPTER 1

Beyond Stereotypes and Myths

Faith is the great cop-out, the great excuse to evade the need to think and evaluate evidence. Faith is belief in spite of, even perhaps because of, the lack of evidence.
    —Richard Dawkins, evolutionary biologist and outspoken atheist

Believing in a relatively "young earth" (i.e., only a few thousands of years old, which we accept) is a consequence of accepting the authority of the Word of God as an infallible revelation from our omniscient Creator.
    —Ken Ham, founder of the Creation Museum and outspoken evangelical *

Richard Dawkins is not typical. We wish religious people knew this. Ken Ham is not typical. We wish scientists knew this. You can find books that want to attack and denigrate how religious people view science. You can find books that want to defend or advance a particular religious perspective on science. This book is neither of these. If you are looking for a book that presents religious people as scientifically ignorant, then you will be disappointed. And you will be disappointed too if you are looking for some unmitigated defense of religious people's views on science. This is a book for scientists, for religious people, and for those who inhabit both worlds. It provides insights for each of these groups, while also providing critiques of each group. This book is about the real story of the relationship between science and religion in the lives of real people—based on data that take us beyond the stereotypes we so regularly hear from the media and pundits.

What do religious people think about science? Elaine can remember exactly when the question first popped into her head many years ago. She was in a rural church in the farm country of upstate New York, at a Bible study where she was conducting interviews for research. There, she met a woman who asked what Elaine did for work. When she answered that she was a doctoral student at Cornell University, the woman responded, "Yuck. I wouldn't want my children to attend Cornell." Elaine was surprised. Most people think of Cornell—an Ivy

League school—as a top university. (Perhaps the woman wanted her children to attend Harvard instead!) When Elaine asked the woman to explain her feelings, she said that she wouldn't want her children to attend Cornell because they might be exposed to scientists who would take them away from their faith.

Chris was also in graduate school when he began to wonder about the relationship between religion and science. On a plane to a sociology conference, he started talking to a young woman sitting next to him, an undergraduate college student who was majoring in biology. She seemed quite bright and enthusiastic about her studies, so Chris asked if she was thinking about going on to graduate school. She hesitated and explained that she was interested in this path but also worried, as she was very religious and did not believe in evolution. She was concerned that going to graduate school would be like feeding herself to the sharks.

These encounters elicited questions for both of us. Were these women typical of how religious Americans think about science and scientists? Are all scientists sharks out to eat religious people for lunch? How do religious individuals across the country approach different scientific issues, and see these issues influencing their faith beliefs, identities, and practices?

We started our journey with some background work. We found that Americans are deeply interested in science. Science museums rank as the most popular museums in the nation, and national survey data show that 85% of US adults are interested in new scientific discoveries. We also found that Americans are deeply interested in religion. The same national survey data show that 57% of US adults are moderately or very religious. About 25% of Americans attend a religious service in any given week and more than 90% believe in God.[1]

How do these two interests interrelate? We hear that religious people dismiss or don't understand science. We hear that religious believers are trying to stop the teaching of evolution or block human embryonic stem-cell research. But does this represent US people of faith as a whole?

In this book, we debunk the myths surrounding what religious Americans think about science, showing that they are not nearly the scientifically ignorant, uninterested, or hostile population that they are often made out to be. At the same time, we will not gloss over the tensions between religious Americans and science.

Our message to social scientists is this: In *Religion vs. Science* we argue that the way religious Americans approach science is shaped by two fundamental questions. First, what does science mean for the existence and activity of God? Second, what does science mean for the sacredness of humanity? How these questions—questions with profound moral implications—play out as individual believers think about science both challenge stereotypes and highlight the real tensions between religion and science. We show that the answers to these questions are birthed from key underlying cognitive schemas—what social scientists call the "knowledge structures that represent objects or events and provide default assumptions about their characteristics, relationships, and entailment under conditions of incomplete information"[2]—for religious people. Schemas structure cultural resources, such as beliefs, concepts, and experiences, providing coherence or a shorthand way to think about complex topics, a way for people to put together disparate pieces of information into something that makes sense, disparate information like all of the new scientific discoveries that constantly bombard us.

For example, contrary to the stereotype that religious Americans are hostile to science, we find that they are interested in and appreciate science. Yet people of faith, particularly the Christians, Muslims, and Jews we study here, view science through the lens of concern about keeping a place for an active God in the world. Hence, many religious Americans like Randall—who has a sincere Christian faith as well as a deep love of science, and whom you will meet in chapter 2—have no problem believing science should treat supernatural miracles as very real, because they believe in a God who is completely capable of acting outside of natural laws. Similarly, contrary to what some nonreligious individuals assume, not all religious Americans are young-earth creationists. In fact, religious Americans appear quite flexible in what they are willing to believe regarding creation and evolution, *but* their underlying schemas motivate them to keep some role for God and respect what they see as the sacredness of humans. This means that a theistic evolution is completely palatable to many people of faith.

Our message to scientists is this: Myths are a problem for the scientific enterprise. The majority of Americans are religious.[3] This means religious people pay taxes and vote.[4] If people of faith do not support science research and education, they may not support the federal science funding that our country so desperately needs in order to be a world leader in basic scientific research and applied technologies. It is important for us to move beyond stereotypes to know exactly *why* some religious Americans reject evolution if we hope to help them accept what science teaches about the origin and development of life on earth. And it is important for our national advancement that we understand whether religious Americans support human embryonic stem-cell research, genetic engineering, and reproductive technologies—and, if we find they do not, why.

Our message to people of faith is this: Myths are a problem for faith communities. Science is incredibly influential in our world, and if religious leaders want to see their communities not just survive but thrive, they must learn how to incorporate science and scientists into their faith communities. A recent poll shows that many Christian teens and young adults, for example, perceive tension between science and their faith, leaving them feeling disconnected from their churches, and "many science-minded young Christians are struggling to find ways of staying faithful to their beliefs and to their professional calling in science-related industries."[5] As more and more young people drift away from organized religion, religious leaders will want to understand exactly how and why their congregants are struggling with the compatibility of science and faith, and whether this struggle is driving them away from their faith communities.

And for everyone, these core questions need answers: How do religious individuals view the interface between religion and science? What is their personal relationship to the scientific community? How do a broad variety of evangelicals view science and scientific issues? How do they compare with mainline Protestants, Catholics, Jews, or Muslims?[6] More broadly, how do religious individuals with a background in science compare with other religious individuals in terms of their attitudes toward scientific issues? Are there certain elements of religious belief or practice—such as how a person views God's role in the world—that transcend denominational and educational boundaries and help us better understand why some people of faith view science in a certain way? What are the particular scientific issues and aspects of science that people from specific traditions or with specific beliefs find most troubling? Based on what we learn, are there possibilities for on-the-ground collaboration between faith communities and scientific communities? What is the most productive way forward for scholars, policymakers, scientists, and believers who would like to see more light than heat?

HOW WE CAME TO OUR CONCLUSIONS

To understand how religious communities today view science and scientific issues, we build on the robust work of philosophers, theologians, and historians, but we focus centrally on present-day lived experiences collected through empirical social scientific methods. Between 2010 and 2015, we conducted the largest study ever of how religious people view science. Alongside a large research team, we first spent hundreds of hours observing congregants of different faith traditions. We went inside largely white evangelical churches, historically black churches, and largely immigrant mosques and historic synagogues in both Houston and Chicago. We also conducted nearly 320 in-depth face-to-face interviews with congregants from 23 organizations, to dive deeper into how congregations discuss science and to discover how much the leaders and members of these congregations use their faith in their approach to science. Then, to get a bird's-eye view, we conducted a nationally representative scientific survey of more than 10,000 Americans—the most comprehensive survey to date of how a sample of all Americans (religious and not) view science. We started with a focus on evangelical Christians—the group to which so much attention has been paid with respect to the relationship between science and religion. They are indeed part of the center story of this book. But we also compare the views of evangelicals to groups other scholars have not paid much attention to when it comes to the science and faith interface. We listen to the stories of other Christian groups (both mainline Protestants and Catholics, looking, in particular, into black and Latino congregations). We look at the views of Jews from different traditions (both Orthodox and Reform) (who have historically shown little tension with science) and Muslims, a group of religious Americans who have recently been in the spotlight with regard to science and faith issues.

For those who are interested in more detailed information on our study methods, such as how we think about the relationship between our survey and interview data or why we chose to focus on these particular religious groups and particular scientific issues, you will find an in-depth methodological appendix at the back of the book. The conclusions we come to are based on a wealth of data and information collected over five years that address the most prevalent myths out there about what religious people think about science. During the course of our journey to find out, we met several people who we use as focal characters, those who represent the perspectives of much larger groups and trends.

BOOK AT A GLANCE

Many people think that religious Americans are not interested in science—or, worse, hostile to science. We set the book up according to prevalent myths. In chapter 2, "Religious People Do Not Like Science,"[7] we show that it is a mistake to stereotype religious Americans in this way. Jews, Muslims, and most Christians, for example, show similar or higher levels of interest in science than do nonreligious Americans. Our national survey shows that evangelicals have slightly lower interest levels in science, but this does not mean that they are hostile to science. For instance, when we asked survey respondents if they thought that, "overall, modern science does more harm than good," evangelicals were just as likely to disagree with this statement as anyone else.

In this chapter, you will meet Sue:

> Sue attends a historically black congregation. Until recently, she did not think that science and religion could ever relate, but a YouTube video has inspired her to try integrating science and her faith, which she finds both challenging and exciting.

Through their individual stories and personal experiences, we begin our examination of how religious individuals approach science and scientific issues. For many religious individuals the way they view science and the natural world is influenced by their desire to maintain an active role for God. We asked our survey respondents whether "scientists should be open to considering miracles in their theories and explanations," and 60% of evangelicals agreed with this statement. Nearly half of the evangelicals we interviewed affirmed their belief in the miracles of the Bible. And 15% of Catholics and about 20% of Muslims think they have witnessed a miraculous, physical healing. One homemaker[8] told us, "Once you posit an omniscient God, then I don't have any trouble with miracles."

In chapter 3, "Religious People Do Not Like Scientists," we explore what people of faith think about the people who do science. Do religious believers who think highly of science also think highly of scientists as a group of people? Or do some religious believers who support science have disdain for or distrust of the people involved in the scientific enterprise, in the same way that Americans might speak highly of "democracy" while simultaneously expressing disdain for "politicians" or "voters"? It was clear from our interviews that some religious people think *scientists* are likely to be opposed or hostile to faith. So while it's not true that religious people don't like science, it is true that some of them don't like *scientists*.

Here we meet Janelle, a young university student, who, although she attends a church with many highly educated people, some of whom are even scientists, does not actually know any scientists personally and consequently thinks most scientists are probably atheists and against religious people.

In chapter 4, "Religious People Are Not Scientists," we explore the extent to which religious people enter the scientific profession. There has been research on the religious beliefs of scientists in universities, including Elaine's earlier book, *Science vs. Religion: What Scientists Really Think*, which focused on how elite scientists view religion. This research *does* generally show that university scientists, particularly those who work at the top US universities, are less religious than the general American population. But the idea that there are no religious scientists is certainly a myth. In our survey, we are able to identify a broader swath of individuals working in science outside of universities, and we find that almost three-quarters of these scientists claim a religious identity.

Blythe is one of these scientists. She does studies of the nervous system to figure out defects. For Blythe it was her faith as a Christian that actually laid the groundwork for her pursuit of science.

In our survey data, we find that 48% of all evangelicals say they view religion and science as being in collaboration with each other, and this percentage rises to 73% among evangelical scientists.

In chapter 5, "Religious People Are Young-Earth Creationists," we tackle the topic of evolution. "We have been talking to so many religious people, and many of them believe the earth is 5,000 years old," Bill Maher tells us in his 2009 documentary *Religulous*, which presents his "pilgrimage across the globe" to explore the lives and thoughts of religious people. To emphasize his point, he pays a visit to the Creation Museum in Kentucky, led by Ken Ham. The museum presents a young-earth, biblically literal understanding of life's origins, and it attracts hundreds of thousands of visitors each year.

We find that young-earth creationism *is* the most popular narrative for the origin and development of life among evangelicals—but we find that only about 28% of evangelicals say that only the young-earth creationism narrative is "definitely true." The other 72% of evangelicals are not strong and exclusive adherents to this view of origins. When we turn to our interview data on questions of creation and evolution, we find that Jews and Muslims also employ a number of different narratives in their attempt to maintain a role for God and a special place for humans in creation. Some accept the concept of evolution, but believe God set it in motion. Others see evolution as God's plan. Some draw a distinction between macroevolution and microevolution, while others accept a form of creationism called "intelligent design," whose proponents accept some religiously controversial issues, such as an old earth, while maintaining that God is detectable in observations not yet explained by science.[9]

Here we meet Kurt, a physician, who has never seen a conflict between his faith as a Christian and evolution. For him, evolution is a sign that God always meant life to be interconnected.

And we show too that most religious Americans are surprisingly flexible in their views of creation and evolution. Often, details such as the age of the earth are not that important to them. What is most important are the theological implications—that the broad narrative of life's origin and development leaves room for an active God and respects the sacredness of humanity.

In chapter 6, "Religious People Are Climate-Change Deniers," we puncture myths about how religious individuals view environmentalism. There is a strong perception that religion is a predictor of environmental attitudes and denial of the threat posed by climate change. It has been reported in recent years that religiously motivated activists, who are engaged in fighting the teaching of evolution in their local school districts, are increasingly making climate-change education a target as well. Yet we show that climate change is not an issue strongly tied to views on evolution or religion.

Our survey data show that even among those who hold the view that "God created the universe, the Earth, and all of life within the past 10,000 years," more than 72% acknowledge that the climate is changing and human activity has made at least some contribution to that change. Political conservatism and a lack of trust in the scientific community are much stronger direct predictors of climate-change denial than is religious identity.

In this chapter, we meet Christians, Jews, and Muslims who advocate environmental stewardship based on the tenets and values of their faith traditions. For example:

> Father Joel[10] believes that Scripture calls us to actively care for the planet. He accepts that climate change is real and caused by humans. Faith and Scripture have bred in him a strong sense of environmental concern, which he feels is typical of his congregation.

We do find, however, that some religious Americans, particularly evangelicals, are uncomfortable when they feel environmental concerns elevate the earth above God or deny God's ability to intervene in the world. Worshipping the earth more than God or God's highest creation, humans—whom they see as having dominion over the earth—dampens enthusiasm for some. As a 31-year-old Southern Baptist[11] succinctly explains, "We should be stewards of this earth, but I will also say that our love for fellow humans should be greater than our love for the earth, because God cares more about them than this place where we live."

Chapter 7, "Religious People Are Against Scientific Technology," takes on the myths of how people of faith view technological advances. We focused on three in particular: reproductive genetic technologies (RGTs), in vitro fertilization (IVF), and human embryonic stem-cell (hESC) research. These technologies touch on the two questions we have found to be central to shaping how religious individuals view scientific issues: the role of God and the sacredness of humans.

RGTs comprise a range of medical procedures.[12] We divide them into two broad categories by purpose: those that are aimed at detecting genetic diseases or birth defects in utero, and those that genetically profile an embryo before it is implanted, which allow some detection of genetic diseases and may eventually allow parents to select embryos based on nonmedical traits, such as eye color, sex, or IQ. Americans are much more likely to see selection-focused RGTs as morally wrong than they are to see disease-focused RGTs as morally unacceptable. Yet disease-focused RGTs raise difficult ethical issues and conflicting values for many religious individuals. While these technologies have a lot of potential benefits, they also have implications for another controversial issue—abortion—against which many religious traditions have taken a strict position.[13] Though the majority of evangelicals do not oppose disease-focused RGTs, they are significantly more likely than the overall population to see a moral problem with them.

Research involving human embryonic stem cells also leads to ethical and moral issues for many religious believers. Deriving human embryonic stem cells destroys a fertilized embryo,[14] which many religious groups object to because they view a human embryo as having the same moral status as a human being. Yet cell types from embryonic stem cells may eventually be used to treat a myriad of health problems, including cancer, birth defects, and heart disease. Thus, hESC research forces religious individuals to weigh the sanctity of human life against their responsibility to care for others and alleviate suffering. Here we meet religious believers like Lana:

> For Lana, Islam is a way of life. She loves science but has strong reservations about the use of genetic reproductive technologies. The issue is personal to her since her parents feared—before she was born—that she might have a genetic disease.

In chapter 8, "Beyond Myths, Toward Realities," we discuss the practical lessons learned from our analyses in an effort to help scientists and religious individuals have the kind of radical dialogue that will move beyond the myths and stereotypes to where there is potential, more productive collaborations. Can scientists use these findings to better connect with religious communities? We believe they can. We suggest that religious leaders invite scientists into their congregations to give talks, teach classes, and lead discussions. We suggest that scientists begin by explaining how basic science is applicable to the concerns of religious people, and how scientific and technological knowledge and advances can help us better care for creation and one another. We believe that scientists can begin to build trust with faith communities by first focusing on scientific topics where little tension exists.

If scientists can better understand and speak to the real, specific concerns of religious individuals—and perhaps even show how science can be used to promote religious ideals—they will have a better shot at both building bridges and advancing science in the process.

NOTES

*   Dawkins quote taken from Alister E. McGrath's *Dawkins God: From the Selfish Gene to the God Delusion* (Chichester: Wiley-Blackwell, 2015, p. 60). Ham quote taken from "A Young Earth—It's Not the Issue!" found at https://answersingenesis.org/why-does-creation-matter/a-young-earth-its-not-the-issue/.

1. Data are from the 2012 General Social Survey. See also Hadaway, C. Kirk, and Penny Long Marler. 2005. "How Many Americans Attend Worship Each Week? An Alternative Approach to Measurement." *Journal for the Scientific Study of Religion* 44:307–322.

2. Sewell also discusses schemas in this way (Sewell, William H. Jr. 1992. "A Theory of Structure: Duality, Agency, and Transformation." *American Journal of Sociology* 98(1):1–29). See http://www.pewresearch.org/fact-tank/2016/07/26/key-find-ings-on-how-americans-view-new-technologies-that-could-enhance-human-abilities/, accessed August 31, 2016. See DiMaggio, Paul. 1997. "Culture and Cognition." *Annual Review of Sociology* 23:263–287.

3. See Finke, Roger, and Rodney Stark. 1998. "Religious Choice and Competition." *American Sociological Review* 63(5):761–766; see also Gallup, George Jr., and D. Michael Lindsay. 1999. *Surveying the Religious Landscape: Trends in U.S. Beliefs.* Harrisburg, PA: Morehouse; Chaves, Mark. 2011. *American Religion: Contemporary Trends.* Princeton, NJ: Princeton University Press.

4. And sociologists have shown that what Americans think about religion and science maps onto what they think about other important social issues. See work by sociologists Shiri Noy and Timothy L. O'Brien. 2016. "Science, Religion, and Public Opinion in the United States." *Socius*, doi: 10.1177/2378023116651876.

5. Barna Group. 2011. "Six Reasons Young Christians Leave Church." Retrieved March 24, 2015, https://www.barna.org/barna-update/teens-nextgen/528-six-reasons-young-christians-leave-church#.UyFvXI0x-2y.

6. Note that when we are reporting survey results we often refer to members of "non-Western traditions." This is not ideal; we do this because there are too few members of these groups (i.e., Hindus and Muslims) to represent them individually in more sophisticated statistical analysis. We recognize there are vast differences among Muslims, Hindus, and Sikhs, for example, so we categorize them according to the broad-est category that accurately describes the commonality among these traditions, namely that they originate primarily outside the West.

7. See Granger, Maury D., and Gregory N. Price. 2007. "The Tree of Science and Original Sin: Do Christian Religious Beliefs Constrain the Supply of Scientists?" *Journal of Socio-Economics* 36:144–160.

8. Mid-High SES Evangelical Church Chicago Int7, conducted June 22, 2012.

9. See Dembski, William A., and Jonathan Witt. 2010. *Intelligent Design Uncensored: An Easy-to-Understand Guide to the Controversy.* Downers Grove, IL: InterVarsity; Evans, John H., and Michael S. Evans. 2008. "Religion and Science: Beyond the Epistemological Conflict Narrative." *Annual Review of Sociology* 34:87–105.

10. High SES Mainline Church Houston Intl, conducted July 14, 2011.

11. Mid-High/High SES Evangelical Church Houston Int9, conducted July 29, 2011.

12. See Robertson, John A. 1994. *Children of Choice: Freedom and the New Reproductive Technologies.* Princeton, NJ: Princeton University Press. See also Stock, Gregory, and John H. Campbell. 2000. *Engineering the Human Germline.* New York: Oxford University Press.

13. See Evans, John H. 2002. *Playing God? Human Genetic Engineering and the Rationalization of Public Bioethical Debate.* Chicago: University of Chicago Press. See also Emerson, Michael O., and David Hartman. 2006. "The Rise of Religious Fundamentalism." *Annual Review of Sociology* 32:127–144. See Hoffmann, John P., and Sherrie Mills Johnson. 2005. "Attitudes Toward Abortion among Religious Traditions in the United States: Change or Continuity?" *Sociology of Religion* 66(2):161–182; Petersen, Larry R. 2001. "Religion, Plausibility Structures, and Education's Effect on Attitudes Toward Elective Abortion." *Journal for the Scientific Study of Religion* 40(2):187–203; Sullins, D. Paul. 1993. "Switching Close to Home: Volatility or Coherence in Protestant Affiliation Patterns?" *Social Forces* 72(2):399–419; Munson, Ziad W. 2009. *The Making of Pro-life Activists: How Social Movement Mobilization Works.* Chicago: University of Chicago Press.

14. National Institute of Health. 2010. "What Are Embryonic Stem Cells?" Retrieved August 7, 2014, http://stemcells.nih.gov/info/basics/pages/basics3.aspx.

CHAPTER 2

Religious People Do Not Like Science

Randall[1] is a tall, thin man with salt-and-pepper hair and a graying mustache. We meet him during a Sunday morning service at his evangelical congregation outside of Chicago. Following the sermon, he taps Chris on the shoulder and asks if it is our first time at the church. We introduce ourselves as the researchers mentioned in the church bulletin, and Randall immediately volunteers to be interviewed.

Religion has been an important part of Randall's life since he was young. Growing up, he had a strained relationship with his parents and would often seek refuge in church. Throughout his life, Randall has thought deeply about his faith. "The object of life is really fellowship with God," he says. "Jesus didn't do his work in order to make us happy pagans or good pagans. He didn't do it to make us [appear] good before God. He did it so that we could have fellowship with God."

Randall is also interested in science. Although he ended up pursuing work as a music teacher, in college he took a course on geology and says, "I loved it! I loved it. The geology course let me understand a lot more about everything that I look at around me." He understands science as "the study of physical things to see how they operate in relationship to one another." In Randall's sense of things

> you study further and further how things work together and the way things work physically. And science has, by its own agreement, decided to use certain procedures, which limit it to what we can see physically. So it has to do with what we can touch and taste and measure, . . . measure and put together in a rational way, that's part of it. . . . So you extend your eyes with things like electron telescopes and you extend your eyes with instruments, which can measure different wavelengths of light in order to see how stars are moving and that sort of thing.

Randall also seems to understand how the process of science works, pointing out that you have to have some kind of control because one person sees one thing and another person sees another thing, and so part of the object is that you need to be able to do some sort of experiments and then replicate them again and again. Because if one person sees it that way, and nobody else can, it isn't much use.

"Science is fantastic and I thank God for this," Randall says. "It isn't as if He didn't want us to find out about His incredible creation."

MYTH: RELIGIOUS PEOPLE DO NOT LIKE SCIENCE

What do religious people think of science? If you posed this question to someone who is not religious, the first response would probably be "They do not like science" or "They have a lot of conflicts with science." Yet, in our conversations with religious Americans, we encounter over and over again people like Randall who challenge this assumption. So where do we get the myth that religious people hate science?

There are historical events, like the Catholic Church's supposed persecution of Galileo,[2] and recent news stories that seem to support this idea, such as religious parents trying to remove evolution from the school curriculum or religious groups opposing human embryonic stem-cell research. The idea is also propagated by vocal writers who appear antireligious, writers who are often scientists. In a 2011 essay for the *Huffington Post*,[3] for example, Sam Harris, a neuroscientist, philosopher, and outspoken atheist, wrote that

> the difference between science and religion is the difference between a willingness to dispassionately consider new evidence and new arguments, and a passionate unwillingness to do so. . . . The difference between science and religion is the difference between a genuine openness to fruits of human inquiry in the 21st century, and a premature closure to such inquiry as a matter of principle.

If religion makes someone closed to scientific inquiry "as a matter of principle," then we suppose it makes sense that religious people do not like science. They must be too busy filling their ears with balled-up pieces of scripture.

The belief that religious people do not like science is not isolated to atheist communities. A team of social psychologists led by Kimberly Rios conducted a study in which they asked individuals to rate their perceptions of how different groups are stereotyped regarding competency and trust in science.[4] Participants in the study said Christians, in particular, are seen as less trusting and less competent in science than the average person. What was most interesting is *that even the Christian participants in the study recognized this stereotype.*[5] On the other hand, the participants stereotyped atheists as more trusting of and more competent in science.[6]

When they were asked about their *personal* beliefs on these issues (i.e., does the study participant actually believe the group is less competent or trusting in science?) non-Christians said they personally *do* believe that Christians are less competent and trusting in science. Christians, on the other hand, did not rate themselves as *actually* less competent or trusting in science, even though they recognized that others stereotyped them as such.[7]

It is fair to ask whether there is evidence to support the stereotype that religious people do not like science. To answer this question, we must first break this stereotype down into its several potential meanings. "Religious people do not like science" could mean that religious people actively dislike science and view it as the enemy. This is obviously the most combative version of the "religious people do not like science" idea and the one that gets reinforced by frequent public attention to alleged conflicts between religion and science. More passively, "religious people do not like science" could simply mean that they are not that interested in science relative to other activities, in the same way that some people might not particularly like basketball yet do not actually hold deeply negative feelings toward the sport. Of course, even such passive lack of interest might be a point of frustration and anger for those who place great importance on science. Finally, the idea that "religious people do not like science" is often tied, by implication, to an assumption that religious people are not knowledgeable about or competent in science (hence the reason Rios raised the competency issue in her stereotype study).

The sociologist Darren Sherkat addressed the competency issue by conducting an analysis of a 13-question true-false science quiz that was included in a national survey of adults.[8] This quiz included questions like "True or False: All radioactivity is man made." On first pass, he found that conservative Protestants, those who are part of denominations such as "Baptists, Pentecostals, Church of Christ, Nazarenes, etc.," got 55% of these questions correct compared with 65% of Catholics, 68% of other Protestants and non-Christians, and 72% of the religiously unaffiliated. The scores for conservative Protestants and Catholics were lower even after adjusting for differences in education, age, and other demographic factors among the groups, suggesting that the gaps are uniquely and directly a product of religion. Sherkat concluded that,

> given the low levels of scientific literacy prevalent among fundamentalist and sectarian Christians, they may have difficulty understanding public issues related to scientific inquiry or pedagogy, and they may have a limited capacity to understand technical information regarding their own health and safety.

Based on this determination, it seems amazing that such individuals can get through their day-to-day activities without encountering some mishap due to their incompetence.

The story becomes more nuanced when we look at another sociologist's analysis. John Evans separated the same quiz questions in that same national survey into those representing what he called uncontested and contested scientific facts.[9] Questions about uncontested facts asked things like whether "electrons are smaller than atoms" and whether "antibiotics kill viruses as well as bacteria." Evans argues that uncontested facts tend to concern issues that are directly observable, or at least perceived as directly observable. On the other hand, questions about contested facts are those that a person may very well know the correct answer to from the perspective of a science textbook, but the answer is rejected because the person's faith offers a clear alternative to the scientific assertion. Contested facts are often based on what Evans calls "unobservable abstractions."[10] For example, the science quiz asked whether "the universe began with a huge explosion" and whether "human beings, as we know them today, developed from earlier species of animals."[11] These questions refer to the "big bang" and "evolution," scientific theories that some religious individuals, particularly conservative Christians, take issue with due to the tenets of their faith.

Evans found no real differences between religious groups and the nonreligious when it comes to their knowledge of uncontested scientific facts—or in their understanding of scientific methods, their likelihood of having been a science major in college, or their likelihood of currently working in a scientific occupation. Yet his analysis did show that Protestants and conservative Catholics are more likely to answer questions about *contested* facts incorrectly from the perspective of science. He concludes that a "more subtle epistemological conflict may arise when scientists make claims that explicitly contradict theological accounts. Findings indicate that Protestants and Catholics differ from the comparison group only on the very few issues where religion and science make competing claims."[12] Beyond those few issues (like evolution and the big bang), religious people have very little conflict between religion and science.

MYTH: RELIGIOUS PEOPLE SEE SCIENCE AS THE ENEMY

Our data also show a more complex portrait of religious Americans' views on science. We too cannot wholeheartedly support the view that religious people see science as an enemy in conflict with their religious faith.[13]

We asked our survey respondents a direct question about the relationship between science and religion: "Which of the following BEST represents your view. 'For me, personally, my understanding of science and religion can be described as a relationship of . . . '"

- Conflict —I consider myself to be on the side of religion.
- Conflict—I consider myself to be on the side of science.
- Independence—They refer to different aspects of reality.
- Collaboration—Each can be used to help support the other.

Responses to this question are shown in table 2.1. This table presents unadjusted and adjusted percentages. Adjusted percentages account for any influence from differences in education, political ideology, income, sex, age, region of residence, marital status, and race. The tables also indicate whether a particular percentage is statistically different from the overall population and from evangelical Protestants. This is important because each percentage comes with an underlying margin of error. If the difference between two percentages is statistically significant, then we can be confident that the percentages really are different from each other after taking into account that margin of error. Statistical significance is a function of the size of the difference between the two percentages and how confident we can be in the accuracy of each percentage. That accuracy, in turn, is a function of how many people are in each group. So, a small difference might be statistically significant if there are many people in each group. Alternatively, a large difference might not be statistically significant if one group is small. Overall, 27% of the individuals we surveyed said they view the science and religion relationship as one of conflict—with 14% siding with religion and 13% siding with science. Thirty-five percent said they view science and religion as independent of each other, while the remaining 38% said they see religion and science as collaborating and supporting each other. Despite the dominance of the conflict narrative in the media and public discourse, *in reality most Americans actually do not perceive religion and science as being inherently in conflict.*

When we break down the results by religious affiliation, we find that those most likely to hold a conflict view are the religiously *unaffiliated* (52%) and evangelicals (31%).[14] Not surprisingly, almost all evangelicals who hold a conflict perspective on science and religion say they side with religion (29% out of the 31%), while almost all of the religiously unaffiliated who hold the conflict perspective say they side with science. About twenty percent of mainline Protestants and Catholics view science and religion as in conflict, but these individuals are more evenly divided between those who side with religion and those who side with science. About 23% of Jews, as well as Muslims and adherents of other non-Western religions, also hold a conflict view, but *almost all of these*

TABLE 2.1 Perception of the Relationship Between Religion and Science

"For me personally, my understanding of science and religion can be described as a relationship of . . ."		All Respondents (a)	Evangelical Protestants (b)	Mainline Protestants	Percentage of Respondents Catholics	Jews	Non-Western Religions	Atheists, Agnostic, Unaffiliated
Conflict—I consider myself to be on the side of religion.	Unadjusted	14.3%	29.4%[a]	12.9%[b]	12.1%[ab]	1.5%[ab]	3.4%[ab]	0.7%[ab]
	Adjusted	10.8%	21.0%[a]	9.9%[ab]	10.3%[b]	2.0%[ab]	4.2%[ab]	0.8%[ab]
Conflict—I consider myself to be on the side of science.	Unadjusted	12.9%	1.3%[a]	7.2%[ab]	6.5%[ab]	21.9%[ab]	19.3%[b]	51.7%[ab]
	Adjusted	9.3%	1.5%[a]	6.5%[ab]	5.5%[ab]	14.2%[b]	17.2%[b]	41.0%[ab]
Independence—They refer to different aspects of reality.	Unadjusted	34.9%	21.1%[a]	38.2%[ab]	41.6%[ab]	44.3%[ab]	43.8%[b]	34.3%[b]
	Adjusted	34.6%	22.2%[a]	38.1%[ab]	41.3%[ab]	43.9%[ab]	39.8%[b]	32.7%[b]
Collaboration—Each can be used to help support the other.	Unadjusted	38.0%	48.2%[a]	41.7%[ab]	39.7%[b]	32.3%[b]	33.5%[b]	13.3%[ab]
	Adjusted	37.6%	47.3%[a]	42.2%[ab]	39.7%[b]	30.0%[b]	31.6%[b]	13.0%[ab]

a = Difference between percentage and all other US adults is statistically significant (p < .05).
b = Difference between percentage and percentage for evangelical Protestants is statistically significant (p < .05).
Source: Religious Understandings of Science, 2014. Adjusted percentages account for any influence from differences in education, political ideology, income, sex, age, region of residence, marital status, and race between the religious groups. Percentages may not total to 100% due to rounding.

individuals say they side with science. This is our first piece of evidence that any broad claim about what religious people think about science is going to miss significant variation across religious traditions. There are big differences in where various religious groups stand on the conflict between religion and science, and these differences remain even after we take into account other social and demographic factors. If we were to imagine a war between science and religion, most evangelicals on the front line will be standing on the side of religion, alongside a substantial minority of mainline Protestants and Catholics. A significant number of mainline Protestants and Catholics, however, will be standing on the other side of this line, alongside Jews, Muslims, Hindus, Buddhists, and the religiously unaffiliated.

But focusing on this metaphorical war misses the much bigger story in our findings: *A strong majority of the US population and a strong majority of every religious group we studied view science and religion as being either independent of each other or in collaboration with one another. The only group that is dominated by a conflict perspective is the religiously unaffiliated.* So while a minority of the population faces off in a war between science and religion, the majority of religious individuals are standing off to the side asking, "What are you all fighting about?" This includes evangelicals, *who are actually significantly more likely than the general population and significantly more likely than any other religious group to see religion and science as having a collaborative relationship.*

When we talked with religious individuals face-to-face, we found relatively few who were looking for a fight with science. The strongest responses in support of the conflict perspective came from evangelicals. "I guess I do feel that scientists have an agenda of trying to disprove God," one evangelical[15] told us with a laugh. Another evangelical Christian said, "I think that especially in [science] people would be more apt to find a bone in the ground and say this is the missing link, this is what proves evolution, we can finally shut up those rotten Christians." It is important to note here, however, that even though we asked individuals about the relationship between religion and science as abstract concepts, they ended up talking about *scientists* rather than science itself, a point we return to in depth later in the next chapter.

In support of our survey data, most of the religious individuals we spoke with saw science as supporting their faith rather than as a threat to it. These individuals were represented among the Protestants, Muslims, Catholics, and Jews we interviewed. An Episcopalian[16] in Chicago put it this way:

> Science . . . has made me really appreciate the complexity and beauty in life. And to me that makes me more spiritual, if anything. A lot of people say, "Well don't you see a lot of conflict between what you've read in the Bible, and what you see in science." I guess for me, I don't . . . the method versus the destination. We don't know the methods He used to create this.

An evangelical[17] in Houston explained his perspective like this:

> I think that the more wonders that scientists discover every day makes me believe that [science] must be created by God because nobody else could ever think of anything like that, nobody could make it all work. It all fits together and works together smoothly and has for millions of years. I think He [God] is the only one that could do that.

When we began to discuss the religion and science relationship with Sue,[18] a retired banker, who is deeply involved in her wealthy African American congregation in the South, she enthusiastically recounted how she recently watched a YouTube video that made her think religion and science are not at "different ends of the spectrum." The clip was about brain scans, which revealed that the thought and speech centers of the brain are not active when people speak in tongues, what some see as a supernatural phenomenon allowing a believer to commune better with God and others by using a language the speaker does not actually know.[19] For the first time, Sue—who also mentioned that she has prayed for and received physical healing from illness—said she realized she might be able to connect science and religion:

> I thought that, OK, there is the scientific whatever and then there's [theology]. . . . God lived, God created. . . . And my mind wants to think that they are separate, even though my mind really couldn't understand how they were separate if God created everything.

She believes God used the video clip to help her develop a more compatible view between faith and science. "You know, God was mad that I had that conflict in my own mind," she said. "But I'm glad that I saw that."

MYTH: RELIGIOUS PEOPLE ARE NOT INTERESTED IN SCIENCE

Perhaps we can now agree that the religious population is not necessarily dominated by the attitude that science is its mortal enemy. But maybe "religious people do not like science" should be interpreted as meaning that religious people simply are not interested in and do not value science, even if they do not actively hate it.

To explore this possibility, we asked those who took our survey a series of questions about how interested they are in "new scientific discoveries." The percentage of respondents saying they are "very interested," overall and by religious tradition, is shown in table 2.2.[20] When we look at the results, we see that evangelicals, at 22%,

TABLE 2.2 Percentage of Respondents Saying "Very Interested" by Religious Tradition

	All Respondents (a)	Evangelical Protestants (b)	Mainline Protestants	Catholics	Jews	Non-Western Religions	Atheists, Agnostic, Unaffiliated
Very interested: New scientific discoveries Unadjusted	31.5%	21.8%[a]	27.9%[ab]	30.6%[b]	42.5%[ab]	52.4%[ab]	47.1%[ab]
Adjusted	29.8%	24.3%[a]	27.0%[a]	28.4%[b]	32.5%[b]	47.5%[ab]	39.6%[ab]
Very interested: New medical discoveries Unadjusted	40.5%	37.4%[a]	39.1%	41.8%[b]	53.2%[ab]	49.5%[b]	43.4%[b]
Adjusted	39.9%	39.3%	38.4%	40.0%	46.0%	47.6%	41.5%

a = Difference between percentage and all other US adults is statistically significant (p < .05).
b = Difference between percentage and percentage for evangelical Protestants is statistically significant (p < .05).
Source: Religious Understandings of Science, 2014. Adjusted percentages account for any influence from differences in education, political ideology, income, sex, age, region of residence, marital status, and race between the religious groups.

report the lowest level of interest in new scientific discoveries. At 28%, mainline Protestants also show a significantly lower level of interest in new scientific discoveries than do other religious groups. On the other end of the spectrum, about 52% of Buddhists, Hindus, and Muslims, 47% of the religiously unaffiliated, and 43% of Jews say they are very interested in new scientific discoveries. Catholics, at 31%, are not significantly different from the overall US population when it comes to their interest level. As we will note throughout this book, the findings show that broad claims about how religious people view science are problematic.

When we look at the adjusted percentages for high interest in new scientific discoveries, we see that the gaps between the different religious groups shrink after we take into account demographic, educational, and other social differences. Even still, however, we find that Protestants are less likely than the general US population to say they are very interested in new scientific discoveries, while adherents of non-Western religions and the religiously unaffiliated are more likely to express a high level of interest than the overall population.[21] This finding would seem to lend support to the stereotype that Protestants, at least, are not particularly interested in science.

But the case becomes more complicated when we look at the responses to the question asking about interest in "new medical discoveries." Looking first at the unadjusted percentages, we find much smaller differences across the religious groups. At 37%, evangelical Protestants are the least likely to say they are very interested in new medical discoveries, but the gap between this group and the overall US population, at 41%, is smaller than what we saw with "new scientific discoveries." Once we account for social and demographic differences, all of the groups become statistically equal. *This means that religious tradition has no direct effect on interest in new medical discoveries.*

Why do we find clear religious differences when we look at interest in new scientific discoveries, but little religious difference when we examine interest in new medical discoveries? The finding could suggest that the relationship between religious affiliation and interest in science differs depending on whether we are talking about more basic science (pure research done without knowledge of how it might help others) or more applied science (science done with a specific technological or medical goal in mind).

Our survey directly asked respondents how much they agreed with the statement "Scientific research is valuable even when it doesn't provide immediate tangible benefits." Overall, 20% of our respondents strongly agreed with this statement.[22] At 40% and 38%, respectively, Jews and the religiously unaffiliated were the most likely to strongly agree that scientific research is valuable, regardless of immediate tangible benefits. Evangelicals (12%) and mainline Protestants (16%) were the least likely to strongly agree with this statement. Catholics (19%) and non-Western adherents (22%) were similar to the overall percentage.

We find other evidence of a division between basic science and applied science in our survey data. For example, we asked individuals how willing they would be to recommend that a child enter a certain occupation. When we asked about occupations that represent pure or basic science, like "biologist" and "physicist," we find Protestants and Catholics are significantly less likely than the religiously unaffiliated to say they would recommend these careers.[23] When we asked about more applied science careers, such as "physician" or "high school chemistry teacher," Protestants and Catholics are no less likely than anyone else to say they would recommend a child enter those occupations.[24] It is clear that these religious groups do not have some explicit distaste for all things related to science.

Rather, religious people show lower levels of interest in basic science activities and careers because such activities and occupations are not as clearly connected to the values and goals that their religious traditions emphasize.[25] For instance, if your faith tradition emphasizes the importance of life or the importance of helping other people, then "physician" might be more easily seen as a "spiritual" profession than "biologist," even if both actually serve to promote the values of your faith.[26] In the same way, it would be easier to see "new medical discoveries" as spiritually connected to the ideals of faith than it would be to see "new scientific discoveries" as promoting faith ideals.

The good news is that Americans, regardless of religious tradition, are primed and ready to be persuaded about the benefits of science. We asked our survey respondents whether they agree or disagree that, "overall, modern science does more harm than good."[27] As seen in table 2.3, *only 15% of Americans agree with this statement*; very few people think science has a negative impact on society. When we look across religious traditions, there are only a couple of groups that are statistically more likely than the general population to agree that science does more harm than good: adherents of non-Western religions (23%) and the religiously unaffiliated (16%).[28]

We also asked our survey respondents whether they agree with the statement "Because of science and technology, there will be more opportunities for the next generation." Overall, 71% of Americans agree with this statement. Jews (83%) and the religiously unaffiliated (79%) are significantly more likely than the general population to agree with this statement, while evangelicals, at 67%, are a bit less likely to agree. These gaps, which are quite small to begin with, largely disappear in the adjusted percentages (those that take into account demographic differences, like gender and social class), although the religiously unaffiliated remain significantly more likely than the general population and evangelicals to say that science and technology will provide more opportunities for future generations. If we take a big-picture view here, we see that the majority of religious Americans think we have a great deal to gain from investing in science and technology.

Quite often, this generally positive attitude toward science's contributions to society came out in our one-on-one discussions. For example, one evangelical man in Houston[29] took a stand strongly in favor of human embryonic stem-cell research,

TABLE 2.3 Percentage of Respondents Saying "Agree" or "Strongly Agree" That Modern Science Does More Harm Than Good, by Religious Tradition

		All Respondents (a)	Evangelical Protestants (b)	Mainline Protestants	Catholics	Jews	Non-Western Religions	Atheists, Agnostic, Unaffiliated
Agree: Overall, modern science does more harm than good.	Unadjusted	14.9%	13.9%	14.2%	13.5%	17.5%	23.4%[ab]	16.4%[ab]
	Adjusted	14.5%	14.7%	14.4%	13.0%	15.3%	19.6%	15.5%
Agree: Because of science and technology, there will be more opportunities for the next generation.	Unadjusted	71.3%	66.6%[a]	70.3%[b]	72.4%[b]	82.8%[ab]	77.3%[b]	78.5%[ab]
	Adjusted	72.3%	70.6%	71.6%	73.4%	78.6%	73.2%	76.0%[ab]

a = Difference between percentage and all other US adults is statistically significant (p < .05).
b = Difference between percentage and percentage for evangelical Protestants is statistically significant (p < .05).
Source: Religious Understandings of Science, 2014. Adjusted percentages account for any influence from differences in education, political ideology, income, sex, age, region of residence, marital status, and race between the religious groups.

which has great potential benefits but is particularly divisive within some religious communities because of its implications for when life begins and our responsibilities to protect life: "We are not killing babies, these are cells," he said. "Research that thing, find out. Cure muscular dystrophy, cure dementia." A middle-aged Reform Jewish man,[30] also in Houston, expressed a similar sentiment when he told us,

> I know there's a lot that science can do to help the human race and to help us. Do I want them to make it where I can live to be 300 years old? No. No. I think nature needs to take its course. But to help with a disability or coming up with a cure for cancer . . . I am all for it.

Religious people are concerned, however, about the possible moral implications of scientific research and technologies. Many individuals we spoke with wanted to put limits on science, fearing the consequences of unfettered scientific advancement. One evangelical man[31] said, "There probably needs to be limitations on science because I think science can be used to do evil things. Like the Nazis did." In fact, more than 30 of the 319 people we interviewed referenced the Nazis when warning of an ethical slippery slope when science is given too much power.

Another common criticism was science's role in militarization. One Reform Jewish doctor[32] put voice to the feelings of many when he said,

> From an educational standpoint, science has certainly driven our civilization. . . . We sit in air conditioning in comfort and I can make tea and things like that. Without a certain kind of experimentation and scientific knowledge, that would not have happened. In terms of society, it has been very much to its benefit and its detriment because, on the one hand, it's like the best of our world, having our ability to feed everybody, to clothe everybody, and the worst of our world is because of the technology of weapons, for instance, which allows humans to, on the other hand, rampage each other and prevent that from occurring. In terms of society, it's been a blessing and a curse.

So far, we have painted a pretty rosy picture of the relationship between religion and science. Americans, regardless of religion, overwhelmingly see science as providing tangible benefits to society. Religious Americans *are* interested in science, especially when science has beneficial applications to human lives. It is true that evangelicals are the most likely of any religious group to say that religion and science are in conflict with each other, but it is also true that *almost 70% of evangelicals do not view religion and science as being in conflict.* We would be remiss, however, if we did not also focus on the real tensions and problems that result from religious Americans' orientation toward science. At the heart of these tensions lie strong views (what we introduced in chapter 1 as moral schemas or interpretive frameworks) about the nature of God and the place of humans in the world.

REALITY: GOD AND THE ISSUE OF MIRACLES

In their faith lives, religious Americans face several key questions concerning God. Is God active in daily life? Does God care about my personal well-being? Can God change the course of events? Can God act outside the laws of nature? The answers to such questions sometimes differ among various religious groups, and at other times they transcend faith traditions. For example, among the three major monotheistic religions, we find Muslims, Christians, and Jews who share similar views on God's activity in the world and God's interest in our personal well-being (or lack thereof).[33] How religious Americans view God influences how they approach science. Social scientists find that different images of God underlie some differences in attitudes and behaviors, above and beyond differences in religious tradition.[34]

Conceptions of God relate to ideas about miracles. One definition of a miracle is an event that defies the laws of nature and is generally attributed to God or another supernatural force.[35] For many religious individuals, miracles are the fingerprints of God, and their existence—or at least the possibility of their existence—provides evidence of God's intervention in the world and thus a grounding for their faith and sense of purpose. The prospect of miracles is fundamentally important to their view of life and human affairs. This is particularly true for evangelicals and some Catholics, who worship a personal and active God.

Indeed, nearly half of the evangelicals[36] we spoke with affirmed their belief in the miracles of the Bible. The veracity of miracles is expressed through the broader framework of God's authority and dominion over the natural world. "I think there are miracles," one evangelical homemaker in Chicago[37] told us, explaining that "once you posit an omniscient God, then I don't have any trouble with miracles." Most evangelicals also made it clear that their acceptance of miracles as described in the Bible is unlikely to be swayed by scientific evidence. In our survey, we asked Christian respondents if they would be more likely to believe the Bible or science if "some scientific discovery appeared to contradict something in the Bible." Almost two-thirds of evangelicals (63%) say they would be "much more likely" to believe the Bible. This is more than double the percentage of mainline Protestants (25%) and Catholics (19%) who say the same. Another 18% of evangelicals say they would be "somewhat more likely" to believe the Bible. So, in all, more than 80% of evangelicals would uphold the Bible even if it appears to contradict science.

Among evangelicals, acceptance of miracles did not stop at those miracles described in scripture. Randall, whom we met at the beginning of this chapter, talked about a miraculous healing he believes happened at a church in his town. Others we talked with also discussed miracles as occurring today, especially overseas, as a sign of God's comfort and hand in places of extreme conflict or suffering. An evangelical Christian who works as a radiologist[38] told us,

> I believe that miracles happen today. I don't see a lot of miracles like what we would think of as a miracle in my life. I think, [however,] if you go and you talk to people who live in Iran, Christians [I mean]—[those in] Iran, China, Syria, Pakistan—a lot of the troubled, troubled places in the world, you see [miracles]. They are a lot more numerous. If you look at the Biblical record, a lot of the miracles that happened, happened in troubling times. I'm not saying they can't happen, but I think in America, we are definitely on a spiritual decline, and I think we basically have given God the middle finger in many ways.

It is not only evangelicals who express raw confidence in the existence of miracles. Several Catholics discussed the Devil's Advocate, a canon lawyer whose job it is to argue against the canonization of a saint by looking for evidence to challenge the miracles supposedly performed by the potential saint.[39] The Catholic Church "is fastidious about gathering documentation in the cases of miracles because it requires two miracles to be performed in order for a person to be declared a saint," one Latino Catholic who works in eldercare[40] told us, adding that, in doing so, the "Church works very closely with medical people. The fact that miracles do take place is indisputable." Catholics, we find, are open to the idea that science has the ability to support the existence of the miraculous and divine.

Most Muslims we spoke with also feel science can explain the miraculous or divine because God can act outside the laws of nature. As one Imam[41] explained:

> God is the ultimate creator, the source, so God is not bound by the laws of nature. He has created the laws of nature and the laws of nature are the norm. In 99.99[% of] cases, if this child has cancer, he will die because this is the law of nature. But God can intervene. God can intervene, and he can change the laws of nature, he can suspend the laws of nature.

Across all faiths, some individuals reported personal experiences involving miracles and God's intervention. As seen in table 2.4, about 20% of Americans say they have witnessed a "miraculous, physical healing," and another 15% say they have personally experienced such a miracle. Yet evangelicals are about twice as likely as the general population to say they have witnessed or received miraculous physical healing, while—unsurprisingly—the religiously unaffiliated are the least likely to report such experiences.

TABLE 2.4 Percentage Reporting Miraculous Experiences

		All Respondents (a)	Evangelical Protestants (b)	Mainline Protestants	Catholics	Jews	Non-Western Religions	Atheists, Agnostic, Unaffiliated
Yes: I witnessed a miraculous, physical healing.	Unadjusted	19.9%	39.2%[a]	17.2%[ab]	14.9%[ab]	8.6%[ab]	19.9%[b]	2.9%[ab]
	Adjusted	17.9%	35.1%[a]	15.4%[ab]	13.7%[ab]	10.8%[b]	20.5%[b]	3.2%[ab]
Yes: I received a miraculous, physical healing.	Unadjusted	14.9%	27.5%[a]	13.0%[ab]	11.1%[ab]	11.5%[b]	7.1%[ab]	4.0%[ab]
	Adjusted	12.4%	23.2%[a]	10.5%[ab]	9.2%[ab]	14.9%	6.5%[b]	4.1%[ab]

a = Difference between percentage and all other US adults is statistically significant (p < .05).
b = Difference between percentage and percentage for evangelical Protestants is statistically significant (p < .05).
Source: Religious Understandings of Science, 2014. Adjusted percentages account for any influence from differences in education, political ideology, income, sex, age, region of residence, marital status, and race between the religious groups.

Ideas about miracles can create tensions between religious believers and scientists. "Any belief in miracles is flat contradictory not just to the facts of science
but to the spirit of science,"[42] the evolutionary biologist Richard Dawkins has
said. Most scientists would agree with him, arguing that science has no ability to
account for supernatural events, nor does it have any desire to do so. Yet, when
we asked our survey respondents whether they agreed or disagreed that "scientists should be open to considering miracles in their theories and explanations,"
38% of Americans agreed with this statement, while 21% disagreed and 41% had
no opinion. Among evangelicals, *60% agreed that scientists should be open to
considering miracles.*[43]

We now must wonder about the 48% of evangelicals who believe religion and
science have a collaborative relationship. What exactly do they mean by "collaboration"? If they mean that scientists should be open to incorporating miracles
into their theories and explanations, it seems safe to say that this is a kind of collaboration to which most scientists would not be receptive. In fact when we told
a science journalist that our research shows many religious individuals believe
in miracles and think scientists ought to allow for miracles, he replied without
missing a beat, "Are you crazy?"

LESSONS

Connect Science to Helping People

The idea that religious people do not like science is a myth, and yet there
are some very real tensions surrounding the relationship between religion
and science. As we've seen in this chapter, many religious individuals tend
to prioritize values over facts—which may explain their greater interest in
applied science than in pure or basic science. In one sense, this finding leaves
a clear path forward: If we want to generate more interest in science among
people of faith, then framing basic scientific research as having clear benefits
for humanity—and hence potential connections to the values and ideals of
faith—is a fruitful strategy.

We recognize that scientists might see the idea of "selling" the practical
benefits of science in order to appeal to religious believers as problematic and
offensive for a number of reasons. It is not always immediately clear how basic
scientific research can ultimately be applied, and some research might not translate into practical benefits in any direct way. There is a long tradition of politicians and other observers critiquing scientific research that they perceive as a

waste of money or time, usually because they do not see any obvious practical application or benefit (often, it should be said, these studies do in fact have such applications and benefits).[44]

In another sense, we support Americans placing more value on science, knowledge, and discovery for its own sake, regardless of whether it would provide so-called practical benefits. Science should be valued as a form of beauty for its own sake. But waiting for this cultural shift to happen has historically led to frustration and disappointment. The physicist Neil deGrasse Tyson, for example, has discussed the frustration of "space zealots" who bemoan the public's lack of appreciation for NASA's exploration.[45] These zealots cannot understand why the enthusiasm surrounding the Apollo missions cannot be re-created. Tyson points out that the enthusiasm of that time had little to do with excitement about science and discovery per se and much more to do with the geopolitics of the Cold War. In the absence of such a "practical" motivator, support for NASA's science and exploration efforts disappeared. Tyson argues that it is possible to regain some of the past excitement not by appealing to the pure goals of science and exploration, but instead by using "tools of cultural navigation that link space exploration with science literacy, national security, and economic prosperity."

Similarly, scientists might employ "tools of cultural navigation" that link basic scientific research with helping people and improving lives in order to develop keener interest among religious communities.

Allow the *Potential* for God to Act in the World

Many religious Americans strongly view God as being active in the world and in their lives, and this is especially so among evangelicals. This translates into how they view science and how they think science should work. They want science to allow for the possibility of a natural world in which God intervenes and miracles occur—a world in which natural laws can be broken.

There are some scientists who allow for the possibility that God could act in the world through natural processes. Some religious scientists, like Francis Collins, are willing to go further, believing that it is possible for God to violate natural processes. Collins has said,[46]

> If you're willing to answer yes to a God outside of nature, then there's nothing inconsistent with God on rare occasions choosing to invade the natural world in a way that appears miraculous. If God made the natural laws, why could He not violate them when it was a particularly significant moment for him to do so?

Yet, while individual scientists, in their personal view, may allow for the possibility of miracles or divine intervention, science does not include or consider the supernatural in its theories and explanations. Scientists seek to explain events through natural causes and universal laws. Here is where compartmentalization of science and faith might actually be helpful. For scientists who want to engage religious Americans in science, it may be helpful for them to stress that when it comes to questions about divine intervention or the potential of miracles, science actually does *not* provide answers.

NOTES

1. Mid-High SES Evangelical Church Chicago Int9, conducted June 23, 2012.

2. Numbers, Ronald, ed. 2009. *Galileo Goes to Jail and Other Myths About Science and Religion.* Cambridge, MA: Harvard University Press.

3. Harris, Sam. 2011. "Science Must Destroy Religion." *Huffington Post,* May 25. Retrieved April 1, 2015, http://www.huffingtonpost.com/sam-harris/science-must-destroy-reli_b_13153.html).

4. Rios, Kimberly, Zhen Hadassah Cheng, Rebecca R. Totton, and Azim F. Shariff. 2015. "Negative Stereotypes Cause Christians to Underperform in and Disidentify with Science." *Social Psychological and Personality Science* 6(8):959–967.

5. See, for example, Barbour, Ian. 1971. *Issues in Science and Religion.* New York: HarperCollins College Division. See also Lindberg, David C., and Ronald L. Numbers, eds. 1986. *God and Nature: Historical Essays on the Encounter Between Christianity and Science.* Berkeley: University of California Press.

6. Muslims were also rated as being stereotyped as less competent in and trusting of science. Atheists were rated as being stereotyped as more competent in and trusting of science, as were Jews.

7. Such stereotypes can become a self-fulfilling prophecy. The same team of researchers conducted a follow-up study in which some individuals were first presented with a fake news story discussing (also fake) results of a survey finding that people viewed Christians as being bad at science. All individuals were asked to answer a number of questions about their interest and confidence in science. Christians who first received the fake news article had significantly lower scores on these measures of identification with and confidence in science. In short, if Christians are told that they are bad at and uninterested in science, then they actually start to feel uninterested in and bad at science.

8. Sherkat, Darren E. 2011. "Religion and Scientific Literacy in the United States." *Social Science Quarterly* 92(5):1134–1150. Quote is from p. 1146.

9. Evans, John H. 2011. "Epistemological and Moral Conflict Between Religion and Science." *Journal for the Scientific Study of Religion* 50(4):707–727.

10. Regarding the issue of observables versus abstractions, we asked our survey respondents their level of agreement with the statement "Science can only truly explain what can be seen and touched." Overall, 6% of respondents strongly agreed with this statement, while 21% agreed, 42% neither agreed nor disagreed, 21% disagreed, and 12% strongly disagreed. The differences across religious groups was fairly small. Among evangelicals, for instance, 7% strongly agreed, 23% agreed, 41% neither agreed nor disagreed, 20% disagreed, and 10% strongly disagreed. Jews and the religiously unaffiliated were more likely to strongly disagree with this statement, at 20% and 19%, respectively.

11. Distinguishing such items is seen as controversial among scientists. In 2010 the annual report of the National Science Board regarding scientific literacy in the United States removed questions about evolution and the big bang from its analyses, saying that the questions "conflated knowledge and belief." Scientists such as the physicist Lawrence Krauss criticized this decision as discarding scientific facts due to religious beliefs. See 2010. "Faith and Foolishness: When Religious Beliefs Become Dangerous," *Scientific American*, August 1, p. 340.

12. See J. Evans 2011.

13. This corresponds to other surveys as well. Baker found that "a relatively small proportion of American adults perceive incompatibility between science and religion." Baker, Joseph. 2012. "Public Perceptions of the Incompatibility Between 'Science and Religion.'" *Public Understanding of Science* 21(3):340–353.

14. A recent survey by the Pew Research Center confirms that it is the nonreligious who are the most likely to view religion and science as inherently in conflict. Funk, Cary, and Becka A. Alper. 2015. "Perception of Conflict Between Science and Religion." Pew Research Center, October 22. Retrieved April 27, 2015, http://www.pewinternet.org/2015/10/22/perception-of-conflict-between-science-and-religion/.

15. Low/Mid-Low SES Evangelical Church Houston Int5, conducted September 4, 2013.

16. High SES Mainline Church Chicago Int11, conducted July 21, 2013.

17. High SES Evangelical Church Houston Int3, conducted July 18, 2012.

18. Mid-High/High SES Evangelical Church Houston Int15, conducted October 2, 2013.

19. See Marina, Peter. 2013. *Getting the Holy Ghost: Urban Ethnography in a Pentecostal Tongue-Speaking Church*. Lanham, MD: Lexington.

20. Our survey included a couple of other questions that measure aspects of interest in science. For instance, one question asked respondents, "In the last month have you read in print or online any science-focused magazines, such as *National Geographic, Discover, Smithsonian, Popular Science*, or *Scientific American*?" Overall, 19% of respondents stated that they had read such a magazine in the past month. This percentage was lower among evangelical Protestants (15%) and Catholics (15%) and higher among the religiously unaffiliated (26%). These differences remained statistically significant even after controlling for other social and demographic factors, including education.

21. We utilized an ordered logistic regression analysis predicting the outcome measures controlling for age (measured continuously), sex, race (five categories: Non-Hispanic White, Non-Hispanic Black, Non-Hispanic Other, Hispanic, and Multi-racial), and region of residence (four categories: Northeast, Midwest, South, West).

22. Another 48.2% chose the "agree" response, 27.6% said that they neither agree nor disagree, 2.6% disagreed, and 1.6% strongly disagreed.

23. The Protestant effect here refers to white Protestants.

24. This analysis can be found in full at Scheitle, Christopher P., and Elaine Howard Ecklund. 2016. "Recommending a Child Enter a STEM Career: The Role of Religion." *Journal of Career Development*, doi: 10.1177/0894845316646879.

25. The sociologist Lisa Keister has connected this line of thinking to socioeconomic differences across religious groups. For instance, in talking about the lower wealth accumulation of conservative Protestants and higher wealth accumulation of Jews, she says that "literal Bible interpretation can . . . lead to the conclusion that wealth accumulation should be avoided" (p. 181) while "Jewish families encourage this-worldly pursuits including actual accumulation of wealth and other activities that lead to wealth accumulation such as high income occupations" (2003, p. 179). "Religion and Wealth: The Role of Religious Affiliation and Participation in Early Adult Asset Accumulation." *Social Forces* 82(1):173–205.

26. Other research corresponds to this idea. For instance, in an analysis of a survey of college students, Scheitle found that students in education and professional fields (primarily health-related fields) scored the highest on measures of religious commitment. Teaching and medicine reflect so-called helping professions that might correspond to religious messages regarding helping others. 2011. "Religious and Spiritual Change in College: Assessing the Effect of a Science Education." *Sociology of Education* 84(2):122–136.

27. This is a question that has been asked previously in other surveys, such as the General Social Survey.

28. There may be differences in the strength or salience of this question across religious traditions, however. For example, only 22% of the religiously unaffiliated said that they "neither agree nor disagree" with this statement compared with 46% of evangelical Protestants. The difference between these is shifted to the "disagree" responses. For instance, 60% of the religiously unaffiliated disagree with this statement compared with 40% of evangelical Protestants.

29. High SES Evangelical Church Houston Int17, conducted October 28, 2012.

30. High SES Reform Jewish Synagogue Houston Int15, conducted September 26, 2013.

31. High SES Evangelical Church Houston Int22, conducted June 25, 2013.

32. High SES Reform Jewish Synagogue Houston Int4, conducted June 25, 2013.

33. See Brooke, John Hedley, and Ronald Numbers, eds. 2011. *Science and Religion Around the World*. New York: Oxford University Press. Note that Hindus and those who do not have a monotheistic version of a god or those faith traditions for which the concept of any god is not relevant may see things in an entirely different way. Brooke and Numbers make this excellent point in the introduction to their edited volume.

34. See Bader, Christopher, and Paul Froese. 2005. "Images of God: The Effect of Personal Theologies on Moral Attitudes, Political Affiliation, and Religious Behavior." *Interdisciplinary Journal of Research on Religion* 1:1–24.

35. Wikipedia. "Miracle." Retrieved October 1, 2014, http://en.wikipedia.org/w/index.php?title=Miracle&oldid=626889308.

36. High SES Evangelical Church Houston Int1, Int2, Int5, Int7, Int8, Int10, Int11, Int12, Int15, Int17; High SES Evangelical Church Chicago Int2, Int3, Int4, Int6, Int7, Int8, Int9, Int12, Int13, Int14.

37. Mid-High SES Evangelical Church Chicago Int7, conducted June 22, 2012.

38. High SES Evangelical Church Chicago Int1, conducted July 15, 2013.

39. See, for example, Wikipedia. "Devil's Advocate." Retrieved July 1, 2015, https://en.wikipedia.org/wiki/Devil's_advocate.

40. Low SES Catholic Church Houston Int2, conducted August 6, 2013.

41. Mid-High SES Sunni Muslim Mosque Chicago Int1, conducted July 13, 2013.

42. Van Biema, David. 2006. "God vs. Science." *Time*, November 5. Retrieved October 1, 2014, http://content.time.com/time/magazine/article/0,9171,1555132,00.html.

43. Similarly, in a different question, we asked respondents whether they agreed or disagreed with the statement "We trust too much in science and not enough in religious faith." Fifty-six percent of evangelicals agreed with this statement, which is much more than the rate of agreement among mainline Protestants (28%) and Catholics (27%).

44. See, for instance, Greenfieldboyce, Nell. 2011. " 'Shrimp on a Treadmill': The Politics of 'Silly' Studies." National Public Radio. August 23.

45. Tyson, Neil deGrasse. 2012. *Space Chronicles: Facing the Ultimate Frontier.* New York: W. W. Norton.

46. Van Biema 2006.

CHAPTER 3

Religious People Do Not Like Scientists

Janelle is a university student in her early twenties.[1] She attends a mainline Protestant congregation, primarily because the congregation is near her school and she doesn't have a car, even though she considers herself more of an evangelical. Different from many of the older people we interview, Janelle is dressed in what look like workout clothes: a T-shirt and shorts coupled with sneakers. When asked what role faith plays in her life, she does not hesitate before saying "a big role." She underscores the significance of faith in her life by saying, "I try to read the Word [the Bible] every day. It doesn't happen every day but that is what I would like. Then prayer. Prayer is something I do every day. And then just weekly church; actually going to the [church] service." She believes that "Jesus is the son of God." She goes on to say,

> He, God, and the Holy Spirit are a trinity and through all three of them . . . that's how we express our beliefs. . . . You know God loves everybody, if they are Christian or not Christian. Once you are saved, you are saved and you are going to heaven. That's my brief overview.

She has a hard time telling us what her image of an ideal scientist might be; she finally says that a scientist needs to be smart and objective. A good scientist would "not be ignorant about what other people think. . . . There is really rocky territory in terms of the ethics that go on with science and the religion that goes on with science . . . and I think a good scientist needs to be able to understand that it's not just black and white and there is a gray area between the two." She doesn't seem to know any scientists like this. Most of her experiences with scientists involve medicine. It's then that she tearfully describes a cancer diagnosis in her family. When we ask her about specific scientific issues, Janelle says that certain issues are taboo to talk about at church; she mentions evolution, for example. Even though Janelle was encouraged by her parents to love science from a young age, when pressed, she told us that there is a clear conflict between science and religion. According to her, there always will be groups of people who believe in science *or* religion, putting them as completely separate ways of viewing the world. Her church is progressive compared with some, yet she says they rarely touch on scientific issues. In her ideal world, she would like to see a formal discussion of faith and science in her congregation. There isn't one now. Janelle tells us she thinks "there will forever be scientists who just don't believe in God." Near a university, her congregation is filled with highly educated people, and we know from our interviews that several are scientists. Yet Janelle says she does not know any scientists personally.

MYTH: RELIGIOUS PEOPLE HATE SCIENTISTS

In the previous chapter, we examined how religious individuals think and feel about science. What about scientists themselves? What do people of faith think about the people who do science? Do religious believers who think highly of science also think highly of scientists as a group of people? Or do some religious believers who support science have disdain for or distrust of the people involved in the scientific enterprise, in the same way that Americans might speak highly of "democracy" while simultaneously expressing disdain for "politicians" or "voters"?

In popular culture, scientists are often depicted in unflattering ways. Studies of books, television shows, and other media indicate that scientists are presented "as obsessive and socially maladjusted."[2] According to one review of how scientists are portrayed on TV, viewers see scientists as "well-meaning but obsessed with the pursuits of knowledge. Amoral rather than immoral, the media and the broader public sometimes seems to perceive scientists as those who will stop at nothing to find the missing link of information they need to know. He will not let human sensitivities stand in his way."[3] Is this what Americans, and religious believers more specifically, think scientists are like?

Indeed a large body of research has been built on asking children or students of any age to write an essay or to draw a picture representing their image of a scientist.[4] This research generally reveals that young children and adults alike have a fairly stereotypical image of a scientist, one of an older man, often with a beard and glasses, who is in a chemistry lab wearing a white coat. And this attitude was borne out among those we interviewed. When asked what images come to mind when she thinks of "a scientist," a woman who attends a largely African American church[5] quips that "I guess it's some little man in a white coat with little glasses in a lab."

Past surveys that looked at attitudes and perceptions toward scientists have produced a number of findings. A 1950s survey found that the US public at that time had generally positive views of scientists as individuals. Almost all of those who responded to the survey agreed that "most scientists want to work on things that will make life better for the average person." About 70% of respondents agreed that "scientists work harder than the average person." When we look a little more closely, however, we find hints of more negative views of scientists. For instance, 40% of respondents also agreed with the statement "scientists are apt to be odd and peculiar people." Twenty-five percent agreed: "Scientists always seem to be prying into things they really ought to stay out of."[6]

Fast forward to 2012, when the General Social Survey asked US adults a number of questions about their perceptions of scientists. Some of the questions replicated those in the 1950s study, and the 2012 findings led to fairly similar conclusions. In 2012, most respondents still felt scientists are good people who are working to help society. Ninety-nine percent of US adults agreed with the statement "scientists are helping to solve challenging problems," and more than 90% thought "scientific researchers are dedicated people who work for the good of humanity."

Yet again, there were hints that the public did not entirely view scientists positively. For example, 36% of US adults surveyed in 2012 thought that "scientists have few other interests but their work." About the same proportion thought that "scientists are apt to be odd and peculiar people" and that "scientists are always prying into things that they really ought to stay out of."

As these findings highlight, the feelings people have toward scientists, like any group, can be complex. And as we saw in the previous chapter, religious people are pretty positive about the work that scientists are doing. But how do we examine the more personal dimension of what religious people think of and how they relate to scientists? In other words, how do we figure out if religious people actually dislike scientists?

The Self-Sorting of Like-Minded People

Figuring out whether religious people like scientists starts with understanding how people sort themselves into different kinds of groups. Back in 2008, the Pew Research Center found that 59% of Americans said they would rather live in a community where there are many different religious groups, while 25% said they would prefer to live in a community where many people share their religion. Among religious individuals, 40% of white evangelicals, 42% of Hispanic Catholics, and 38% of those who attend religious services at least weekly said they would rather live in a community where many people share their religion.[7] Researchers also find that individuals with strong political identities are more likely to say that their closest friends share their political views and that they would prefer to live around people who share their views.[8] Conservatives take great pains to interact mainly with other conservatives, and liberals take great pains to interact mainly with other liberals. America is becoming increasingly polarized, as our communities become more homogeneous. The journalist and book author Bill Bishop calls this clustering of Americans into like-minded communities "the big sort."[9]

If Americans are increasingly sorting themselves into communities of like-minded individuals, what might this mean for interactions between scientists and religious people? Our survey included a question that allows us to assess whether people who are religious spend time with people who are scientists. We asked those who took our survey to, "first, think of your five closest friends." Then we asked them how many of these close friends work in a science-related occupation. Table 3.1 shows the percentage of respondents who stated that at least one of their closest friends works in a science-related occupation. About 31% of all US adults say they have at least one close friend working in a science-related occupation. Evangelicals (29%) and Catholics (27%) fall slightly below this overall percentage. Adherents of non-Western religions (61%), Jews (43%), and the religiously unaffiliated (37%) are more likely than the general American population to say they have a close friend working in science.

When we adjust the percentages to account for differences in education, political ideology, income, race, region of residence, and other factors, we find that Catholics are still slightly less likely than the other groups to report having a close friend working in science, while adherents of non-Western traditions are somewhat more likely. Yet, between Protestants, Jews, and the religiously unaffiliated, there is no significant difference. Thus, it seems factors other than religion are contributing to the differences across religious traditions on this question. Average education levels across religious traditions, for example, likely affect the probability of a religious person having a close friendship with a scientist because scientists tend to be more highly educated and, hence, tend to work with, interact with, and be friends with others who are also more highly educated.[10] If religious individuals, *particularly evangelical Protestants*, truly had a personal distaste for scientists, then we would have expected that they would be less likely than other people in the general population to have friends working in science. This does not seem to be the case.

Myth: Religious People Do Not Understand Who Is a Scientist

When we asked religious individuals whether they had a close friend in science, how did they determine who is a scientist and who is not? Do religious

TABLE 3.1 Percentage Who Have a Close Friend Working in Science

		All Respondents (a)	Evangelical Protestants (b)	Mainline Protestants	Catholics	Jews	Non-Western Religions	Atheists, Agnostic, Unaffiliated
At least one of five closest friends works in science-related occupation.	Unadjusted	31.2%	28.7%[a]	29.8%	26.5%[a]	43.3%[ab]	61.2%[ab]	36.8%[ab]
	Adjusted	28.4%	29.8%	28.4%	24.9%[ab]	32.3%	41.1%[ab]	27.6%

a = Difference between percentage and all other US adults is statistically significant (p < .05).
b = Difference between percentage and percentage for evangelical Protestants is statistically significant (p < .05).
Source: Religious Understandings of Science, 2014. Adjusted percentages account for any influence from differences in education, political ideology, income, sex, age, region of residence, marital status, and race between the religious groups.

people define "scientist" the same way the general public does? Or could it be that religious people use different criteria to decide what makes someone a scientist? Our survey asked respondents how scientific they think various occupations are. These occupations included some that were clearly in the natural and social sciences as well as some that were more applied or technical in nature. In table 3.2, we show the percentage of respondents who said that a particular occupation is "very scientific."[11] To make the table easier to understand, we show only the adjusted percentages, which account for the influence of social and demographic differences between the groups we studied.

Overall, "biologist" was the occupation rated most scientific; about 70% of Americans say that the work of a biologist is very scientific. Being a physicist is close behind, with just under 61% of respondents saying that it is a very scientific occupation.[12] Despite differences of a few percentage points, members of all religious traditions think the occupations of biologist and physicist are by far the most scientific occupations on our list. At 66%, Catholics fall just slightly below the overall percentage of individuals who think "biologist" is a very scientific occupation. At 78%, the religiously unaffiliated are more likely than the general population to say biologists have a very scientific job. If we look at the bottom of the table, we see that only 1.6% of US adults think a pastor, minister, or clergyperson has a very scientific occupation. At about 2.2%, evangelicals as well as those who practice a non-Western religion (like Hinduism) are only slightly more likely than the general population to say religious leaders have a very scientific job. Members of the other religious groups are less likely than the general population to see pastors, ministers, and clergypersons as having a very scientific occupation. That is to say, only a tiny proportion of people from any religious tradition view the work of religious leaders as very scientific.

Overall, then, across all of the occupations we looked at, there is general consensus about which jobs are very scientific. Determining whether an occupation is scientific does not seem tremendously dependent on a person's religious identity. We do not find any evidence that religious individuals are using a different metric than anyone else in defining who is or is not a scientist.

When we examine other questions from our survey data, however, *we do find some evidence for real and potentially personal tensions between religious individuals and scientists.* These tensions result, in part, from how religious individuals think scientists view them, as well as from the belief of some religious individuals, especially evangelicals, that scientists should not be the only voice in conversations about science.

TABLE 3.2 Percentage Rating Different Occupations as "Very Scientific"

Percent Saying Occupation Is "Very Scientific" (Percentages)	All Respondents (Adjusted Percentages) (a)	Evangelical Protestants (b)	Mainline Protestants	Catholics	Jews	Non-Western Religions	Atheists, Agnostic, Unaffiliated
Biologist	69.7%	67.9%	69.4%	66.1%[a]	72.2%	67.0%	77.8%[ab]
Physicist	60.8%	59.2%	59.6%	56.8%[a]	67.1%	52.8%	70.4%[ab]
Physician/doctor	38.7%	39.3%	38.1%	39.2%	43.4%	44.3%	37.6%
TV weather forecaster	25.9%	26.9%	25.9%	26.7%	25.7%	30.2%	22.2%[ab]
Psychologist	16.3%	16.8%	16.2%	15.7%	18.8%	16.8%	14.9%
Plumber	3.5%	3.6%	2.9%	3.7%	4.9%	5.8%	3.0%
Pastor, minister, clergyperson	1.6%	2.2%[a]	1.2%[b]	1.4%	1.3%	2.2%	1.6%

a = Difference between percentage and all other US adults is statistically significant (p < .05).
b = Difference between percentage and percentage for evangelical Protestants is statistically significant (p < .05).
Source: Religious Understandings of Science, 2014. Adjusted percentages account for any influence from differences in education, political ideology, income, sex, age, region of residence, marital status, and race between the religious groups.

Reality: Some Religious Believers, Particularly Evangelicals, Suspect That Scientists Hate Them (or at Least Their Religion)

In our survey, we asked respondents whether they agreed that "most scientists are hostile to religion." The pattern of responses to this question is shown in table 3.3. Twenty-two percent of all respondents agree with the statement. Mainline Protestants, Catholics, Jews, and the religiously unaffiliated are significantly *less likely* than the overall population to agree that scientists are hostile to religion. The religiously unaffiliated are the least likely to believe scientists are hostile to religion. At first blush, this finding may seem surprising. Earlier we saw that the religiously unaffiliated are the group most likely to view science and religion as being in conflict, and almost all of the religiously unaffiliated individuals who hold this conflict perspective say they side with science. As a result, we might expect nonreligious people to be the most likely to think that scientists are hostile to religion. But the results in table 3.3 suggest that the nonreligious do not feel the conflict between science and religion is a function of how scientists think and feel about religion or religious individuals.

But we do find that evangelical Protestants, at 36%, are *much* more likely than the religiously unaffiliated and other religious groups to believe scientists are hostile to religion. This result holds even when we take other social and demographic influences into account. Interestingly, this view of scientists does not seem highly dependent on whether the evangelical respondent views religion and science as being in conflict. We find, for instance, that 38% of evangelicals who think religion and science have a collaborative relationship also feel most scientists are hostile to religion. Among evangelicals who view religion and science as being in conflict, the percentage rises only slightly: 42% of evangelicals who hold the conflict perspective think most scientists are hostile to religion.

It is interesting to note that while evangelicals are more likely than other religious groups to say scientists are hostile to religion, they are as likely as other religious groups to say they have close friends working in science. At first we could not figure this out: If you have close friends who are members of the scientific community, why would you think that community is hostile to your belief system? Conversely, why would you be close friends with someone who you think is hostile to your most deeply held beliefs? As we thought about this further, we came to the conclusion that our evangelical survey respondents may think their scientist friends are exceptions to the rule. In their minds, the highly vocal scientists they see dominating the news, rather than their personal friends, are representative of most scientists—and these scientists appear to be very hostile to their religion.

Case in point: We asked the respondents to our survey whether they had ever heard of two scientists, Richard Dawkins and Francis Collins. Both are highly accomplished. Dawkins, a well-known evolutionary biologist and former chair

TABLE 3.3 Percentage Who Agree That "Most Scientists Are Hostile to Religion"

		All Respondents (a)	Evangelical Protestants (b)	Mainline Protestants	Catholics	Jews	Non-Western Religions	Atheists, Agnostic, Unaffiliated
Percentage agreeing that "most scientists are hostile to religion."	Unadjusted	22.0%	36.1%[a]	18.6%[ab]	19.5%[ab]	13.4%[ab]	25.1%[b]	10.7%[ab]
	Adjusted	20.3%	33.6%[a]	19.0%[ab]	16.5%[ab]	15.1%[b]	21.4%[b]	10.6%[ab]

a = Difference between percentage and all other US adults is statistically significant (p < .05).

b = Difference between percentage and percentage for evangelical Protestants is statistically significant (p < .05).

Source: Religious Understandings of Science, 2014. Adjusted percentages account for any influence from differences in education, political ideology, income, sex, age, region of residence, marital status, and race between the religious groups.

of the Public Understanding of Science at Oxford University, is a vocal atheist and author of a *New York Times* best-selling book, *The God Delusion*. Collins is currently the director of the National Institutes of Health, the former director of the Human Genome Project, and an outspoken Christian who wrote *The Language of God: A Scientist Presents Evidence for Belief*. In public debates, the two have been pitted against each other as representing opposing views on the relationship between science and religion.[13]

Based on our survey results, we find that Americans are five times more likely to have heard of Dawkins than Collins (21% to 4%). It would thus be fair to assume that they are more likely to have heard Dawkins's antireligion views than Collins's message of reconciliation between science and religion.

We assumed Collins would be more highly recognized among Christians, since his views speak to their faith, but we found only 3% of Protestants (including evangelicals and Mainline Protestants) and Catholics are familiar with Collins. Although Collins is a public figure who writes books and participates in national debates, it would seem his message is not reaching the people who need it most.

We do in fact find that many religious people—especially conservative Christians—seem to think scientists (at worst) are against them and (at best) have forgotten God. A woman in her early fifties[14] who attends a largely African American congregation explains:

> I don't put scientists too far from doctors. [But] If they're not careful they become gods themselves. Because when God has given you the ability to do things, if you're not careful you begin to get prideful. And when you get prideful you begin to take credit for that which you have accomplished. In other words you take the glory.

Later in our discussion she goes on to explain the risk in scientists taking matters into their own hands and denying God.

> And case in point . . . I was just watching television one day. . . . [T]here was this couple they had been trying to have a baby for . . . a long time. And they kept trying and they finally found these doctors and they had a boy and a girl. Some kind of way the scientists had manipulated and it was amazing. These children were in elementary school and the boy had the characteristics and emotions of a girl, and the girl had the characteristics and emotions of a boy. . . . So there's no question as far as God's concerned as to what's going to come about in the children that you have. But when we manipulate with science and . . . bring forth children, then we create something that we can no longer make decisions about and help control. Because we'll never be able to put those kids in their right mind.

Not all of those who thought scientists were against them were evangelicals. For example, a Muslim woman from Houston[15] told us,

Our physics teacher, actually, he was adamantly atheist and couldn't understand why we believe in God because you couldn't prove it. And I said: Well, if everything had to be proven, it'd be a crazy world to live in because you have to say that everything I do is proven. I'm like: That's OK, but when I'm having a hard day or I feel like the weight of the world is too much, who do I turn to? And he's like, "Well, yourself." And I'm like, "That's too much for me to handle." So my reliance and the way I was brought up is that for something too much you can't handle, well give it to God. . . . So by the time the discussion [had ended], he was almost like smirking like "Oh you poor kid, you have no idea what you're talking about."

And an Orthodox Jew[16] from Chicago said,

I see a bias in that anything that [scientists] think could possibly be used to confirm anything that a religious scholar might have said at any time in the past, they will completely bend over backward and do somersaults to make sure that that is not how the evidence presents itself.

And it's worth repeating from the last chapter the quote from the woman who attends a largely white congregation in Houston[17] who said, "I think that [scientists] would be more apt to find a bone in the ground and say this is the missing link, this is what proves evolution, we can finally shut up those rotten Christians." This congregant was not the only one to suggest that many scientists might be misusing science, as one Catholic woman[18] said, "I think that there are a lot of scientists that are misled, and they feel like they have to be that way . . . because they get so caught up into figuring out very specific things, but I don't think that that's what God intended science to be." In fact, some respondents drew parallels between religious commitment and scientific inquiry, as one mainline Protestant respondent[19] told us: "I think there are scientists for whom science is the religion." Religious leaders often articulated similar views about the nature of science, as one evangelical pastor[20] said, "[Scientists] try to rationalize away from God, those who [are] atheistic in their science. But, true science, I've seen more scientists who favor true science that believes in God than I have those who are atheistic with their science, they're trying to disprove."

In many cases, the concerns about science functioning like a religion for many scientists went further. For instance, an evangelical Christian we talked with[21] brought up concerns about scientists trying to play God:

I guess [scientists] don't believe that God created this stuff, because they can manipulate it, they can look at it . . . if they have new species, but they can make—they can create and destroy so . . . in some ways think that they're God because they are Creators and manipulators and destroyers, but they're not really creating anything that God didn't already put here, you know.

Another evangelical[22] admitted that he had believed that atheism and science were synonymous by saying, "Really, I thought all scientists were atheists. And because I work now with science teachers, I know now that . . . you can be Christian and a scientist, but before I did not know that, I thought you had to be an atheist in order to be in science."

Reality: Evangelicals Are Much Less Likely Than Other Religious Groups to See Scientists as the Sole Authority on Science Issues

In our survey, we also asked respondents how likely they would be to consult a variety of sources "if [they] had a question about science."[23] Overall, respondents said they are most likely to consult a "general Internet source, such as Wikipedia." This finding held true for all religious groups. This is not particularly surprising, since so many of our daily thoughts and inquiries lead us to search Google. But we asked respondents too how likely they would be to consult "a religious leader" if they had a question about science. Table 3.4 shows the percentage of people who said they would be somewhat or very likely to do so. About 17% of all US adults say they would be at least somewhat likely to ask a religious leader if they had a science question. This percentage doubles to 34% among evangelicals, which is much higher than the percentages for mainline Protestants, Catholics, and the other religious groups. Even though, as we saw before, evangelicals do not think religious leaders are actually scientists *but* they still often approach their faith leaders to ask questions about science.

Note that we intentionally did not specify whether the question about science they asked the religious leader would be technical, moral, or otherwise. We also intentionally did not specify what scientific topic they would be asking about, or whether the question would be about a religiously controversial issue, such as evolution. And using this approach allows us to measure whether respondents broadly perceive certain sources of information as relevant to discussions about science. We find that evangelicals strongly view religious leaders as having a place in conversations about science.

We also find that religion is a much stronger positive predictor of seeking out religious sources for scientific information than it is a negative predictor

TABLE 3.4 Percentage Who Would Consult a Religious Leader with a Question about Science

Somewhat or Very Likely to Consult About a Science Question		All Respondents (a)	Evangelical Protestants (b)	Mainline Protestants	Catholics	Jews	Non-Western Religions	Atheists, Agnostic, Unaffiliated
Religious leader	Unadjusted	16.5%	34.1%[a]	11.8%[ab]	15.0%[b]	6.8%[ab]	13.0%[b]	2.5%[ab]
	Adjusted	14.4%	30.1%[a]	10.6%[ab]	12.6%[ab]	9.1%[b]	11.8%[b]	2.7%[ab]

a = Difference between percentage and all other US adults is statistically significant (p < .05).
b = Difference between percentage and percentage for evangelical Protestants is statistically significant (p < .05).
Source: Religious Understandings of Science, 2014. Adjusted percentages account for any influence from differences in education, political ideology, income, sex, age, region of residence, marital status, and race between the religious groups.

of seeking out scientific sources. Interest in science, which we might assume would lead an individual to turn to scientific sources of information, has no influence on the likelihood of turning to a religious source for scientific information.

The findings in table 3.4 demonstrate that, while evangelicals recognize that being a pastor is not a scientific occupation, evangelicals still view pastors and religious leaders as having a potentially important role in conversations about science.

Reality: Some Religious Believers Think Scientists View Themselves as God-Like or Worship Science as a God

"A scientist is someone who sometimes wants to believe more than God. Because he believes that with the intelligence that he has, he believes that he is more than God," a woman who goes to a largely Latino Catholic church[24] told us in Spanish. "Sometimes," she later added, "I feel like scientists want to be more than God."

To some religious believers, scientists seem like "know-it-alls" who see themselves as God-like. A woman in her early fifties[25] who attends a largely African American congregation explained, like Janelle, whom we met at the beginning of this chapter, many religious believers think scientists today tend to value science above all else. When asked if she thought scientists were hostile to religion, a home-school teacher[26] who attends a largely African American church in Houston said,

> I think it depends on what period of history I'm thinking of, because Sir Isaac Newton was a devout Christian and an incredible scientist, of course. We owe a large bulk of our present knowledge to him. But when I think of a modern-day scientist, I think of a person who thinks that their knowledge is their God. And that's what I also think of, is that they think they can reason away God.

What, then, would an "ideal" scientist think and believe? Many religious individuals we talked with felt that the "ideal" scientist strives for objective knowledge, but they doubt whether scientists can ever fully escape their biases. A middle-aged evangelical engineer,[27] who considers himself a scientist, told us he hopes scientists are objective, but they are "people too. So, they have faults

like the rest of us do. So they may not be entirely objective, although that is supposedly the goal."

Those who are most suspicious of scientists believe scientists today are far
from following the objective ideal: that they will simply disregard information
that does not support their pet theories and instead cherry-pick data to support their views. Randall,[28] whom we met in the previous chapter, said that even
though he felt scientists strive for objective knowledge, they often fall short of
that ideal. Their own inclinations often shape their work and accounts of the
world, and it is impossible for them to be completely free of bias. In his words,

> Scientists are flawed human beings like everybody else. So, science as the sort
> of ideal ... isn't always done that way; which is one of the reasons that it's really
> important to replicate things.... . When you want things to be a certain way,
> there's a tendency to see them that way, and to be careful about what sorts of
> things you accept and don't accept, and that's going to skew results. And we're
> human beings, we're going to do that kind of stuff.

Other religious believers we spoke with expressed the idea that the ideal scientist is one who is open or sympathetic to religious beliefs. One evangelical in
Chicago we interviewed[29] said,

> I don't know who the ideal scientist is. Isaac Newton was sort of [it] for me. Again
> they say that Isaac Newton's journals, on one page were his scientific notes and on
> the opposite page were notes from the Bible. And his approach to science, he said,
> was: "I am thinking God's thoughts after Him."

Another evangelical man in Houston,[30] who expressed a similar sentiment, said,

> I believe that a true scientist is a man of infinite curiosity, who loves to learn, who
> is a lifelong student of the creation and all that that means around him. I believe
> he is a man who has not divorced the secular and the sacred, which is never
> meant to be divorced. Science and the world of the spirit should exist in won-
> derful harmony because God has created everything that is. God is the original
> scientist. If you look at a nebula, if you look into a microscope at an atom, you
> will see God working in both of those places. Science commits itself to inquiry,
> rigorous inquiry, through process.... . Science and the world of the spirit are at
> odds only to the degree that men of science and women of science do not see
> their harmony. And I think one of the great challenges of the brilliant people who
> devote themselves to the world of science is to continue in great humility to see
> the hand of God behind everything.

LESSONS

Increase Positive Interactions Between Religious Believers and Scientists

We have found that religious believers in the United States are more likely to have heard of Richard Dawkins, a scientist who crusades against religion, than they are to be aware of Francis Collins, who sees his scientific work as compatible with his belief in God and Christian faith. We also found that a number of religious believers think scientists as a group are hostile to religion. Would that change if more of these believers were aware of Collins and his views? Not necessarily. *Greater awareness of Collins alone, without being able to point to a number of other scientists, whom they actually know personally and seem open to religious ideas, might not be all that helpful in changing perceptions.* If religious individuals are given the impression that Collins is a special case, it might serve to reinforce or even amplify their perception that most scientists are hostile to religion.

Instead, religious believers need their faith leaders to celebrate the scientists within their congregations, and they need these scientists to speak out about how scientific knowledge is not a threat to their faith. The lesson from this chapter is that those looking to build bridges between religious believers and scientists must not necessarily change how religious people perceive scientists, but rather how religious people think scientists perceive them.

Religious communities must also develop avenues through which religious people have greater access to scientific sources of information. As we have seen, religious identities and beliefs do not inherently turn individuals away from consumption of scientific information, yet a number of religious individuals approach their faith leaders with questions about science. Educational programs are needed to help faith leaders develop a foundational fluency in scientific topics. New mechanisms are needed to expose religious leaders to scientists and scientific sources of information, so that they are better equipped to guide their congregants on scientific questions. Scientists and science communicators can also help by expanding their venues for science outreach to religious communities and congregations. For example, the results here suggest that in a highly religious context such as the United States, places that are not typically thought of as a venue for science education—evangelical churches—may be an important venue for reaching new audiences. New mechanisms, such as partnering with religious leaders who receive questions from their congregations, may provide a new basis for outreach.

While the risks are high, so too may be the reward for expanding our conception of where people turn to learn about science. There may be a deep sense of awe and beauty as well as an appreciation of wonder that people of faith and scientists share. According to one man who attends an African American church,[31]

[Scientists] are just individuals who are, I like to say, "blessed" with a sense of curiosity; . . . So you say, OK why is there a [beautiful] rainbow in the sky? So in the Biblical sense . . . it's God's covenant with Noah that "I will never flood the earth again." And then you say, "OK, well, that's fine, but why is the rainbow there? Why do you have different colors?" And then you go to Isaac Newton who discovered a prism, so that it reflects white lights into the different light spectrums of different colors. . . . So mathematics is a precise aspect of things, but—mathematics is [also] something that's revealed to me [by God].

NOTES

1. High SES Mainline Church Houston Int24, conducted November 11, 2012.

2. Schibeci, R. A. 1986. "Images of Science and Scientists and Science Education." *Science Education* 70(2): 139–149.

3. Garfield, E. 1978. "Scientists' Image in Movies and TV Programs." *Current Contexts* 10:5–12.

4. For a review of this research, see Finson, Kevin D. 2002. "Drawing a Scientist: What We Do and Do Not Know After Fifty Years of Drawings." *School Science and Mathematics* 102(7):335–345. The classic study in this area is Margaret Mead and Rhoda Metraux's 1957 article, "Image of the Scientist Among High-School Students: A Pilot Study," in *Science* (Vol. 126, pp. 384–390).

5. Mid-High/High SES Evangelical Church Houston Int2, conducted July 25, 2012.

6. Withey, Stephen B. 1959. "Public Opinion About Science and Scientists." *Public Opinion Quarterly* 23(3):382–388.

7. See http://www.pewsocialtrends.org/2008/12/02/americans-say-they-like-diverse-communities-election-census-trends-suggest-otherwise/, accessed November 25, 2016.

8. See "Political Polarization in the American Public." 2014. Pew Research Center. Accessed at http://www.people-press.org/2014/06/12/political-polarization-in-the-american-public/.

9. See Bishop, Bill. 2008. *The Big Sort: Why the Clustering of Like-Minded America Is Tearing Us Apart.* Boston and New York: Mariner Books of Houghton Mifflin Harcourt.

10. See McPherson, Miller, Lynn Smith-Lovin, and James M. Cook. 2001. "Birds of a Feather: Homophily in Social Networks." *Annual Review of Sociology* 27:415–444.

11. The full question wording was "How scientific do you view each of the following occupations?" Respondents were then provided 13 occupations to rate: biologist, engineer, plumber, anthropologist, TV weather forecaster, high school chemistry teacher, psychologist, physician, pastor/minister/clergyperson, electrician, sociologist, and nurse. The respondent rated each occupation as either very scientific, somewhat scientific, a little scientific, or not at all scientific.

12. It might be surprising to some readers that the percentages for biology and physics are not even higher. This is likely a function of some survey respondents being hesitant to pick more extreme responses, which is called the central tendency bias. So, even though respondents might see physics and biology as clearly the most scientific occupations, they feel the need to hedge their responses somewhat.

13. Van Biema, David. 2006. "God vs. Science." *Time,* November 5. Retrieved October 1, 2014, http://content.time.com/time/magazine/article/0,9171,1555132,00.html. See also Scheitle, Christopher P., and Elaine Howard Ecklund. 2015. "The Influence of Science Popularizers on the Public's View of Religion and Science: An Experimental Assessment." *Public Understanding of Science,* doi: 10.1177/0963662515588432.

14. Mid-High/High SES Evangelical Church Houston Int9, conducted August 16, 2012.

15. Mid-High SES Sunni Muslim Mosque Chicago Int2, conducted July 16, 2013.

16. Mid-High SES Orthodox Jewish Synagogue Chicago Int10, conducted July 21, 2013.

17. Mid-High/High SES Evangelical Church Houston Int5, conducted July 5, 2011.

18. Mid-High/High SES Catholic Church Houston Int8, conducted October 16, 2013.

19. High SES Mainline Protestant Church Houston Int12, conducted March 16, 2012.

20. Low/Mid-Low SES Evangelical Church Houston Int1, conducted August 15, 2013.

21. High SES Evangelical Church Houston Int3, conducted July 18, 2012.

22. Mid-High/High SES Evangelical Church Houston Int16, conducted December 8, 2011.

23. We offered nine sources overall and the respondents rated their likelihood of consulting each as very, somewhat, not very, or not at all likely. The nine sources were (1) a general Internet source, such as Wikipedia; (2) a scientific magazine, such as *National Geographic, Discover, Smithsonian, Popular Science,* or *Scientific American*; (3) a book written by a PhD scientist; (4) a person working in a scientific occupation; (5) a teacher at a local school or college; (6) a friend of a family member; (7) a religious text; (8) a religious leader; and (9) other people at your religious congregation.

24. Mid-Low SES Catholic Church Chicago Int4, conducted June 22, 2012.

25. Mid-High/High SES Evangelical Church Houston Int9, conducted August 16, 2012.

26. Mid-High/High SES Evangelical Church Houston Int17, conducted December 13, 2011.

27. High SES Evangelical Church Houston Int5, conducted July 22, 2012.

28. Mid-High SES Evangelical Church Chicago Int9, conducted June 23, 2012.

29. Mid-High SES Evangelical Church Chicago Int5, conducted June 21, 2012.

30. High SES Evangelical Church Houston Int6, conducted July 23, 2012.

31. Mid-High/High SES Evangelical Church Houston Int8, conducted August 16, 2012.

CHAPTER 4

Religious People Are Not Scientists

Religion is based on dogma and belief, whereas science is based on doubt and questioning. In religion, faith is a virtue. In science, faith is a vice.

—Jerry Coyne*

Science without religion is lame, religion without science is blind.

—Albert Einstein**

We first meet Blythe early one Sunday morning at a woman's Bible study group. She stands out—about 10 years younger than the other women and wearing nearly black lipstick. She doesn't say much during the class, so we are surprised when she volunteers to speak with us in depth about her experiences negotiating her Christian faith and her work as a scientist.

Blythe is a professor and a neurophysiologist, which means she conducts high-level studies of the nervous system in order to figure out defects. She grew up in a rural community where going to church "was just kind of what everyone did," she says. "Both of my parents were in leadership positions in the church." For Blythe, church "was a positive experience," and her faith laid the groundwork for her pursuit of science. Today, she sees her faith as influencing her understanding of science, explaining,

> You look at DNA or at neurologic systems and you look at the amount of order that is actually in those systems, it's just remarkable.... Things generally become less ordered, they degrade and they become more random ... so to think that things become more ordered ... goes against one of the basic premises of science, and so you have to think, "How did this just happen? How did all this order occur randomly?" Because it's not how we think of things working. And so, somebody who doesn't have a faith background doesn't really understand that perhaps there's a creator, someone who created all the order.

Blythe also understands that "you have to leave your biases behind whenever you do science and you really have to look at the data for what the data is, and you can't bring [in] any kind of preconceived ideas when you do studies."

As Blythe sees it, faith and science can be deeply integrated, and yet she sometimes feels that she cannot talk openly about her work as a scientist inside her church. In particular, she expresses frustration at fellow members of her congregation whose understanding of their faith causes conflict with scientific knowledge:

> [T]here are some people in the church that are very dogmatic. They say the Bible says [the earth] was [created] in one day, two days, three days and those are 24-hour days and they're very dogmatic about that. . . . [B]ecause there's no science to say that dinosaurs and man coexisted . . . the dinosaurs would have been created on the fourth day and man would have been created on the sixth day, and so you would have to say that the dinosaurs lived for 48 hours, which is just kind of ridiculous. . . . Some people get so hung up on the words.

Blythe approaches the biblical story of creation differently, seeing the "days" of creation as what she calls "creative periods." Yet, even though she disagrees with the more "dogmatic" views of some members of her church, she can understand where they are coming from. "I think a lot of people have the fear that, you know, [finding out about evolution] is going to degrade the basis of what they believe in, and that's frightening for a lot of people because they've been taught these things their whole life and put their stock in them," she says. "It's hard to let go of that."

MYTH: RELIGIOUS PEOPLE AREN'T SCIENTISTS

To many observers, both religious and nonreligious, Blythe represents an oxymoron: religious scientist. Yet when we look back in history, we see that many early modern scientists were Christians—for example, faith and belief in God were motivating factors for Copernicus, Faraday, Galileo, and Newton.[1] Considerable research has also shed light on the flourishing pursuit of science in the early centuries of Islam.[2] Vital contributions to astronomy, algebra, geometry, and medicine are credited to prominent Islamic scholars such as Al-Khwarizmi, Al-Kindi, Omar Khayyam, and Ibn al-Nafis. So where did the idea that "religious people aren't scientists" come from?

The assumption that religious individuals do not go into science occupations—or do not remain religious after they gain scientific knowledge—can be seen as the natural consequence of the presumption that "religious people do not like science" and that "religious people do not like *scientists*." After all, why would someone pursue an education or career in something that they are not interested in or view as an enemy to the beliefs and behaviors they hold so dear? Yet the intellectual roots of the assumption that religious people aren't scientists go deeper and are more complex than they might at first seem.

The myth that scientists are all atheists—or should be atheists—has deep roots in history. When asked why they think there might be a conflict between being religious and being a scientist, both religious individuals and scientists mention Galileo, who discovered that the earth revolved around the sun, not the other way around. For this theory, which the Catholic Church felt contradicted Scripture, some believe Galileo was persecuted and found guilty of heresy.[3]

In the early 20th century, scholars who championed the myth that religious people aren't scientists sought support for this view through surveys of particular groups of scientists. The psychologist James Leuba argued that religion was a creation of the human imagination rather than a rational response to a divinely ordered cosmos, and he reasoned that scientists—as those who know the most about the natural world—would be the first to apprehend this truth. Consequently, they would be the least likely to believe in God or attend church. Surveying the members of the National Academy of Sciences, the most elite scientific body in the United States, Leuba did indeed find that these scientists were generally much less religious than other Americans. He reasoned that it was only a matter of time before science would overtake religion.[4]

Today, there are a number of prominent scientists—many of them prolific writers who belong to the New Atheist movement—who support the idea that religion is irrational and incompatible with science. And this idea sells. *The God Delusion*, by the well-known evolutionary biologist Richard Dawkins, stayed on the *New York Times'* list of top 10 best-selling titles for 16 weeks. The neuroscientist Sam Harris's *Letter to a Christian Nation* was on a *New York Times* list of best-selling hardcover books for 7 weeks, while his previous book, *The End of Faith*, was on the *New York Times'* best-selling paperback list for 29 weeks. When we interviewed university scientists for a separate research study, we found they too often think being religious is inconsistent with being a scientist. As one biology professor[5] expressed,

> I guess my own bias is [that religious scientists] might be a little closed off to certain possibilities because they have some preformed possibilities. Whereas as

a scientist, I think you need to have a very open mind to look at all the data and interpret it no matter which direction it's going to take you. So, if I had evidence saying that the Earth was a certain age and I'm faced with that evidence, but I have a bias that the Earth cannot be that age, then I think the nonreligious person would probably consider the possibility that the data is saying what it's saying [but a religious person might not].

Similarly, other scientists referenced specific colleagues whose faith convictions become problematic for their scientific work. For instance, one graduate student in biology[6] told us about a colleague who is seen as

all about God all the time, and Jesus; all Jesus all the time. She is very vocal about it and often she will say how God is great or like, "thank you, Jesus," for like doing blah, blah, blah thing or she'll read an interesting paper and she will say, "Oh, this biochemical process is really interesting and it just shows how God's work is just so good." And I'm, like, it makes no sense [*laughs*], because I would not come to that same conclusion if I read that paper. . . . [Scientists who are religious] are either very quiet because they know their colleagues will ridicule them or will question their scientific work and their objectivity or they're like her where they just don't question their own objectivity and they don't think [their faith] affects their direct line of work . . . but I definitely see that there's a conflict in how she's able to understand things. Her work is good for what it is, but it's never going to get past some level of reflection because of [her faith].

Can a scientist be deeply religious? As we see, not all scientists are atheists. But how common are religious scientists? Are the majority cold and hyperrational, with zero interest in or high levels of hostility toward religion? Answering these questions is somewhat tricky.

REALITY: THERE ARE RELIGIOUS SCIENTISTS (ESPECIALLY OUTSIDE OF ELITE UNIVERSITIES)

It is actually fairly difficult to define who counts as a "scientist." Does having a particular educational degree make one a scientist? If so, what degree level counts (i.e., is a master's degree enough, or does one need a doctorate)? And which specific disciplines count? Or is it the actual occupation or work performed that makes someone a scientist? If so, which occupations count? These questions produce much debate but little agreement. As a 2014 Congressional Research Service report noted, "Most experts agree that there is no authoritative definition of which occupations comprise the science . . . workforce."[7]

Elite University Scientists

Let us start with a fairly restrictive definition of who counts as a scientist: individuals with doctorates working as professors in elite universities in the three natural science fields—physics, biology, and chemistry. This is the definition that has been used by most past research, including our own earlier work, that looked at scientists' religiosity. When we conducted a large survey that looked at religiosity among American elite university scientists[8] compared to the general US population, the differences between the two groups were fairly stark. Only 11% of chemists, 7% of biologists, and 6% of physicists stated they have no doubts about God's existence compared with 63% of US adults. At the other extreme, slightly more than 40% of physicists and biologists and about 27% of chemists said they unequivocally do not believe in God compared with about 2% of US adults. So not all natural scientists at US elite universities are atheists, but they certainly are quite religiously different from the general population, at least on traditional measures of what it means to be religious.

It may be that religious individuals who enter science occupations do not end up in elite professor positions. Surveys of professors more broadly reveal that professors in the humanities (e.g., English, history) and social sciences (e.g., psychology, political science) are just as irreligious as those in the natural sciences, and in some disciplines they are even less likely to be religious.[9] *This suggests that irreligiosity among elite US academic scientists could be more a function of who reaches elite university professor positions than a specific dynamic between religion and science.*[10]

It is also important to recognize that just because scientists at elite universities are less religious then the general public, it does not mean that they are actively hostile toward religion. Across our studies—which include surveying more than 14,000 scientists and interviewing nearly 900 scientists over 10 years—we can count on two hands the number of atheist scientists we met who have the same attitude toward religious people as Richard Dawkins or Sam Harris has. Their views on religion are not typical. And it is also important to note that when we ask them about their backgrounds and religious histories, nonreligious scientists rarely point to science itself as the main reason they are not religious.

Scientists Who Are Spiritual

In our survey of elite university scientists, we not only asked what they believe about God, but also asked, "Do you consider yourself a spiritual person?" We found that more than 22% of atheist scientists and more than 27% of agnostic scientists are still interested in spirituality. In other words, many scientists who are not religious in the traditional sense or do not believe in God still see themselves as spiritual. According to one,[11]

> If anything my own spirituality might be closer to almost an Eastern kind of tradition than a Western tradition, even though I was raised a Catholic. I feel a little more comfortable with certain Eastern ideas about individuality as an illusion. When I think about death, for example, I think about it's the end of me, but whatever me was before it was me is going to go back to that. I like this parable of the water going over the waterfall and all these droplets pop out of the water and as they're going down the waterfall they're individual droplets; when they get to the bottom, they go back to the stream. And so these kinds of ideas give me comfort when I think about mortality, but they're not really ideas about a god or anything. But they are ideas about before and after and meaning of life as it is being lived now and that sort of thing.

In our interviews we learned that many of these scientists also saw their work exploring the mysteries of the natural world and the cosmos as spiritual in one way or another. As one physicist[12] said, "The spirituality part of it . . . is why you do the work. I mean I'm interested in understanding how the universe began, possibly what its long-term future is going to be. I think those are certainly spiritual questions." Some scientists even suggest that *not* believing in God allows them to admire and exalt the natural world in this way.

Religion in Scientific Work

Our research on scientists at elite universities also found that there is a sizable minority of scientists—about 20%—who think that, although the scientific method ought to be value-neutral, religion is potentially helpful in understanding the moral implications of scientific work (providing a justification for fighting poverty or global warming, for example). They also think their students ought to understand religiously based forms of science ethics alongside ethical-moral value systems derived from naturalism. One scientist[13] we spoke with, who described herself as Jewish, believes university students have to learn to "take responsibility for the ways in which their beliefs and values affect other people," and they must understand how other people's beliefs and values might affect their research. She strongly believes this kind of dialogue should begin among communities of scientists in the academy, who ought to have "discussions and debates about how we might better address the kinds of things that religion brings up."

Rank-and-File Scientists

What if instead of looking at elite academic scientists we look at individuals who are educated and trained in science and who work in science-related occupations but are outside universities? We might think of these individuals as "rank-and-file" scientists.

Our survey of US adults included a couple of questions that might be utilized to identify rank-and-file scientists. One question asked survey respondents whether they think their "current occupation is science-related?" As seen in table 4.1, about 14% of US adults view their occupation as science-related. Jews, adherents of non-Western faiths, and the religiously unaffiliated are significantly more likely than the general population to have this perception. Mainline Protestants and Catholics are slightly less likely than the general population to say they are in a science-related occupation, while evangelicals do not *statistically* differ from the overall percentage, although their percentage is superficially slightly lower. Once we adjust for differences between the religious groups, particularly in educational attainment, we find that the members of different religious groups are equally likely to say they are working in a science-related occupation.[14] In other words, if we were to compare two similarly educated individuals (e.g., both college educated) from two different religious groups, we would not have reason to expect that one would be more likely than the other to say they are working in a science-related occupation. Religion may *indirectly* play a role by influencing the level of education an individual receives and, hence, whether that person is qualified for a science-related occupation— but religion does not seem to directly influence whether a person goes into a science-related occupation.

Our survey respondents also chose 1 of 29 occupational sectors to best represent their specific occupation.[15] Several of these classification options represent "scientists" in a broad definition of the word. One option was "Life, Physical, and Social Sciences." Beyond this sector, there are many occupations—such as doctor, engineer, nurse—that involve a great deal of science in their education and training requirements and day-to-day activities. For that reason, we consider four other occupational sectors: the Computer and Mathematical, the Architecture and Engineering, the Medical Doctor, and the other Health Care Practitioner sectors. The percentage of individuals

TABLE 4.1 Measures Used to Identify Rank-and-File Scientists by Religious Group

		All US Adults (a)	Evangelical Protestants (b)	Mainline Protestants	Catholics	Jews	Non-Western Religions	Atheists, Agnostic, Unaffiliated
"Would you say your current occupation is science-related?"—Yes	Unadjusted	13.8%	12.4%	11.9%[a]	11.6%[a]	20.6%[ab]	31.1%[ab]	18.6%[ab]
	Adjusted	9.6%	10.6%	9.1%	8.7%	11.9%	10.3%	9.6%
In one of five science-related occupational sectors	Unadjusted	7.6%	5.8%[a]	6.4%[a]	6.1%[a]	10.9%[b]	21.3%[ab]	13.1%[ab]
	Adjusted	3.0%	2.7%	2.8%	2.8%	2.9%	4.5%	4.0%[ab]

a = Difference between percentage and all other US adults is statistically significant (p < .05).

b = Difference between percentage and percentage for evangelical Protestants is statistically significant (p < .05).

Source: Religious Understandings of Science, 2014. Adjusted percentages account for any influence from differences in education, political ideology, income, sex, age, region of residence, and race between the religious groups.

in one of these five occupational sectors across religious groups is shown in table 4.1. The patterns are fairly similar to what we saw with the questions asking whether the survey respondent thinks of their occupation as science-related. Jews, the religiously unaffiliated, and adherents of non-Western religious traditions are all more likely than the general US adult population to be in these science-related sectors, while Christians are slightly less likely to be in these sectors.

For our purposes here, we're going to define "rank-and-file scientists"[16] as those who think of their occupation as science-related *and* who are working in one of these five occupational sectors. If a person works in one of the five scientific sectors but does not see the job as related to science, then we do not consider that person a scientist. Similarly, an individual who works in the food industry would not be considered a scientist by our definition, even if the person thinks the job is a science-related occupation.

The percentage of individuals we define as rank-and-file scientists in the general US population and within each religious group is shown in table 4.2. Among all of our survey respondents, just over 4% qualify as rank-and-file scientists based on our definition.[17] Similarly, we see that about 3% to 4% of Christians qualify as rank-and-file scientists. Members of other religious groups are significantly more likely to be rank-and-file scientists—Jews (8%), adherents of non-Western faiths (14%), and the religiously unaffiliated (about 7%). As we see when we look at the adjusted percentages, however, these differences are mostly a result of other social and demographic differences between the groups, especially discrepancies in education.

Another interesting way to analyze the data in table 4.2 is to flip the rows and columns so that we can see the distribution of religions within rank-and-file scientists. In other words, instead of asking what percentage of evangelicals are rank-and-file scientists, we now ask what percentage of rank-and-file scientists are evangelicals. This view is shown in table 4.3. In this table, we see that Jews, adherents of non-Western religions, and the religiously unaffiliated are more highly represented among rank-and-file scientists than we would expect them to be based on their share of the survey respondents. For instance, adherents of non-Western religions are 2% of all survey respondents but 7% of rank-and-file scientists. We also see that evangelicals, mainline Protestants, and Catholics are somewhat *underrepresented* among rank-and-file scientists. Evangelicals, for example, comprise 24% of all survey respondents but 21% of rank-and-file scientists. These patterns are not surprising and—as we noted with table 4.1—these differences are mostly explained by differences in education level and other social and demographic factors between the religious groups.

TABLE 4.2 Summary Measure of Rank-and-File Scientists by Religious Group

		All US Adults (a)	Evangelical Protestants (b)	Mainline Protestants	Catholics	Jews	Non-Western Religions	Atheists, Agnostic, Unaffiliated
Percentage that are rank-and-file scientists	Unadjusted	4.4%	3.7%	4.0%	3.2%[a]	8.3%[ab]	14.1%[ab]	6.5%[ab]
	Adjusted	1.0%	1.1%	1.0%	0.8%	1.1%	1.6%	1.0%

a = Difference between percentage and percentage for all US adults is statistically significant (p < .05).
b = Difference between percentage and percentage for evangelical Protestants is statistically significant (p < .05).
Source: Religious Understandings of Science, 2014. Adjusted percentages account for any influence from differences in political ideology, education, income, sex, age, region of residence, and race between the religious groups. A rank-and-file scientist is defined as identifying as working in a science-related occupation and working in one of the five sectors identified in the text.

TABLE 4.3 Religious Composition of Rank-and-File Scientists Compared with the Overall Population

	Rank-and-File Scientists	All Respondents	Difference
Evangelical Protestant	21%	24%	−3%
Mainline Protestant	26%	30%	−4%
Catholic	18%	26%	−8%
Jewish	4%	2%	+2%
Non-Western adherent	8%	2%	+6%
Atheist, agnostic, unaffiliated	24%	16%	+8%

Source: Religious Understandings of Science, 2014. A rank-and-file scientist is defined as identifying as working in a science-related occupation and working in one of the five sectors identified in the text.

All in all, 65% of rank-and-file scientists are Christians, and almost 21% identify as evangelical. We also find that 16% of rank-and-file scientists identify as "very religious" compared with 19% of the general population. Rank-and-file scientists are also similar to the general population on other religious measures: 19% of these scientists read a religious text weekly or nearly weekly compared with 22% of the overall population, and 41% of rank-and-file scientists pray several times a week or more compared with 52% of the general population. We see the biggest gap when it comes to certainty of belief in God. Forty percent of rank-and-file scientists state they have no doubts about their belief in God compared with 57% of the general population. But overall the religiosity of the American science community looks very different (*and much more like the general population*) when we look at rank-and-file scientists rather than the scientists working at elite universities.

REALITY: RELIGIOUS SCIENTISTS ARE OFTEN STUCK BETWEEN OTHER HUMANS AND GOD

Our past research surveying and interviewing religious scientists who work at the top universities shows they often face challenges in dealing with their religious peers as well as their scientific peers. Forty-nine percent of religious scientists at elite universities feel their scientific colleagues do not view religion positively. "I think universities are not always very accepting environments," one physicist[18] told us, explaining, "It is really hard to be a religious academic because the public opinion is such that you're either religious or you're a scientist! To say you are religious might mean other scientists would question your work."[19]

And religious scientists also find they are more questioning and less open about their faith than the people they sit alongside in the pews. "I think some of my fellow Roman Catholics might accept many things at face value . . . finding religious imagery in natural phenomena . . . [whereas] being a scientist makes me want to raise objections like, 'Well, does this grilled cheese sandwich really look like Jesus?' " said a chemist.[20] When Elaine's own congregation recently tried a program called Scientists in Congregations, designed to encourage scientists to talk openly about their work in the context of their congregations,[21] concerns were expressed almost immediately by the scientists in the congregation. They feared some in the church would get angry and defensive about what they perceived to be threats to their views about the Bible, especially the creation story of Adam and Eve. These scientists wondered whether some congregants would think the materials were too "pro-science" and not "pro-faith" enough. In particular, one scientist on the planning committee said he was concerned that, even in this highly educated community, if congregants really knew what he does as a scientist, some might distance themselves from him, assuming he has different faith beliefs.

Many religious scientists do not feel comfortable discussing their scientific work within their congregations, nor do they feel comfortable talking about their faith within their work environments. This results in a level of secrecy that can lead to the perception that there are no religious scientists.

When we look at our survey data, we find evidence that evangelical rank-and-file scientists are in fact often distinct from both their religious and scientific peers. As noted in the previous chapter, when we asked our survey respondents whether they saw science and religion as being in conflict, independent of each other, or in collaboration with each other, we found that 14% of US adults view science and religion as being in conflict and see themselves as on the side of religion. Among evangelicals, the percentage of those who share this view more than doubles—to 29%. But, as seen in table 4.4, when we look at evangelicals *who are also scientists*, we find that this group is half as likely as the general evangelical population to see themselves on the religion

TABLE 4.4 Relationship Between Religion and Science Among Four Groups

	US Adults (a)	Rank-and-File Scientists (b)	Evangelical Protestants (c)	Evangelical Rank-and-File Scientists (d)
Conflict—I'm on the side of religion.	14%[bc]	4%[acd]	29%[abd]	14%[bc]
Conflict—I'm on the side of science.	13%[bcd]	21%[acd]	1%[ab]	2%[ab]
Independence— They refer to different aspects of reality.	35%[cd]	34%[cd]	21%[ab]	17%[ab]
Collaboration— Each can be used to help support the other.	38%[cd]	41%[d]	48%[ad]	67%[abc]

a = Percentage is significantly different from US adult percentage (p < .05).
b = Percentage is significantly different from rank-and-file scientist percentage (p < .05).
c = Percentage is significantly different from evangelical Protestant percentage (p <. 05).
d = Percentage is significantly different from evangelical rank-and-file scientist percentage (p < .05).
Source: Religious Understandings of Science, 2014. A rank-and-file scientist is defined as identifying as working in a science-related occupation and working in one of the five sectors identified in the text.

side of a science and religion conflict.[22] But it is most important to notice that *evangelical rank-and-file scientists are significantly more likely than all rank-and-file scientists and all evangelicals to say that they see religion and science as in collaboration with each other.* (This makes sense from a psychological perspective. If a person holds both a religious identity and a scientific identity, then the individual will likely want to see those identities as working together rather than being in conflict.)

Our interviews confirmed that religious rank-and-file scientists often see, or at least desire, collaboration between science and faith. "I think that the church needs basically to drop its fear of science. Both the church and science are interested in the truth," one evangelical scientist said. "Now, they are a little bit different aspects of the truth, but I don't think that either side needs to view the other antagonistically. And I understand how science feels because of some of the past oppressions from the church. So, maybe there needs to be a little forgiveness . . . on both sides."[23]

And when asked about the relationship between religion and science, a Reform Jewish scientist told us, "I think there's room for both in the explanation of biological or chemical or physical processes. It's a way that religion can be the missing link or the explanation for the scientific occurrences that we cannot explain. So I think they're compatible."[24] Another Jewish scientist, from an Orthodox synagogue, said that "religion tells you what should be done and why—namely, that you have to take care of the poor and the sick. Science provides techniques for doing that."[25]

Do evangelical scientists have different ideas about how religious people view science and how scientists view religion? As seen in table 4.5, 19% of all US adults agree that most religious people are hostile to science and 22% agree that most scientists are hostile to religion. Rank-and-file scientists as a whole actually mirror these percentages, while evangelicals are significantly less likely to agree that religious people are hostile to science (11%) and significantly more likely to agree that scientists are hostile to religion (36%). Like their evangelical peers, evangelical rank-and-file scientists are also less likely to agree that religious people are hostile to science. *But* they are significantly more likely than their evangelical peers to think that scientists are hostile to religion.

At first blush, this seems somewhat surprising. We might suppose that religious scientists would be less likely to think scientists are hostile to religion—not only because they are religious themselves, but also because they likely work closely and develop personal relationships with other scientists. It is possible, though, that evangelical scientists have heard negative comments or observed certain actions that give them the impression their colleagues are hostile to religion. When we asked our survey respondents if they have ever "felt discriminated against in [their] work life because of [their] religion?" 17% said they have experienced at least some workplace religious discrimination, as seen in table 4.5.[26] Evangelicals, at 25%, are significantly more likely to report workplace religious discrimination than the general population. Among rank-and-file scientists as a whole, 25% say they have experienced religious discrimination at work. When we zoom in on evangelical rank-and-file scientists, we find that this group claims even higher levels of workplace religious discrimination at 35%.

TABLE 4.5 Comparing Perceptions of Hostility and Discrimination Across Four Groups

	US Adults (a)	Rank-and-File Scientists (b)	Evangelical Protestants (c)	Evangelical Rank-and-File Scientists (d)
Strongly agree or agree: Most religious people are hostile to science.	19%[cd]	21%[cd]	11%[ab]	9%[ab]
Strongly agree or agree: Most scientists are hostile to religion.	22%[cd]	23%[cd]	36%[abd]	48%[abc]
Ever discriminated against due to religion at work?	17%[bcd]	25%[ad]	25%[ad]	35%[abc]

a = Percentage is significantly different from US adult percentage (p<.05).
b = Percentage is significantly different from rank-and-file scientist percentage (p < .05).
c = Percentage is significantly different from evangelical Protestant percentage (p < .05).
d = Percentage is significantly different from evangelical rank-and-file scientist percentage (p < .05).

Source: Religious Understandings of Science, 2014. A rank-and-file scientist is defined as identifying as working in a science-related occupation and working in one of the five sectors identified in the text.

LESSONS

Broaden the Definition of "Scientist"

The idea that religious people are not scientists is a myth. Historically, when researchers have studied religiosity among American scientists, they have focused on professors at elite universities. This research, including our own work, has indeed shown that such scientists are much less personally religious than the general US public.[27] However, our research also shows that it is actually fairly difficult to find university scientists who are strongly antireligion. What's more, a closer look at scientists at elite US universities reveals that many have substantial interest in spirituality and see themselves as spiritual.[28] There is also evidence that the irreligiosity among scientists at elite universities is not really a function of the direct relationship between science and religion.

We also find that when we broaden the definition of a scientist to include individuals working in scientific occupations outside of universities, who have generally been ignored in past research, we find they are much closer to the general population when it comes to traditional measures of religiosity. More research is needed to examine the religious views of these rank-and-file scientists, and to explore how they differ from their religious and scientific peers in their religious beliefs and practices and in their views on the religion and science relationship.

Religious Scientists Need to Serve as Bridge Builders

We also find through our interviews that religious scientists often face scrutiny, judgment, and unfair assumptions from their colleagues and fellow congregants. Both religious individuals and scientists need to play a role in addressing the myths surrounding how scientists approach religion. Religious scientists, despite their hesitancy and concerns, can serve as a bridge between the two communities. Consider the Scientists in Congregations program, which we mentioned earlier. We described the fears that scientists expressed about sharing their scientific knowledge and faith beliefs with their fellow congregants. But what came of those fears?

Over three years, the congregation ran a series of programs aimed at youth and adults. Scientists within the congregation did share the work they do and their views on science and faith. The congregation also brought in top-notch scientists from around the world to speak about a number of hot-button issues: God and origins, evolution and creation, what it means to be alive, what it means to be human, and how—and why—we should think about the relationship between science and faith.

Despite the initial fears, the program was successful on multiple levels. The turnout to adult-education classes tripled during the time of the initiative. Youth participants brought up for discussion very real tensions between faith and science. Even the most theologically conservative congregants were open to the program and were willing, at worst, to civilly agree to disagree.

One church member said that wrestling with divisive issues related to science and faith during the program provided her with models she can use to "stay in the conversation without walking away" when faced with potentially divisive issues in the future. According to her, the experience was particularly meaningful because "the scientists were also church members, people we know and trust."

A scientist on the planning committee said the experience was life-changing for him. "I always thought of my work [as a scientist] as completely separate from my actual faith or something that needed to 'be dealt with,'" he explained. "But through presenting my own perspective on the compatibility, for me, between science and Christian faith, I came to see how my work and my Christian faith can be deeply integrated." The ultimate lesson of the program was this: While the congregation had invited some of the very best scientists in the world to discuss compatibilities between science and faith, the best ambassadors of the program and its efforts were not the scientists brought in from outside but rather the scientists in the pews. Religious scientists can help dispel myths other religious people hold about how scientists view religion by speaking up within their congregations, sharing their personal experiences, struggles, and successes integrating their science and faith. Synagogues, mosques, and churches also need to reach out to the scientists in their midst, inviting them to be leaders in adult religious education, to preach sermons and give teachings, and to have other public roles that will provide them with a more prominent voice in their faith communities.

Knowing One Scientist

We end with the story of Dellarobia Turnbow, a character in Barbara Kingsolver's[29] novel *Flight Behavior.* Dellarobia is a 28-year-old discontented housewife living in a small town in Appalachia. It's the kind of place where religion—a particular kind of conservative fundamentalism—reigns supreme, and science (if it is thought about at all) is devalued and even derided as being against religion, the kind of place where no one would think that a scientist could be a person of faith. The novel follows the story of this young woman as she learns more about science through her relationship with one scientist. Dellarobia is the first to discover millions of monarch butterflies that—because of global warming—have erroneously migrated to the Appalachian Mountains rather than Mexico. Dellarobia must suddenly negotiate the tension between the scientists who now flock to her small town to study the butterflies, who show her the power of science, and her church community, who believes she has witnessed the power of a miracle. This tension, between science and faith and the idea that if Dellarobia learns more about science she must let go of faith, is held together in Kingsolver's tale through Dellarobia's relationship with one scientist, Ovid Bryon. Ovid is a university professor who studies the monarchs. He doesn't poke fun of Dellarobia's faith, even accepting it. But he also warns that the butterflies are a disturbing symptom of climate change. In the end, Dellarobia keeps her faith, deciding that it is faith itself that ultimately motivates her to know the beauty of science in order to save the monarchs.

NOTES

* Connor, Steve. "For the Love of God . . . Scientists in Uproar at £1m Religion Prize," *The Independent*. Retrieved January 15, 2015, (http://www.independent.co.uk/news/science/for-the-love-of-god-scientists-in-uproar-at-1631m-religion-prize-2264181.html).

** See Jammer, Max. 2002. *Einstein and Religion: Physics and Theology*. Princeton, NJ: Princeton University Press.

1. For a more complicated discussion of one such scientist, see ibid. For a comprehensive account of the historical relationship between science and Christianity, see Lindberg, David C., and Ronald L. Numbers, eds. 1986. *God and Nature: Historical Essays on the Encounter Between Christianity and Science*. Berkeley: University of California Press.

2. See Lapidus, Ira M. 2014. *A History of Islamic Societies, Third Edition*. New York: Cambridge University Press. See also Sabra, A. I. 1996. "Situating Arabic Science: Locality Versus Essence." *Isis* 87(4):654–670.

3. See Machamer, Peter, ed. 1998. *The Cambridge Companion to Galileo*. Cambridge: Cambridge University Press. This volume contains a special focus on Galileo's relationship to the church. In addition, Maurice A. Finocchiaro persuasively dispels the myth that Galileo was incarcerated and tortured for his scientific work. See Finocchiaro, Maurice A. 2009. "Myth 8. That Galileo Was Imprisoned and Tortured for Advocating Copernicanism": pp. 68–78 in *Galileo Goes to Jail and Other Myths About Science and Religion*, edited by Ronald Numbers. Cambridge, MA: Harvard

University Press. It should be noted here that Richard J. Blackwell has argued that this view is an "oversimplified and false view ... [when] the church had understandable reasons for refusing to reinterpret the Bible in Galileo's favor" (Ferngren, Gary B. 2002. *Science and Religion: A Historical Introduction*. Baltimore, MD: Johns Hopkins University Press, p. 105). There is a growing literature that challenges the conflict narrative. See, for example, Giberson, Karl, and Mariano Artigas. 2006. *Oracles of Science: Celebrity Scientists Versus God and Religion*. Oxford: Oxford University Press; Evans, John H., and Michael S. Evans. 2008. "Religion and Science: Beyond the Epistemological Conflict Narrative." *Annual Review of Sociology* 34:87–105; and Collins, Francis S. 2007. *The Language of God: A Scientist Presents Evidence for Belief*. New York: Free Press.

4. Leuba, James H. 1934. "Religious Beliefs of American Scientists." *Harper's Magazine*, August, p. 300. See also Ecklund, Elaine Howard. 2010. *Science vs. Religion: What Scientists Really Think*. New York: Oxford University Press.

5. RASIC US BIO 41—Female, Biology, Professor, conducted April 3, 2015.

6. RASIC US BIO 03—Female, Biology, Graduate Student, conducted March 2, 2015.

7. Sargent, John F. Jr. 2014. "The U.S. Science and Engineering Workforce: Recent, Current, and Projected Employment, Wages, and Unemployment." *Congressional Research Service* R43061.

8. This study also surveyed social scientists in psychology, economics, and sociology. We do not include them here simply because we are aware that some would question whether these should be considered "pure" scientists, and we are starting here with the most restrictive definition we can.

9. See, for instance, Gross, Neil, and Solon Simmons. 2009. "The Religiosity of American College and University Professors." *Sociology of Religion* 70(2):101–129. This research also showed that professors in education, business, and health-related disciplines have higher levels of religiosity compared with the social sciences, humanities, and natural sciences. This corresponds to research on the religiosity of undergraduates, such as Christopher P. Scheitle's 2010 study, "Religious and Spiritual Change in College: Assessing the Effect of a Science Education" in *Sociology of Education* 84(2):122–136. This research found that undergraduates in business, education, and professional fields (primarily health-related) scored higher on measures of religious commitment compared with the overall student population. Students in natural sciences, however, were comparable to the overall student population. The only students that experienced a significant reduction in religious commitment over the course of their college studies were those in the arts and humanities.

10. Some have argued the conflict between religion and science does extend more broadly than just the natural and physical sciences. For example, the sociologist Rodney Stark (1963) argued that "the qualities of thought associated with science are characteristic of modern scholarship in general, and not limited to the traditional sciences. The criteria by which a historian identifies causes and tests hypotheses are not different in kind from those of a physicist. Similarly, the approach taken to data by philologists, literary

historians, and even modern Bible critics, is in this same style, grounded in skepticism and empirical rules of evidence" (p. 4). See "On the Incompatibility of Religion and Science: A Survey of American Graduate Students." *Journal for the Scientific Study of Religion* 3(1):3–20.

11. RAAS Psyc15, conducted October 19, 2005.

12. RAAS Phys5, conducted July 12, 2005.

13. RAAS PS 21, conducted October 6, 2005.

14. Twenty-three percent of our evangelical respondents have a bachelor's degree or higher compared to 27% of mainline Protestants, 26% of Catholics, 58% of Jews, 59% of non-Western adherents, and 40% of the religiously unaffiliated.

15. This measure comes from GfK's Core Profile data that each panel member completes upon joining the panel.

16. Our survey also asked those who said that their occupation was science-related whether they worked at a college or university. Given that we are trying to identify individuals outside of colleges, we exclude these people from our definition of a "rank-and-file" scientist (N = 78 of the 688 qualifying as a rank-and-file scientist).

17. N = 616. The 4% represents the weighted estimate.

18. RAAS Phys 29, conducted March 15, 2006.

19. While this was a real fear for many religious scientists and a critique from some of the nonreligious scientists, Elaine found in her study of scientists working at elite US research universities that being religious did not translate into a rejection of science in favor of religious explanations. For example, 94% of the elite scientists surveyed agreed that evolution provides the best explanation for the emergence of life on earth.

20. RAAS Econ 35, conducted June 8, 2006.

21. Scientists in Congregations. Retrieved July 25, 2016, www.scientistsincongregations.org. See also Ecklund, Elaine Howard, and Jeff Smith. 2015. "Congregational Conversations." *Christian Century*, August 5, pp. 26–29.

22. N = 127.

23. High SES Evangelical Church Houston Int5, conducted July 22, 2012.

24. High SES Reform Jewish Synagogue Houston Int7, conducted June 30, 2013.

25. Mid-High SES Orthodox Jewish Synagogue Chicago Int8, conducted July 19, 2013.

26. There were four response options: very often, sometimes, rarely, never. Here we combined the first four responses to represent "more than never."

27. See Leuba 1934: 300. See also Ecklund 2010.

28. See Ecklund, Elaine Howard, and Elizabeth Long. 2011. "Scientists and Spirituality." *Sociology of Religion* 72(3):253–274.

29. Kingsolver, Barbara. 2012. *Flight Behavior*. New York: HarperCollins.

CHAPTER 5

Religious People Are All Young-Earth Creationists

We meet Kurt,[1] an emergency room doctor, early one morning at a local café. Because of his hectic schedule, it took us more than six months to schedule an interview with him after being introduced at his Presbyterian church. The church has always held an important place in Kurt's life. "My father was a pastor, as was his father, as was his father, so there *is* a tradition," he says with a small chuckle. He describes his faith as centered around a "deity that's benevolent. I believe in a deity that has connected with us well . . . a belief in Jesus, as Christ, and as a savior, and that he came and presented Himself to heal and reconcile." Kurt also has "an interest in science that was certainly encouraged and appreciated" from a young age, he says, and he "was involved, even in high school, in the National Science Foundation program, studied science, and was very interested in doing graduate work in science as an undergraduate." He went to the Massachusetts Institute of Technology, where he developed, he says, "a very strong understanding and appreciation for science, the role of science and discovery, and the specific processes in a variety of disciplines in science."

What does someone like Kurt, an evangelical with a good understanding of science, think about evolution? "Great question!" he says. "For me—and my background is primarily biological sciences—so evolution just means fundamentally that we're related to each other . . . [w]hich to me is a beautiful description."

Kurt goes on to explain that

> evolution, and evolution of the world, or creation of the world, and the evolution of life and human beings, has informed my understanding of biblical creation stories. I think I can interpret the Bible, and I think that the Bible will continue to have valuable messages and meanings that concern humans for at least hundreds of years, if not thousands of years to come. Will those understandings change? Yes. But they've changed before, and they'll continue to change. . . . I fully recognize that 10 years, or 100 years from now, we may have a very different date on the age of the earth, on the age of the universe, and I think that both the scientists and religious people are going to have to adjust to those things.

Kurt recalls finding a clipping his father had saved and stuck in a book:

> My dad loved to read, and not just books, but newspapers and science articles, and I remember discovering a book he had, which had to be from the early '50s, when [Louis] Leakey [a pioneer in the study of early human evolution][2] was discovering some of the early humanoids. . . . Leakey was being interviewed; I don't know whether it was *Time* or *National Geographic*. He was talking about how he never considered any of his discoveries to be particularly in conflict with any biblical tradition or religious views, [but that we have] a God-given ability . . . to discover the world around us and interpret it. And it augmented [Leakey's] belief in religion rather than contradicting it.

MYTH: RELIGIOUS PEOPLE ARE ALL YOUNG-EARTH CREATIONISTS

How did we get here, and how did life develop on earth? For some, like Jerry Coyne, a well-known evolutionary biologist, answers to these questions are a matter of science alone—and religion often stands in the way of accepting these answers. Coyne writes,[3]

> American resistance to accepting evolution is uniquely high among First World countries. This is due largely to the extreme religiosity of the United States, which is much higher than that of comparably advanced nations, and to the resistance of many religious people to the facts and supposed implications of evolution. The prevalence of religious belief in the United States suggests that outreach by scientists alone will not have a huge effect in increasing the acceptance of evolution, nor will the strategy of trying to convince the faithful that evolution is compatible with their religion. Because creationism is a symptom of religion, another strategy to promote evolution involves loosening the grip of faith on America.

Due to the long history, current state, and high profile of the evolution-creation debate in the United States, we are led to believe religious people writ large simply do not accept evolutionary theory.[4] We are also led to believe that nonreligious people must be strict adherents of a purely evolutionary view of life's origins. For more than 30 years, Gallup polls have asked samples of Americans the following question:

"Which of the following statements comes closest to your views on the origin and development of human beings:

- Human beings have developed over millions of years from less advanced forms of life, but God guided this process.
- Human beings have developed over millions of years from less advanced forms of life, but God had no part in this process.
- God created human beings pretty much in their present form at one time within the last 10,000 years or so."

The first time Gallup asked this question, back in 1982, only 9% of Americans chose the second option, representing a nontheistic, purely evolutionary perspective. Forty-four percent of Americans chose the third option, representing the young-earth creationist perspective. This percentage has been remarkably stable. The last time Gallup asked this question, in 2014, 42% of Americans chose the creationist option.[5] And cross-national surveys reveal that the US population is among the lowest in accepting evolution.[6]

When it comes to social issues, two clearly opposite positions are usually pitted against one another (e.g., pro-choice versus pro-life, pro-gun versus anti-gun). This is often because those with the most extreme positions are usually the most invested in the issue and, as a result, are the most organized and vocal. Yet, in reality, public attitudes about these issues are rarely neatly dichotomized. Sure, there are people who are *always, totally, and completely* anti-[issue] or *always, totally, and completely* pro-[issue]. But when social scientists dig deeper, we almost always find that positions on an issue are much more varied and nuanced than it might appear from looking at picket signs. Evolution is no exception. Many religious individuals are not easily classified as simply young-earth creationists. Instead, as we uncover in our survey, their views on evolution and creation are complex.

A Few True Believers and Everyone Else

In our survey, we offered individuals *six* potential narratives on the origins of life. These narratives are shown in figure 5.1. They vary along several dimensions, including the time period involved, the role of supernatural forces, the name given to those forces (i.e., "God" or "Intelligent Force"), and the place of humans within the process. At one end of the spectrum is a narrative that corresponds to the young-earth creationist perspective, the belief that "God created the universe, the Earth, and all of life within the past 10,000 years." At the other end of the spectrum is a narrative that corresponds to a purely evolutionary model, which holds that "the universe and Earth came into being billions of years ago;

Young-earth creationism	• God created the universe, the Earth, and all of life within the past 10,000 years.
Recent human creation	• God created the universe and the Earth billions of years ago; plants and animals evolced over millions of years from earlier life forms, but God intervened to create humans within the past 10,000 years.
God-guided evolution	• God created the universe and the Earth billions of years ago; God started and has guided human evolution over millions of years.
Intelligent design	• The universe and Earth came into being billions of years ago, and humans evolved over milloins of years according to the design of an Intelligent Force.
God-initiated evolution	• God created the universe and the Earth billions of years ago; but all life, including humans, evolved over millions of years from earlier life forms due to environmental pressures to adapt and without any guidance from God or an Intelligent Force.
Natural evolution	• The universe and Earth came into being billions of years ago; all life, including humans, evolved over millions of years from earlier life forms due to environmental pressures to adapt; there was no God or Intelligent Force involved in either the creation or evolution of life.

FIGURE 5.1 Six creation-evolution narratives

all life, including humans, evolved over millions of years from earlier life forms due to environmental pressures to adapt; there was no God or Intelligent Force involved in either the creation or evolution of life."

Different from some other researchers, we did not force those who took our survey to pick only one narrative, recognizing that people are sometimes unsure what they think or report views that appear inconsistent. We also asked individuals to note whether they think a narrative is "definitely" or "probably" true or false, or whether they are not sure, so that we could assess the certainty of their belief in that narrative. We have thus produced a much more nuanced picture of Americans' views on human origins than much of the previous research on this topic.[7]

Let us consider a person who says *only one* of these narratives is "definitely true." We might label this person a "true believer" in that narrative. How many such true believers are there? The first row of percentages in table 5.1 provides the answer. Here we see that evangelicals, at 40%, are the most likely to say that only one narrative is "definitely true." The next row in the table shows what narrative is most popular among the "true believers" in each religious group. Among evangelical true believers, the most popular narrative is young-earth creationism.

A strong rejection of evolution is not limited to evangelical Christians, however. When asked about evolution, a member of an Orthodox Jewish congregation told us, "That's a big no-no for us. . . . That's a direct conflict between creating Adam from dust and then Eve from the rib. So you have that versus the monkey theory."[8] And a Muslim woman we interviewed told us she did not "think [evolution] could be compatible with the teachings of the Quran."[9]

Despite the fact that creationist beliefs can be found in other religious traditions, it is clear that evangelicals are unique in the strength and clarity with which they hold and express a young-earth creationist perspective. Some of the religious individuals we talked with recognized this distinction in their responses to questions about evolution and creation, defining their own perspective in contrast to what they perceive as evangelicalism's focus on scriptural belief. For example, a member of a conservative Jewish congregation in Houston, who was studying geology, told us,[10]

> The Torah has flexibility on a lot of different things to be able to find leniencies for certain things under certain circumstances and to accept different interpretations of how the world works. Christianity . . . because you have to take it literally, you don't have that flexibility. That makes it much harder to corroborate the two.

Similarly, a Muslim in Chicago stated that, in his view, "Christians are far more dogmatic about not believing in science than Muslims are."[11]

The sociologist Jeffrey Guhin argues that creationist beliefs represent an identity or boundary marker for evangelicals in a way that it does not for other religious groups. In one study, Guhin finds that students and teachers in both evangelical Christian and Muslim schools in New York City say they do not believe in evolution. The difference comes in the importance placed on those beliefs. Creationist beliefs are not as salient or important for Muslims, who derive their identity more from religious practice (e.g., prayer) than strict adherence to scriptural belief.

In analyzing public opinion data, the sociologist Joseph Baker finds that higher education tends to lead to more pro-evolution attitudes—except in the case of individuals who hold a "literalist" view of how the Bible should be read.[12] And among young adults, the sociologist Jonathan P. Hill finds that religion is a strong predictor of maintaining creationist beliefs in the face of educational attainment—but only if the young adult's social network is full of many similarly religious peers.[13] "The most important takeaway here," he writes about his study, "is that individual theological beliefs, practices, and identities are important, but they only become a reliable pathway to creationism or atheistic evolutionism when paired with certain contexts or certain other social identities."[14]

TABLE 5.1 Description of Responses to Origin Narratives

	All Respondents (a)	Evangelical Protestants (b)	Mainline Protestants	Catholics	Jews	Non-Western Religions	Atheists, Agnostic, Unaffiliated
Percentage saying only one of the origin narratives is "definitely true"	26.5%	39.8%[a]	20.9%[ab]	18.8%[ab]	21.9%[ab]	21.5%[b]	30.6%[ab]
Most popular narrative among this group	Creationism 43.3% of the 26.5%	Creationism 71.1% of the 39.8%	Creationism 43.8% of the 20.9%	God-guided evolution 34.0% of the 18.8%	Natural evolution 63.2% of the 21.9%	Natural evolution 58.0% of the 21.5%	Natural evolution 88.1% of the 30.6%
Percentage saying none of the origin narratives are "definitely true"	57.5%	39.3%[a]	64.0%[ab]	60.5%[ab]	69.7%[ab]	65.9%[ab]	63.9%[ab]
Percentage saying more than one of the origin narratives is "definitely true"	16.0%	20.9%[a]	15.1%[ab]	20.7%[a]	8.4%[ab]	12.6%[b]	5.5%[ab]
Total	100%	100%	100%	100%	100%	100%	100%

a = Difference between percentage and all other US adults is statistically significant (p < .05).
b = Difference between percentage and percentage for evangelical Protestants is statistically significant (p < .05).
Source: Religious Understandings of Science, 2014. Unadjusted percentages.

If we look back at table 5.1, we see a larger story about beliefs in evolution and creation. The second row of this table shows there are significant segments of every religious group that are unwilling to say that *any* of the origin narratives is "definitely true." Among evangelicals, almost 40% are unable or unwilling to commit as a "true believer" to any single perspective on the origin of life. Outside of evangelicals, the majority of individuals in every religious group hold multiple perspectives on origins. This could be because the narratives we offered are unsatisfactory in some way. Our interpretation, however, is that large segments of the religious population are unsure what they think about the origin of life—or at least they are not sure enough to commit fully to any particular explanation.

The last row of table 5.1 shows the percentage of individuals in each religious group that selected *more than one* of the origin narratives as being "definitely true." Respondents who profess to be "true believers" of multiple narratives are interesting, because most of the narratives contain elements that appear contradictory in the timeframe or mechanism. One possibility is that these individuals are readily willing to accept various accounts of creation as long as they address key theological issues. Other researchers have observed this same flexibility. In that same work interviewing teachers and students in Muslim schools in New York City, Guhin spoke with a teacher named Sheikh Yusuf who strongly rejected any idea of evolution as "dangerous and wrong." Yet, Guhin writes, when he asked the teacher how he would feel "about someone believing Allah had guided evolution, his whole expression changed.[15] 'Oh,' he said, 'this is fine, they're trying to accommodate the theory, and they are trying to be scientific, well they evolved, and God is the one who is behind the evolution.' Sheikh Yusuf did not believe theistic evolution was possible, but when it was suggested, he was not threatened by the idea."[16]

Findings like these suggest that the technical details of an origin narrative can often matter less than the underlying meanings and theological implications of the narrative. We found in our interviews that for many religious believers, it is not scientific facts—which they properly understand—that lay at the heart of their concerns about evolution, but rather what one person we interviewed called the more "ultimate question[s]."

The Ultimate Questions

At major US universities, it is hard to find a scientist—religious or nonreligious—who would dispute that evolution is *the* key explanation for the "development of life on earth."[17] It is also important to note that the scientific view of evolution focuses on purely *natural processes*. Science gives us no ultimate end goal, divine master plan, or master purpose in evolution. Yet, for many religious individuals, naturalistic evolution seems to have implications for God's creative powers and the specialness, or sacredness, of humans.[18] In our conversations with Christians, Muslims, and Jews, concerns about evolution focused on its implications for these two questions: (1) Is there a God and is God active in the world? and (2) How does evolution alter the sacredness of humanity?

REALITY: IS THERE A GOD, AND IS GOD ACTIVE?

Does evolution inherently rule out the existence of God or God's active role in the world and human lives? This is the biggest question and concern for many people of faith, including evangelicals, Catholics, Jews, and Muslims. For a number of religious individuals, the timeline of human origins—10,000 years or millions of years—does not matter as long as there is room for God. A medical student who attends an evangelical church in Houston[19] gives voice to this perspective when she says she doesn't worry much about the timeframe of evolution but thinks the

> idea of a Creator—"Was a Creator behind evolution?" or "Is there a Creator or not?"—is more important. Could a Creator have used evolution as a means to create man or something? Sure. Why not? But I think "Is there a creator?" is a much more important question.

The true importance of the biblical creation story, a religion teacher at a Reform Jewish congregation in Chicago[20] asserted, is what it says about the powers of God:

> So the world was created in six days? That's ridiculous; there wasn't even a sun and a moon until the third day! . . . So how long was the first day? What do I care? What that story tells me is there was nothing, and now there's all this, and God did it.

"Sure things are evolving. That's fine with me," a Muslim professor of engineering, who regularly participates in his mosque in Chicago, told us,[21] "but I want to look at who programmed the DNA. Who's the master programmer? So, we have to incorporate that into the big picture. If I remove the programmer from that picture, then there's some problems."

In our survey data, we find strong evidence of a connection between a respondent's view of creation and a respondent's view of God, which comes as little surprise. Let's compare those who believe in God to varying degrees. Among those respondents who said, "I know God exists and I have no doubts about it," 36.1% also said the young-earth creationist narrative we offered is "definitely true." Among those who said, "While I have doubts, I feel that I do believe in God," the percentage drops significantly; only 7.2% are "true believers" in the young-earth creationist narrative. And among those who stated, "I find myself believing in God some of the time, but not at others," the percentage dropped even further, with 5.2% saying they are certain the young-earth creationist narrative is true.

While many religious individuals from different faith traditions share an interest in maintaining an active role for God in the origin and development of life, there is variation in how they view God's role in the process.

Evolution with a Divine First Cause

Some religious individuals accept evolution but maintain a role for God in creation by seeing God as the initial cause that set in motion the development of life on earth. We found this view among individuals from different religious traditions. For example, one Orthodox Jewish woman in Chicago[22] gave almost a textbook answer when asked to define evolution:

> Evolution is that in any given generation of any life form there are a certain number of those life forms born with various mutations, some of which are positive—will positively impact the life of the life form—and some of which will negatively impact the life of the life form and some of which won't change its reproductive outcome at all. So evolution is the weeding out of the negative outcome.

When we asked this woman if she feels evolution offers the best explanation for the development of life on earth, she said that, in her view, "it offers the best explanation for everything after the original start. It cannot explain how we got to life forms in the first place." When we asked her to explain "how we got here," she said, in no uncertain terms, "God."

A middle-aged woman in an Episcopal congregation in Houston[23] also articulated an approach to the origins of life that argues for God as the first cause:

> OK, there is nobody who knows how any of this got here. There was nothing and there was something. What happened between nothing and something? You have

to start with something to evolve into something else. So where did the some-thing come from? It didn't evolve out of nothing. It started. Evolution requires a starting point. You can't change something that isn't there.

Some individuals expressed a similar view with regard to the creation and devel-opment of the universe, accepting the idea of the big bang but seeing God as its divine first cause. As a church leader at an African American evangelical con-gregation in Houston told us,[24]

> I took a group [of youth] to a science center and they had this great exhibit on the big bang theory, and [the youth] were really upset about it. And I said . . . well . . . what if it was a big bang? I'm OK with that. I'm OK with there being a big bang. I think as a believer, though, *we know who lit the fuse* [emphasis hers].

A Catholic woman in Houston[25] expressed the same idea, arguing that

> you can think of all different kinds of theories, but they have to come from some-where. Something had to happen first. Or something had to be put into motion. I mean, even if you believe in the big bang theory—like, the gases and the random matter and all that kind of stuff had to exist at some point before they collapsed and then created the big bang.

For a number of religious individuals, the scientific explanations are not enough when it comes to understanding the creation of the universe and the world we live in. In their view, there are certain ideas that lie beyond the purview of sci-ence. We asked our survey respondents whether they agree or disagree with the statement "Given enough time, science will be able to provide a natural expla-nation for everything." Of course, a person need not be religious to believe there are limitations to science. When we look at the data, however, we find that evangelicals are particularly skeptical of science's ability to fill every gap in our knowledge. As we see in table 5.2, just about 50% of evangelicals don't believe science will be able to provide a natural explanation of everything.[26] This com-pares with 30% of mainline Protestants, 24% of Catholics, and 16% of the reli-giously unaffiliated.

God's Ongoing Involvement in Evolution

In our survey, we asked our respondents whether they agree or disagree with the statement that God is "directly involved in the affairs of the world." Overall,

TABLE 5.2 Percentage Disagreeing That Science Will Be Able to Provide a Natural Explanation for Everything by Religious Tradition

Given enough time, science will be able to provide a natural explanation for everything.		All Respondents (a)	Evangelical Protestants (b)	Mainline Protestants	Catholics	Jews	Non-Western Religions	Atheists, Agnostic, Unaffiliated
Percentage who disagree	Unadjusted	31.0%	49.7%[a]	29.7%[b]	24.2%[ab]	26.5%[b]	9.7%[ab]	15.8%[ab]
	Adjusted	29.3%	46.1%[a]	29.2%[b]	23.8%[ab]	24.9%[b]	10.5%[ab]	16.4%[ab]

a = Difference between percentage and all other US adults is statistically significant (p < .05).

b = Difference between percentage and percentage for evangelical Protestants is statistically significant (p < .05).

Source: Religious Understandings of Science, 2014. Adjusted percentages account for any influence from differences in education, political ideology, income, sex, age, region of residence, marital status, and race between the religious groups.

45% of our respondents agree with this statement. The percentage is roughly the same among mainline Protestants (43%), Catholics (43%), and Muslims, Hindus, and other practitioners of non-Western traditions (42%). At 24%, Jews are much less likely to agree with the statement. Evangelicals, on the other hand, at 70%, are much more likely to agree that God is actively involved in the world.

A number of religious individuals we interviewed talked about viewing evolution as God's plan, a plan that God is *consistently involved in executing.* Here's how one Episcopalian in Houston sees God's potential involvement in evolution:[27]

> Well, evolution to me is really a broad term; you could look at all animal and plant life and things change over time and they adapt. . . . And I'm not struggling too much with that. If it had to be my guess, that's what God planned, and that we didn't just evolve one day and that was it. That there's been an evolutionary process and we're part of it. And instead of fighting it, I think it's really fascinating how it's come about. And did one day God really suddenly inject knowledge in a way that allowed us to evolve in a different way? Maybe. I'm just not too worried about answer[ing] that. I think God's here.

Similarly, a Catholic man who works for an oil and gas company in Houston explained that he sees God as the initiating and ongoing force behind evolution (which he realizes is a somewhat controversial position among conservative Catholics).[28] "For me, it's ultimately all the evolution goes back to God," he said. "It's God's work. That's why the world is evolving and people are evolving."

REALITY: ARE HUMANS SACRED?

In our interviews, many religious individuals also discussed what evolution means for the specialness or sacredness of humans and, in turn, the implications for human meaning and purpose. The idea that humans are made in the image of God is an important doctrine for all branches of Christianity and Judaism and for some branches of Islam.[29] According to the Christian theologian Richard Middleton, "The idea first occurs in the Bible in Genesis 1:26–28, where God creates humanity (both male and female) in his 'image' and 'likeness' (parallel terms)."[30] In our interviews, language about humans being made in the image of God came from Christians, Jews, and Muslims. For example, a rabbinical leader in a Reform Jewish synagogue in Houston[31] told us that when her congregation reads of creation, they "don't get too hung up on any of these specific details," but they "read about a plan—that God had a plan, and being created in the image of God." A man who is part of a Latino Catholic church[32] explained that in his understanding of his religious tradition, "We believe . . . that we are made in the image of God. And when we do this, we are speaking of a birth more spiritual than physical. . . . So, my physical form, or whatever, or the physiology of man, can change over a lifetime and will probably keep doing so. But this doesn't affect anything of who we come from or where we are going." He said, "I'm not going to change my opinion if someone comes and says, 'Well, man was created from nothing.'"

A number of religious individuals separated human evolution from the evolution of other animals to keep from violating the idea that humans were created in the image of God. "As far as humans go," a young Muslim college student in Houston hoping to pursue a career in medicine[33] told us, "humans were never part of the evolutionary process. So those animals, maybe, have been going through evolution all that time, the plants, but as far as humans go, I believe that we were placed on this earth by God."

A Muslim man we interviewed in Chicago[34] similarly accepted the idea that plants and animals evolve, but he rejected the possibility that humans have evolved:

> If we're talking about the theory that life has evolved from simple to complex, OK. But I don't necessarily believe that humans came from single cells. This theory is OK when it's describing how most things came to be, but for humans it leaves out the soul and the spirit. Science can't explain that; it's hard to reconcile. Evolution can probably explain most things, but for humans and the spirit it just falls short.

Macroevolution vs. Microevolution

Some religious individuals make a distinction between macroevolution and microevolution as a way of retaining a special place for humans in creation. Put simply, microevolution involves relatively minor, cosmetic changes to a species. For example, the coloring of a species might become lighter or darker over time if the new color helps it better blend into its environment. While the species has adapted or evolved, it is still the same species. Macroevolution refers to the development of entirely new species though the process of evolution.

Many religious believers have no problem accepting microevolution, *but* macroevolution, which occurs on a much larger timescale, is much more difficult to accept because it appears to have significant implications for who humans are. While many religious individuals accept the idea that species change over time, they reject the idea that humans evolved from other species. The primary motivation behind this view appears to be keeping humans apart from the rest of creation in the evolutionary process, believing this is necessary to maintaining a special relationship between the creator and human beings. Time and time again in our interviews, we heard Christians, Jews, and Muslims trying to maintain, in the face of scientific thinking and evidence, the belief that God created humans as they are now.[35]

"I always separate it out into sort of macro- and microevolution—microevolution being this theory of adaptation to the environment, which is basically like what Darwin saw in the Galapagos Islands," explained an evangelical medical student in Houston.[36] "Changing the environment, the organism responds, some changes in DNA, and sort of 'bird gets new beak!'" She finds macroevolution—which she describes as the "idea that, somehow, there were some original one-celled organisms that became multicelled organisms and . . . *became man* through, however, millions of years"—more difficult to accept. "Have I seen evidence for macroevolution? No," she told us. "I don't think there's any sort of thing in the fossil record that really supports it or something that exists today that's like a half this, half that." We note here that she uses scientific rather than religious language to explain her view.

An evangelical man in Chicago[37] explained that he separates evolution into "microevolution, the variations within the species," which he thinks is clearly true. "And then there's the theory that through mutations, or whatever else, species will begin to evolve and develop new characteristics and become whole new species." This theory does not mesh with his personal view of the development of life on Earth and human origins: "I mean, I believe the Bible in that," he said. "That God just created man. I don't think that species have changed into other species over time."

Another evangelical,[38] who attends a congregation in Houston, similarly drew a distinction between microevolution and macroevolution, maintaining a sacred space for humans in creation:

> I believe it was the sixth day when He [God] created man and He said it was very good. As far as evolution from a scientific perspective, there is no evidence for it. We have never witnessed evolution across the species, that is macroevolution. We have witnessed microevolution within species, but never from one species to another.
>
> *Interviewer*: So you would say you believe in microevolution, not macroevolution?
>
> Yes, yes. I would point to Darwin himself in supporting my beliefs. It's mildly amusing how I see all these different cars around with little fish on the back with feet and then in the middle it says "Darwin." I try to just look at it as amusing

because if I don't, I can become insulted—both as a Christian, but also as someone who appreciates science. We make it all about Darwin when Darwin himself
said that there wasn't enough evidence to support this theory [of macroevolu-
tion] and that it was impossible.

Rejecting Randomness and Its Implications

A common theme among religious believers when discussing evolution was
an objection to seeing life, and humans in particular, as the product of random
forces and processes. Here's how one young evangelical,[39] training to become a
pastor, puts it:

> I got fed evolution . . . from the best professors in the best way possible. And even
> still, I found myself looking at it like, "Really? Like there's still gaps in the fossil
> record. I don't know, is it really so simple?" I think the evolution premise as a
> whole, the idea that random mutations, and like an error here and an error here,
> led to human beings who are so bent on anything but randomness, who are all
> about purpose and meaning and questions of "why?" I just don't see how totally
> random processes could have gotten us here, if that makes sense.

Another man from a nondenominational evangelical congregation[40] drew a
direct line between his view of creation and his sense of purpose. For him, the
random processes of evolution, which scientists describe as purposeless, have
theological implications that strip life of hope and meaning:[41]

> You look at how man started, how man was created, and it also gives you hope,
> you know, because . . . if we all just came from some cellular amoeba mass, and
> just all of a sudden we became this being, right, at some point we're going to be a
> completely different being. Then I think there's really not very much hope or pur-
> pose in any of that. You know, whereas, if I am created by God, in God's image, in
> His likeness, and I'm given a purpose, I have a reason for living. . . . I help other
> people *not* to make myself look better, or to feel better. [I help others] because [I
> want to] glorify the one who created me, in His image.

Another evangelical[42] expressed a similar problem with the random, purposeless, mindless, and heartless processes of evolution:

> Was this just a random product of random particles bouncing together and grow-
> ing from a single cell to complex cells? It could be, but my experience in life doesn't

seem to allude to that kind of idea. And the reason I think—the biggest fingerprint is in—[and] lives inside of every human being, which is the desire to live with a purpose. I think that was planted from creation—that why does it all matter? This idea that why is there good and bad? Why is violence not always good in our human society, yet violence in nature is what rules and dominates? That process of natural selection, it is very violent—that you destroy the weaker beings, and they will die, that there isn't a support of the lower race because then you're just screwing up—the gene pool, right? Yeah, humans. . . . We don't kill every mentally handicapped child, but we care for them. We actually make exceptions. And we sacrifice for them. To me, that's evidence of God's fingerprints . . . we didn't just come from apes. . . . This didn't just happen, but there was a purpose.

And a man who attends a largely African American church in Houston summed up the feelings that many believers expressed toward the origin and development of life, the role of God, and the sacredness of humans:[43]

What's important for me is, God played and is still playing an active role in creation, that we see God's hand in nature, that we are created in the image of God and what that could mean for us.

LESSONS

There are certainly religious individuals who are "true believers" in strict creationism, the idea that God created humans as they are now within the past 10,000 years or so. We encountered these people in our interviews and in our survey; the most prominent among them were evangelicals. However, we also found religious individuals who wholly believe in natural evolution. "Evolution is . . . how we came to be," a self-described "very Darwinian" Reform Jewish woman[44] told us. "I absolutely don't think it's the way it was described in the Bible, at all. Zero. Nothing."

But the views of the bulk of the religious population, including evangelicals, are much harder to pin down. They are not committed to any particular origin narrative; they are open to multiple narratives so long as key theological understandings are not threatened. Many of these individuals understand the scientific details of evolution, but they reject a purely naturalistic view of life's origins due to the perceived implications for their faith. Some reject the idea that their God, whom they pray to when they are ill or need guidance, does not act in nature. Some reject the idea that humans are just the result of purely natural, random processes lacking direction or goals because they think it means their lives have no ultimate meaning or purpose. The majority of them want to leave room for the hand of God and human specialness.

David Masci, a senior writer at the Pew Research Center who focuses on science and religion issues, including evolution, believes that "much of the general public simply chooses not to believe the scientific theories and discoveries that seem to contradict long-held religious or other important beliefs." The data show that "when the two realms offer seemingly contradictory explanations (as in the case of evolution), religious people, who make up a majority of Americans, may rely primarily upon their faith for answers."[45] In one sense Masci is right but his view certainly doesn't describe all religious people, as we have shown, and certainly does not give the deeper reasons and conditions under which people might favor religious over scientific explanations.

The sociologist Peter Berger starts to tap into some of these deeper reasons of "why" when he writes "the nightmare *par excellence*" for a human being occurs when the person "is submerged in a world of disorder, senselessness and madness." Berger recognized the power of religion to create an "area of meaning carved out of a vast mass of meaninglessness, a small clearing of lucidity in a formless, dark, always ominous jungle."[46]

Is there a way for scientists to talk about the evidence and facts of evolutionary theory without ruling out a role for God? Is it possible for scientists to help religious individuals maintain their sense of meaning and purpose in the world without violating scientific principles?

We go back to Kurt, the evangelical Christian doctor whom we introduced at the beginning of this chapter,[47] who told us that evolution "just means fundamentally that we're related to each other . . . the fact that all life, at least that we recognize on this earth, and specifically human life, have very similar common processes. [To me], this is a beautiful description." In other words, he says, "evolution itself means that we have, in a sense, a common ancestor or a common framework that we share with other living things."

And consider the story that Eugenie Scott, the former director of the National Center for Science Education, told the American Humanist Association nearly 20 years ago when she accepted the Isaac Asimov Science Award.[48] In 1995, she recounted, the National Association of Biology Teachers (NABT) defined evolution like so:

> The diversity of life on earth is the result of evolution: an unsupervised, impersonal, unpredictable and natural process of temporal descent with genetic modification that is affected by natural selection, chance, historical contingencies and changing environments.

"As one Christian said to me," Scott went on in her speech, "defining evolution as 'unsupervised' and 'impersonal' implied to many Americans that 'God had nothing to do with it and life has no meaning.'" Two theologians petitioned the NABT to delete those two words, and Scott pushed for the change, which the NABT ultimately made. "We cannot say, wearing our scientist hats," she said later in her speech, "whether God does or does not act."

Does removing words like "unsupervised" and "impersonal" from the definition of evolution appeal to all people of faith? Probably not, but what Scott's story illustrates is that many religious individuals see something other than randomness and purposelessness in the world—and they are more likely to accept evolution if presented in such a way that allows them to maintain a role for God and the sense of meaning and purpose that it provides.

"The evidence supporting that all living things are descended from a common ancestor is truly overwhelming!"[49] the evangelical Christian scientist Francis Collins has said. "But I have no difficulty putting that together with what I believe as a Christian because I believe that God had a plan to create creatures with whom he could have fellowship, in whom he could inspire [the] moral law, in whom he could infuse the soul."

NOTES

1. High SES Evangelical Church Houston Int19, conducted February 13, 2013.

2. See, for example, Leakey Foundation. Retrieved September 28, 2016, https://leakeyfoundation.org/about/the-leakey-family/.

3. See Coyne, Jerry A. 2012. "Science, Religion, and Society: The Problem of Evolution in America." *Evolution* 66(8):2654–2663. Quote is from p. 2654. For a similar view, see also Miller, Jon D., Eugenie C. Scott, and Shinji Okamoto. 2006. "Public Acceptance of Evolution." *Science* 313(5788):765–766.

4. For some excellent overviews of the theological, legal, and historical dynamics of the evolution\creationism debate, see works such as Eugenie C. Scott's *Evolution vs. Creationism: An Introduction* (2009; Westport, CT: Greenwood Press) and Ronald L. Numbers's *The Creationists: From Scientific Creationism to Intelligent Design* (2006; Cambridge, MA: Harvard University Press).

5. See Gallup. 2016. "Evolution, Creationism, Intelligent Design." Retrieved September 28, 2016, http://www.gallup.com/poll/21814/Evolution-Creationism-Intelligent-Design.aspx. Respondents were also allowed to say "no opinion."

6. See Miller, Scott, and Okamoto 2006.

7. See Eckberg, D. L., and A. Nesterenko. 1984. "For and Against Evolution: Religion, Social Class, and the Symbolic Universe." *Social Science Journal* 22(1):1–18.

See also Mazur, Allan. 2005. "Believers and Disbelievers in Evolution." *Politics and the Life Sciences* 23(2):55–61. See Pew Research Center. 2013. "Public's Views on Human Evolution." Retrieved August 26, 2014, http://www.pewforum.org/files/2013/12/Evolution-12-30.pdf.

8. Mid SES Orthodox Jewish Synagogue Houston Int12, conducted October 28, 2013.

9. Generally speaking, the Muslims we interviewed were much more uncomfortable with the idea of human evolution than nonhuman evolution. For instance, one Muslim, when asked about evolution, at first stated that the "Quran is open to many interpretations," but he then later specified that "humans did not evolve but they are created as human" (Mid-High SES Sunni Muslim Mosque Chicago Int1, conducted July 13, 2013). Another Muslim we interviewed, a female healthcare professional, similarly distinguished general evolution from human evolution: "I feel like humans have evolved in size but not cross-species. . . . So I don't believe that once upon a time, we were orangutans or monkeys and then through whatever natural selection and environment pressures, we evolved into human beings" (Mid-High SES Sunni Muslim Mosque Chicago Int2, conducted July 16, 2013).

10. Mid SES Orthodox Jewish Synagogue Houston Int9, conducted October 20, 2013.

11. Mid-High SES Sunni Muslim Mosque Chicago Int3, conducted July 18, 2013.

12. Baker, Joseph. 2013. "Acceptance of Evolution and Support for Teaching Creationism in Public Schools: The Conditional Impact of Educational Attainment." *Journal for the Scientific Study of Religion* 52(1):216–228.

13. See also Hill, Jonathan P. 2014. "Rejecting Evolution: The Role of Religion, Education, and Social Networks." *Journal for the Scientific Study of Religion* 53(3):575–594. In his analysis, Hill finds that religion is a strong predictor of maintaining creationist beliefs in the face of educational attainment among young adults, but only if the young adult has many similarly religious peers in his or her social network.

14. See Hill, Jonathan P. 2014. "The Recipe for Creationism." Retrieved September 20, 2016, http://biologos.org/blogs/archive/the-recipe-for-creationism. See also Hill, Jonathan P. 2014. "Rethinking the Origins Debate," *Christianity Today*, February 4. In the latter work, Hill writes, and we agree, that "surveys like the Gallup poll tend to represent the various views we might label Atheistic Evolution, Theistic Evolution, Intelligent Design, or Young Earth Creationism with position statements that force respondents to select the one that comes closest to their beliefs."

15. This would be similar to the "God-guided evolution" narrative we offered in our survey.

16. Guhin, Jeffrey. 2016. "Why Worry About Evolution? Boundaries, Practices, and Moral Salience in Sunni and Evangelical High Schools." *Sociological Theory* 34(2):151–174.

17. Ecklund found that 87% of scientists at elite US universities "strongly agreed" that evolution is the best explanation for the development of life. Another 7.4% "somewhat agreed" (See here: http://www.thearda.com/Archive/Files/Descriptions/RAAS.asp.)

18. See Roos, J. Micah. 2014. "Measuring Science or Religion? A Measurement Analysis of the National Science Foundation Sponsored Science Literacy Scale 2006-2010." *Public Understanding of Science* 23(7):797–813.

19. High SES Evangelical Church Houston Int23, conducted June 25, 2013.

20. High SES Reform Jewish Synagogue Chicago Int10, conducted June 21, 2012.

21. Mid-High SES Sunni Muslim Mosque Chicago Int4, conducted July 18, 2013.

22. Mid-High SES Orthodox Jewish Synagogue Chicago Int10, conducted July 21, 2013.

23. High SES Mainline Church Houston Int16, conducted June 20, 2012.

24. Mid-High/High SES Evangelical Church Houston Int14, conducted September 27, 2013.

25. Mid-High/High SES Catholic Church Houston Int8, conducted October 16, 2013.

26. The question offered five responses: strongly agree, agree, neither agree nor disagree, disagree, and strongly disagree. About 40% of all respondents chose the "neither agree nor disagree" response.

27. High SES Mainline Church Houston Int5, conducted September 1, 2011.

28. Mid-High/High SES Catholic Church Houston Int5, conducted October 2, 2013.

29. See, for example, Guessoum, Nidhal. 2010. "Religious Literalism and Science-Related Issues in Contemporary Islam." *Zygon* 45(4):817–840.

30. Middleton, J. Richard. 2011. "Image of God," in *Dictionary of Scripture and Ethics*, edited by J. B. Green. Grand Rapids, MI: Baker Academic.

31. High SES Reform Jewish Synagogue Houston Int11, conducted August 8, 2013.

32. Mid-Low SES Catholic Church Chicago Int6, conducted October 26, 2012.

33. Mid/Mid-High SES Sunni Muslim Mosque Houston Int8, conducted October 8, 2013.

34. Mid-High SES Sunni Muslim Mosque Chicago Int5, conducted July 19, 2013.

35. The sociologist Michael Evans talks extensively about the role of intelligent design in public debate. See Evans, Michael S. 2012. "Who Wants a Deliberative Public Sphere?" *Sociological Forum* 27(4):872–895. See also Evans, Michael S. 2016. *Seeking Good Debate: Religion, Science, and Conflict in American Public Life.* Berkeley: University of California Press.

36. High SES Evangelical Church Houston Int23, conducted June 25, 2013.

37. High SES Evangelical Church Chicago Int8, conducted July 20, 2013.

38. High SES Mainline Church Houston Int14, conducted June 9, 2012.

39. High SES Evangelical Church Chicago Int2, conducted July 16, 2013.

40. High SES Evangelical Church Chicago Int5, conducted July 18, 2013.

41. Other research has found similar perceived negative consequences of believing in evolution. For example, see Brem, Sarah K., Michael Ranney, and Jennifer Schindel. 2003. "Perceived Consequences of Evolution: College Students Perceive

Negative Personal and Social Impact in Evolutionary Theory." *Science Education* 87(2):181–206.

42. High SES Evangelical Church Houston Int25, conducted July 8, 2013.

43. Mid-High/High SES Evangelical Church Houston Int14, conducted September 27, 2013.

44. High SES Reform Jewish Synagogue Houston Int2, conducted June 20, 2013.

45. See Masci, David. 2007. "How the Public Resolves Conflicts Between Faith and Science." Retrieved September 25, 2016, http://www.pewforum.org/2007/08/27/how-the-public-resolves-conflicts-between-faith-and-science/.

46. Berger, Peter. 1967. *The Sacred Canopy: Elements of a Sociological Theory of Religion*. Garden City, NY: Doubleday. Quotes from pp. 22–23. Interestingly, Berger once argued that pluralism, science, and other social forces would reduce the plausibility of religion. In recent years, however, he has actually backed away from this argument and concluded that the secularization hypothesis is not valid. See, for instance, his February 2008 article in *First Things* titled "Secularization Falsified."

47. High SES Evangelical Church Houston Int19, conducted February 13, 2013.

48. National Center for Science Education. 2008. "Science and Religion, Methodology and Humanism." Retrieved September 25, 2016, https://ncse.com/religion/science-religion-methodology-humanism.

49. See Beliefnet. 2006. "God Is Not Threatened by Our Scientific Adventures." Retrieved September 25, 2016, http://www.beliefnet.com/News/Science-Religion/2006/08/God-Is-Not-Threatened-By-Our-Scientific-Adventures.aspx.

CHAPTER 6

Religious People Are Climate Change Deniers

We meet Father Joel in his office, where he greets us with a smile and a handshake.[1] An ordained priest for an Episcopal congregation, Fr. Joel has white hair and round, stylish glasses. He has a passion for geology, which he studied in college, and sees science as a tool from God that humans can use to help each other and improve the quality of life. In his role as a priest, though, he prefers to focus on issues that he sees as more connected to social justice.

He tells us that his congregation is actively involved in environmental care; they recycle, buy natural cleaning products, hold Earth Day events, and have held a series of adult-education talks that explore the link between faith and the environment. Fr. Joel believes that human activity has had a role in climate change and that it is our responsibility to be good stewards of the earth. He sees a strong connection between faith and the environment that comes directly from his reading of the Bible:

> In the book of Genesis and the Torah . . . God gave the garden to humankind. Adam is earth, a man of earth, manmade of clay, man of humus, and Eve is mother of all living things. Some theologians think that the garden is the representation of the entire earth. God gave earth to man to care for its part of the *berit*, the covenant. . . . God creates Adam out of the earth. . . . You get living earth, and we're supposed to take care of the earth. What does that include? It includes animals. It includes air. . . . Let me say this: We receive a great deal of inspiration from Scripture about how to be good stewards. We want to be good stewards.

ORIGINS OF MYTH

How do religious beliefs and religious affiliation affect attitudes toward environmental care and beliefs about climate change? Are religious individuals divided

93

on the role and responsibility of God and humans in protecting the environment or are they more like Fr. Joel?

Some scientists and media pundits have pointed to religion, especially evangelical Protestantism, as a central factor in shaping climate-change denial specifically and environmental indifference in general. It is not hard to see where they get the idea that evangelicals do not care much about the environment. After all, we hear politicians like James Inhofe, a current senator of Oklahoma and self-described Christian, telling a radio talk show that

> God's still up there, and the arrogance of people to think that we, human beings, would be able to change what He is doing in the climate, is to me, outrageous.[2]

There is also the Baptist evangelical church in Idaho that produced bumper stickers reading "Forget 'Save the Earth'; What about your Soul? The Earth is Going to Burn; What about You?"[3]

Much of the scholarly work on religion and the environment stems from the seminal 1967 article by the historian Lynn White, which suggests that "what people do about their ecology depends on what they think about themselves in relation to things around them. Human ecology is deeply conditioned by beliefs about our nature and destiny—that is, by religion."[4] In other words, the views people hold on environmental care, like their views on evolution, are shaped by what they think about the role of God in the world and the significance and place of humans.

Although not based on data about actual practices, White argues that Western Christianity's theological beliefs in human dominion over nature and the distinction Christianity makes between humans (made in God's image) and the rest of creation (which many believe is not created in God's image) are partially fostering an ecological crisis. Early studies looked at White's proposed "dominion over nature" or "mastery over nature" theory and found that such beliefs are indeed predictive of environmental apathy.[5]

More recently, however, there is a growing body of research that actually links religion to environmental concern,[6] and there is mounting evidence that religious leaders, like Fr. Joel, from many traditions are becoming interested in environmental issues *and* that individuals from many traditions are also suspicious of climate change.[7] But, increasingly, voices from a variety of religious and spiritual traditions are bringing the link between religion and the environment—and climate change, in particular—to national and international notice, creating what the religion scholar Bron Taylor has called "dark green religion."[8] For instance, in 2014, the World Council of Churches, representing more than 500 million Christians from a range of denominations, began divesting from fossil fuels.[9] And in 2015, Pope Francis devoted an encyclical to "The Care of Our Environmental

Home,"[10] where he delved deeply into the significant problems in the ecological world and the spiritual need for humans to care for the environment.

Here we show that many religious individuals do make quite strong and clear connections to their faith when discussing the environment. Yet this does not always translate into strong environmental action, as three factors tend to put on the brakes. First, many see God as all-powerful in the world and outside of nature, which means they think God will not allow environmental destruction or will intervene to do something about it. Second, individuals of almost all faiths—but especially evangelical Christians—think that caring for hurting humans is more important than caring for the environment, and they do not see how the two imperatives can be connected. Finally, there are religious individuals who worry about pro-environmental views leading them to align with individuals or groups that they view as too extreme, too political, or simply too different from themselves. While these three factors attenuate religious individuals' enthusiasm about environmental care generally, they come together in a perfect storm to impact climate-change views.

MYTH: RELIGIOUS PEOPLE DON'T CARE ABOUT THE ENVIRONMENT

Let us start by examining the connection between religion and environmental attitudes more broadly. We asked our sample of US adults how interested they are in "the environment." As seen in table 6.1, about 33% of Americans overall say they are very interested in the environment, but we see some significant differences across religious traditions. For example, evangelicals are a little less likely than the general public to say they are very interested in the environment. A much larger gap is seen with adherents of non-Western religious traditions, who are much more likely than the general public or any other religious group to say they are very interested in the environment, even after we eliminate other sociodemographic differences. This is perhaps because some non-Western religious traditions, like Hinduism, make a tighter link between representations of the divine and nature.

As the bumper sticker mentioned earlier displays, most of the connection between religion and *lack* of environmental care has focused on evangelicals. But we also find that only 15.6% of evangelicals say they are "not at all interested" in the environment compared with 13.4% of all respondents, which is statistically equivalent. In other words, it is by no means the case that evangelicals have *no* interest in environmental issues. At worst, they have only a slightly lower level of interest in environmental care than other groups.

TABLE 6.1 Interest in the Environment by Religious Tradition

	All Respondents (a)	Evangelical Protestants (b)	Mainline Protestants	Catholics	Jews	Non-Western Religions	Atheists, Agnostic, Unaffiliated
Please tell me how interested you are in the following things: The environment ("Very interested")							
Unadjusted	32.8%	25.9%[a]	32.1%[b]	34.5%[b]	40.3%[b]	46.9%[ab]	36.8%[ab]
Adjusted	32.0%	27.8%[a]	31.2%	32.0%[b]	34.3%	52.7%[ab]	34.1%[b]
I think about the effect on the environment when making shopping decisions . . . frequently							
Unadjusted	17.2%	14.0%[a]	16.3%	15.0%[a]	29.8%[ab]	24.4%[ab]	22.0%[ab]
Adjusted	15.6%	14.8%	14.8%	12.7%[a]	20.8%	28.4%[ab]	18.4%[ab]

a = Difference between percentage and percentage for all other US adults is statistically significant ($p < .05$).

b = Difference between percentage and percentage for evangelical Protestants is statistically significant ($p < .05$).

Source: Religious Understandings of Science, 2014. Adjusted percentages account for any influence from differences in education, political ideology, income, sex, age, region of residence, marital status, and race between the religious groups.

It is fair to ask what "interest in the environment" really means and whether it even matters. Does interest translate into actually making efforts to help the environment?[11] Our survey also asked our sample of US adults how often they "think about the effect on the environment when making shopping decisions." The responses to this question are also shown in table 6.1. Once we account for other social and demographic differences (like age and gender) across the religious groups, we see that Catholics are slightly less likely than the general public to say they "frequently" consider the environment in shopping decisions. Adherents of non-Western faith traditions and the religiously unaffiliated are more likely to say they shop with the environment in mind. While some groups, like Jews, appear to differ from the general population, we cannot be statistically confident that these differences are real given the underlying margins of error for these percentages. When we look at those who say they "never" think about the environment when shopping, we find similar weak or nonexistent differences between religious groups. Overall, 14.4% of American adults say they never think about the environment when shopping. This compares with 16.6% of evangelicals, 15.7% of mainline Protestants, 13.1% of Catholics, 9.3% of Jews, 6.7% of adherents of non-Western religions, and 12.9% of the religiously unaffiliated. These gaps, where they are even statistically significant in the first place, disappear when we account for other differences between the religious groups.

In sum, our survey data do not support the idea that religious individuals do not care about protecting the environment. It is true that evangelicals report slightly lower levels of interest in the environment, but this does not translate into a complete absence of interest.

Theology and Environmental Care

In our interviews, we found that many religious individuals ground their view of the environment in their faith. Christians and Jews from all the traditions we examined freely used the concept of "stewardship" as they talked about caring for the earth, creating a strong rationale for environmental concern.[12] One woman, a church secretary from an African American Baptist congregation,[13] explained, "I feel obligated that it's His creation, and He sent us here as stewards of His creation. And so I believe that definitely we should be caring for what He created." A retired attorney from a Reform Jewish congregation[14] echoed these sentiments, saying, "The Torah says that God made humans last, and that we were to be the stewards, and have dominion over all the animals and over all of the plants and waters of the Earth. And I take that real[ly] seriously."

When asked for whom we are serving as stewards, most point to God. For example, a Catholic man who works as the church administrator for his largely Latino parish in Chicago[15] said,

> As Catholics understand it, God creates man and he entrusted man this place, not only the Garden of Eden, but the whole world, the planet. We are the stewards of the planet, and as stewards of the planet, God is going to ask us: How did you administrate the planet? How did you contribute to the well-being of the planet?

While the religious understanding of stewardship largely holds individuals accountable to God, the secular repurposing of the idea emphasizes accountability to future generations. Some religious individuals have embraced this interpretation of stewardship.

Yet, in our conversations with religious Americans, fewer than 30 people mentioned caring for the earth for the sake of future generations[16]—and many of those who did mention future generations did so in the context of God's wishes. That is, even when religious individuals referenced the secular idea of serving as a steward of humanity, they did so in a way that served God.[17] For example, one Latino Catholic,[18] a member of the religious group we found to be most vocal about a responsibility to future generations, said of caring for the environment,

> We should take care of it because we are failing—if we don't do it, we are failing, we are ruining our planet, we are [leaving] a bad planet for our children or grandchildren, we are doing things that are not in agreement with . . . what the church asks either.

Similarly, a mainline Protestant[19] stated that

> we should care for it. This doesn't belong to us. Not just it doesn't belong to us as it belongs to God, but it belongs to the people who are coming after us. We have no business and no right to be destroying it at all, let alone in the name of profit.

Muslims also framed environmental care in religious terms—expressing a sense of accountability to God and to future generations—although they did not utilize the term "stewardship." One young Muslim student[20] said, "I feel like I'll be held responsible on the Day of Judgment if I don't do certain things to help the environment when I can." Other Muslims pointed to the Quran as informing environmental appreciation and activism, like this other Muslim college student:[21]

> So there's an entire chapter called "Ankabut," like it's literally called "The Spider" . . . and God highlights the spider as a creature, and it says—he called people to witness the spider as one of his creations. . . . There's even some that talk about the bee. There's some that have the ant. There's some about the cow. We don't worship any of those creatures. It's just for you to see as a sign.

In our discussions with both Reform and Orthodox Jews, nearly a quarter specifically invoked the concept of *tikkun olam* in reference to the environment. An Orthodox Jewish primary schoolteacher[22] explained, "There's a saying called *tikkun olam*, that we are supposed to repair the world. We're supposed to be in partnership with God to repair the world." *Tikkun olam* has grown from a minor rabbinic doctrine into a driving concept of modern Jewish social justice theology. The environmental theologian Rabbi Lawrence Troster explains that this theology "sees human freewill, not divine action, as the chief means by which the world will be perfected."[23] Echoing this theological sensibility, a middle-aged woman[24] who is part of a Reform Jewish synagogue and works as a development officer told us,

> [The environment] is a blessing. We should care for it. One of the tenets of Judaism is called *tikkun olam*. . . . And that means repairing the world. And it could mean anything from clothing the naked or feeding the hungry or picking up trash. . . . Pursuing justice doesn't just mean making sure that somebody gets really good representation in court. It means ensuring that trees are planted and that they're cared for and that we be good stewards of our waterways and of our air.

Likewise, a law professor discussed how he sees all of the Jewish faith pointing toward taking care of people and the planet:[25]

> I think that it is absolutely fundamental to the Jewish faith to take care of the earth, to respect it, to not be wasteful, to be appreciative of the bounty, and to try to take care of it as much as possible. You know, we believe very much in . . . issues of justice, and we have a belief called *tikkun olam*, which means heal the world.

Elements of their faith traditions provide Jews, Muslims, and Christians with a rationale or logic for environmental care. As seen in the Jewish concept of *tikkun olam* and the broader Judeo-Christian concept of stewardship, religion can provide an interpretive frame (schema) that would seem to motivate environmental care *actions*. But when we look at what exactly healing the world or serving as God's steward means to religious individuals—in terms of their personal choices, actions, and priorities—the picture is much more complex.

Translating Theology to Action

"The model in God's kingdom is not wilderness; it is garden," one evangelical told us, "the garden that man tends as steward of God himself."[26] Many of the religious individuals we spoke to enthusiastically believe their faith tradition provides a rationale or a responsibility to care for the earth; yet they pulled back when asked if they *do* anything personally to care for the environment. Often, they discussed conservation—sacrificing for the sake of the earth—alongside dominion over the earth. For example, a retired Orthodox Jewish teacher[27] argued that Judaism "says two things":

> Right in the beginning, master [the environment] and conquer it. But also respect it. And they are not incompatible.... We can build cities, and yes, we can build—we can dig mines and whatever. But ... you are supposed to respect the environment, keep things clean.... I'm all for mines and fracking and whatever.... And yet it does say ... you should plant trees so even though you won't be around, the next generation should have them. Yes, both of them. You don't leave behind a dump. You clean it up. You make it look good. So you can have both.

We found that while religious individuals from a variety of traditions connected their faith very directly to caring for the environment, these connections often produced only the most basic environmental practices and fairly muted actions. For example, a Southern Baptist oil company employee[28] told us,

> I like a plastic bottle to drink my Coke out of; that's fine. I shouldn't go throw that plastic bottle in a river, because that's irresponsible of me; I'm not being a good steward of my environment. For me, there's nothing wrong with that plastic bottle because I can actually recycle it, and they can actually make more plastic bottles out of it. So it's a balance.

What makes religious individuals confine their pro-environmental behaviors?

REALITY: FOCUSING ON GOD AND HUMANS

Some individuals struggled with a tension between caring for the natural world and caring for humanity. When thinking about the future of the planet, some people considered the breadth of creation, while others weighed only humanity. A youth minister from a Houston evangelical congregation[29] stated bluntly, "If we have the opportunity, yeah, we should help take care of this planet that we've been given. Having said that, I also believe that the value of human life is higher than the value of a whale, or a species of monkey, or something like that."

A number of religious individuals complained that the environmental move-ment neglects the important place of humans in the schema of creation, which violates a core tenet of their faith tradition. The same youth minister[30] said he was actually angered when people donate to environmental charities rather than humanitarian causes:

> It really makes me kind of upset when you have those commercials for people to donate to, you know, some sort of environmental thing when somebody could be donating to give money toward a starving child, or children with AIDS, that sort of thing. So, I feel like there is a higher value on human life than there is on the planet.

Other individuals placed importance on humanity over the environment based on concern about the Christian "end times." They are less concerned with saving the planet than they are with salvation for the people of the earth. A youth minister at an evangelical congregation[31] in Houston expressed a version of this perspective, based on what he sees as the true mission of Christianity:

> Are we stewards? Yes. Right? It's our responsibility. This is our place. Let's take care of it. But at the same time, do I think we should be running around and try-ing to save every tree we can? . . . I'd rather be interested in people. I think we're given a pretty clear indication of the way everything's going to end, and it's not because of global warming [*laughs*]. And so it's not on the top of my priorities. . . . Jesus' last command before he left Earth was go baptize people. Go tell people, not go save the trees [*laughs*].

And a homemaker in Houston who considers herself an evangelical[32] also framed her *lack* of concern for the environment in terms of a biblically predeter-mined outcome for life on earth, saying,

> We are not the creators, and I think it gets carried away sometimes in folks' minds—in people's minds—and thinking that it's all up to us. [Environmentalists say] "If we don't do this to save the planet, we're all going to be destroyed in so many million years." And I'm thinking we're not going to be here anyway.

What scholars have called a *hierarchy of needs argument*—the idea that basic, pressing needs must be met before a person has room to focus on higher-level issues—was especially salient for some of the African American Christians we interviewed. Acknowledging the general correlation between race and economic status in the United States, the hierarchy of needs viewpoint proposes African Americans are more environmentally apathetic because they disproportion-ately struggle to meet the basic material needs that come before environmental concerns.[33] To be clear, the hierarchy of needs and environmental deprivation perspectives are not specific to African Americans but to individuals low in socioeconomic status. We do not want to completely conflate race and class but do want to recognize that there is often a correlation between the two. A pastor[34] at a black church noted the priority of basic needs for his congregants, explaining,

> If you've ever found yourself in a survival moment, what you thought about was survival.... And so I don't want to say that *environmental thinking is luxury box thinking* [emphasis his], that it is really not on the ground of the world. I mean, it is hugely important. But I just know that when my world is falling apart, I'm not worried about drinking from a [plastic] water bottle, even though I probably should be.

We also found that just as there are some religious individuals who appreciate science but think they are fundamentally different from scientists—who are seen as holding an extreme naturalistic view of the world—there are religious believers who highly value the environment yet perceive environmentalists as culturally and politically different from people of faith. Many religious people we spoke with wanted to distance themselves from "tree huggers" and the modern environmental movement, which they categorized as "extreme." Many thought religious believers ought not to go to "the extreme."

One woman,[35] who called herself an evangelical, discussed how she was uncomfortable with the secular repurposing of the term "stewardship"; she thought it was "very self-righteous." An evangelical from a church in Houston told us, "It makes me a little bit sad, actually, that a lot of the people that are leading environmental care and the voices that lead that are so far from God. Because it's almost like they're worshipping the planet and not God. I'd like to see some awesome Christian guys out there leading it on that front."[36]

Orthodox Jews often joined evangelicals in expressing concern that environmental care not go too far: "Greenpeace is not a Jewish priority; People for the Ethical Treatment of Animals [PETA] is not a Jewish priority. More than likely, Greenpeace and PETA, when you emphasize something over here, you deemphasize other things," explained one Jewish man from a synagogue in Houston.[37] "And by focusing as extremely as they do on things that may or may not be important, it means they are not paying attention to other things that are as, or more, important."

THE PERFECT STORM: CLIMATE CHANGE

These drivers of apathy, suspicion, and even hostility toward environmental issues among religious individuals were most apparent when discussing the issue of climate change.[38] Consider a member[39] of an evangelical church who said of climate change, separately emphasizing each word, "That—is—a—lie!" He went on to tell us,

> I worship the God who is the source of all truth, and as a steward of the environment, I'm going to oppose you [when you say climate change is true]. I'm going to tell you what is true, and I'm going to try to persuade you to get off of this path because it's terribly destructive.

In his view, the real aim of those who advocate climate change is "to shut down the oil business." His statements are noteworthy for several reasons, the first of which is the emotion and passion with which they are delivered. Second, he not only points to faith that God is in control of the climate, but also suggests that the arguments for climate change are driven by ulterior motives that are destructive for the economy and hence the quality of human life. Indeed, there is the strong perception among many individuals that climate change is a Trojan horse for a political or social agenda. Survey data over the past 20 years have shown that views of climate change have become increasingly politicized, with self-identified Republicans or conservatives increasingly rejecting climate change, regardless of how educated they are or how much they understand about climate change.[40] The evangelical climate scientist Katharine Hayhoe recounts that after she gave her first lecture about climate change at Texas Tech University, the first question asked by a student was, "You're a Democrat, aren't you?"[41]

The Al Gore Effect

Without a doubt, the issue of politics—what we have elsewhere called "the Al Gore effect"[42]—came out most clearly in our interviews with regard to climate change. Some individuals think climate change is completely fabricated and a tool of the political left to gain power. The use of carbon credits (national and international efforts to decrease the growth of greenhouse gases)[43] was mentioned and often seen as a tool for personal accumulation of wealth and power. Here's how one middle-aged Catholic man[44] expressed his suspicion of climate change:

> Honestly, I don't believe it. For starters, they used to call it global warming, and now it's climate change. The climate has been changing ever since—you know, you had the Ice Age that happened without—nobody had any kind of vehicles. . . .

[And now] there are ulterior motives for that—if you had somebody like Al Gore who championed climate change. But this whole carbon tax credit—carbon credit . . . I think God made the planet to where it's going to be around until the end of the world.

"You know, you got a general rule in my family that you can agree with Al Gore, or you can act wisely," one evangelical pastor[45] said, jokingly. He went on further: "Any man that's going to tell me that we've got a global problem of killing polar bears while he's flying his jets all around the world; well, there's a disconnect there." Another evangelical man in Houston[46] also expressed serious concerns about the politics surrounding climate change, saying,

I think [climate change] occurs all the time. I think historically it has occurred. . . . I think that any kind of drastic change in percentage of chemicals in the atmosphere is a potential problem. But it seems to me that . . . it's hard to really discern how much of a problem there is because both sides seem to be more politically motivated than scientifically motivated. And I don't know where to go to determine what the truth is on that.

In our survey, we asked our respondents which of four statements best represented their view on climate change:

- The climate is changing and human actions are a significant cause of the change.
- The climate is changing but human actions are only partly causing the change.
- The climate is changing but not because of human actions.
- The climate is not changing.

As seen in table 6.2, relatively few people state that the climate is not changing at all or that *humans have no role in climate change*. The real issue is the extent to which humans are seen as a cause of climate change. For instance, 39% of US adults agree that humans are *partly* playing a role in climate change, but other factors (e.g., natural climate cycles) are also playing a role. In contrast, 43% of US adults agree that the climate is changing and humans are a *significant* cause, accepting the scientific consensus on climate change. When we look at the percentages by religious group, we see that members of non-Western traditions (63%) and the religiously unaffiliated (57%) are the most likely to agree with the scientific consensus, while Catholics are slightly more likely to pick this response (45%) than the general population.

TABLE 6.2 Views on Climate Change by Religious Tradition

		All Respondents (a)	Evangelical Protestants (b)	Mainline Protestants	Catholics	Jews	Non-Western Religions	Atheists, Agnostic, Unaffiliated
The climate is changing and human actions are a significant cause of the change.	Unadjusted	42.5%	29.0%[a]	41.5%[b]	44.8%[ab]	47.7%[b]	62.7%[ab]	56.7%[ab]
	Adjusted	41.8%	34.7%[a]	41.6%[b]	42.4%[b]	43.8%[b]	55.4%[ab]	49.9%[ab]
The climate is changing but human actions are only partly causing the change.	Unadjusted	38.5%	41.2%[a]	40.5%	39.6%	31.9%[b]	24.9%[ab]	32.1%[ab]
	Adjusted	38.2%	38.5%	39.7%	41.0%[a]	30.3%	27.6%[ab]	32.9%[ab]
The climate is changing but not because of human actions.	Unadjusted	12.6%	19.5%[a]	11.9%[b]	11.0%[ab]	14.1%	8.5%[b]	6.7%[ab]
	Adjusted	10.9%	13.6%[a]	10.5%[b]	10.2%[b]	15.3%	9.2%	8.1%[ab]
The climate is not changing.	Unadjusted	6.5%	10.4%[a]	6.1%[b]	4.6%[ab]	6.3%	3.9%[b]	4.5%[ab]
	Adjusted	5.2%	6.7%[a]	5.2%	3.8%[ab]	7.8%	4.5%	5.2%

a = Difference between percentage and percentage for all other US adults is statistically significant (p < .05).

b = Difference between percentage and percentage for evangelical Protestants is statistically significant (p < .05).

Source: Religious Understandings of Science, 2014. Adjusted percentages account for any influence from differences in education, political ideology, income, sex, age, region of residence, marital status, and race between the religious groups.

At 29%, evangelicals are significantly less likely to agree with the scientific consensus on climate change. For those who want to conduct outreach to religious communities on this issue, this suggests that those efforts would be best spent among evangelicals. Once we account for the influence of other social and demographic factors, particularly political ideology, we see that these gaps close somewhat, but evangelicals are still significantly less likely to agree with the scientific consensus. Evangelicals are also more likely to say either that the climate is not changing at all or that the climate is changing but not because of human actions. So, while politics does contribute to lower levels of acceptance of the scientific consensus on climate change among evangelicals, politics does not appear to be the sole factor.[47] So, for those conducting outreach to evangelical communities on this issue, the message needs to reach beyond the political issues to address the distinct faith concerns of evangelicals.

Our interviews point to some of the specifically faith-based reasons for rejecting climate change. Many religious individuals linked their view on climate change to God's sovereignty over the earth or to the idea that we are too small to have an effect on the global climate. A few people said that because of their faith in God, they didn't feel like climate change was something they needed to worry about even if it were occurring. An evangelical college student[48] stated with a laugh that "our world is supposed to end in fire, so that could be the slow process of global warming." An evangelical administrative assistant[49] elaborated on this idea, saying,

> If natural disasters increase, which I believe that God's word says that they will as Christ's return becomes closer, I think it's pretty clear. So that's not surprising to me, first of all. Second of all, I believe the Lord is very clear that He commands us not to live in fear of those things. And so, not to be alarmed, not to be surprised, and not to be afraid. And so I automatically, when I see things happening in the physical world or hear scientific reports, I automatically translate that into what I know the Lord has said, how that correlates with what is happening spiritually.

And an Orthodox Rabbi[50] says with a laugh, when asked about climate change, "I think climate change is, like, the biggest scam ever created!" He is particularly put off by the idea that people have a moral duty to have fewer children for environmental reasons (which, we note, contravenes the divine commandment to go forth and multiply). "So who are you saving the world for? Right?" he asks rhetorically. "So let's all just not have any more children. We'll die out [*he laughs*], and then the world will be there forever for who?" This Rabbi tells us he is sure "God can handle the amount of carbon dioxide that's still in the world. . . . I'm sure God designed the world in such a way that no matter how many humans we have, there's a way to feed everybody."

LESSONS

We believe there is real potential to harness religious beliefs and ideals to promote environmental care among people of faith if environmental concerns are framed in the right way. Both religious leaders and scientists can play a role here.

Caring for the Environment Is Caring for People

While we encountered a number of religious believers who viewed stewardship of the earth as a key way they could care for and protect humanity, we also saw how some individuals shied away from environmental concerns because they felt caring for humanity was the paramount interest of their religious tradition.

First and foremost, scientists and religious leaders need to show religious believers that *caring for the environment is caring for people*. This is especially important for members of congregations with low economic resources, who are particularly likely to think that other needs are more pressing than environmental issues, but are also particularly likely to be located in places that are hardest hit by the forces of environmental degradation, like poor air quality. As a resolution put forth by the National Association of Evangelicals (NAE) in 2015 points out, "A changing climate threatens the lives and livelihoods of the world's poorest citizens."[51] In that resolution, the NAE reaffirmed its belief that there is an "urgent need to relieve human suffering caused by bad environmental practice."[52]

One way to engage religious individuals in environmental care is to use this sort of language—to call attention to the fact that environmental actions have human consequences. As Robert White, a geophysicist and fellow of the Royal Society, writes, "Though we often talk of 'natural disasters,' in reality the vast majority of deaths and suffering can be traced to the behavior of humans."[53]

In this regard, the words of the faith practitioners we talked with are incredibly instructive. For example, a Catholic schoolteacher[54] framed the importance of environmental care this way:

> There's a connection between how we relate to nature and how we relate to other people. So if we mistreat and look at nature as a commodity and as something that we can just exploit, I think that connects to how we treat others.

And a physician,[55] who identifies as an evangelical Christian, linked caring for the environment and caring for humanity in similar terms:

Throughout the world the poor are often victims of environmental degradation. And so one of the most important things that the Bible teaches us [is] that [what] God cares most about, is the poor. And so to the extent that degradation of the environment is harming the poor and making them even worse off, then it is an essential issue for Christians to get engaged in.

Our research shows that if we want to mobilize religious people like Father Joel to really get involved in environment care, it needs to be framed as a social justice issue. *Saving the environment ultimately needs to be about saving people.*

Stop Linking Politics to Climate Change

For those who wish to foster more environmental concern and greater climate-change alleviation efforts among evangelicals in particular, our findings are instructive. Climate-change skepticism may in part be connected to religion, but this connection is weaker and more muddled than, say, the religion-evolution connection.[56] Attitudes on climate change are also strongly influenced by factors like political ideology. Over and over, we found, particularly among evangelical Christians, that environmentalism was tied in their minds to political ideologies they want to distinguish themselves from. Evangelicals are the religious group most likely to be suspicious of scientists, so they need to hear about climate change from voices they trust. Religious leaders can help here, making climate-change action about theology not politics. They need to be vocal about the reality of climate change and endorse climate-change action as a calling for those who are mandated to promote human welfare and protect God's creation.

Move from the Personal to the Collective

We believe religious institutions have a crucial role to play in cultivating environmental action among religious individuals. Congregations not only can draw connections between theology and environmental care, but also can provide *opportunities for members to practice and reinforce environmentally conscious behaviors.* Practices that begin within congregations—for example, community gardening initiatives or environmentally conscious strategies (such as avoiding the use of disposable plates and utensils)—can lead to environmental habits that may be transferable to other settings. (Of course, the specific strategies chosen will depend on the economic resources of the congregation.) It is important to note here that congregations are providing institutional structures that can support environmental action beyond the boundaries of the institution.[57]

Scientists can help make environmental issues more salient for religious believers by focusing on the human impacts of climate change, and religious leaders can use those impacts to provide people of faith with a religious rationale for climate-change action. "It is time to move forward with boldness, confidence, and sound judgment," the climate scientist Katharine Hayhoe and pastor Andrew Farley write at the end of their book *A Climate for Change*, "to build a new and better future for ourselves and for our children."[58]

NOTES

1. High SES Mainline Church Houston Intl, conducted July14, 2011.

2. See Mooney, Chris. 2013. "Why Climate Change Skeptics and Evolution Deniers Joined Forces," *Mother Jones*, November 27. Retrieved February 10, 2015, http://www.motherjones.com/blue-marble/2013/11/why-climate-change-skeptics-evolution-deniers-joined-forces; Harris, Sam. 2006. "Jewry's Big Question: Why Are Atheists So Angry?" *Huffington Post*. Retrieved January 15, 2015, http://www.huffingtonpost.com/sam-harris/jewcys-big-question-why-a_b_35180.html; and Bruenig, Elizabeth. 2015. "Why Do Evangelicals Like James Inhofe Believe That Only God Can Cause Climate Change?" *New Republic*. Retrieved February 10, 2015, https://newrepublic.com/article/120889/evangelical-james-inhofe-says-only-god-can-cause-climate-change.

3. See Zaleha, Bernar Daley, and Andrew Szasz. 2014. "Keep Christianity Brown! Climate Denial on the Christian Right in the United States." Pp. 209–224 in *How the World's Religions are Responding to Climate Change*, edited by R. G. Veldman, A. Szasz, and R. Haluza-Delay. London: Routledge.

4. White, Lynn. 1967. "The Historical Roots of Our Ecologic Crisis." *Science* 155(3767):1203–1207.

5. Hand, Carl M., and Kent D. Van Liere. 1984. "Religion, Mastery-over-Nature, and Environmental Concern." *Social Forces* 63(2):555–570.

6. See Nepstad, Sharon E., and Rhys H. Williams. 2007. "Religion in Rebellion, Resistance, and Social Movements." Pp. 419–437 in *The SAGE Handbook of the Sociology of Religion*, edited by J. A. D. Beckford. Los Angeles: Sage. See also Boyd, Heather H. 1999. "Christianity and the Environment in the American Public." *Journal for the Scientific Study of Religion* 38(1):36–44; Djupe, Paul A., and Patrick K. Hunt. 2009. "Beyond the Lynn White Thesis: Congregational Effects on Environmental Concern." *Journal for the Scientific Study of Religion* 48(4):670–686; Eckberg, Douglas L., and T. Jean Blocker. 1996. "Christianity, Environmentalism, and the Theoretical Problem of Fundamentalism." *Journal for the Scientific Study of Religion* 35(4):343–355; Ellingson,

Stephen, Vernon A. Woodley, and Anthony Paik. 2012. "The Structure of Religious Environmentalism: Movement Organizations, Interorganizational Networks, and Collective Action." *Journal for the Scientific Study of Religion* 51(2):266–285; Hand and Van Liere 1984; Kanagy, Conrad L., and Hart M. Nelsen. 1995. "Religion and Environmental Concern: Challenging the Dominant Assumptions." *Review of Religious Research* 37(1):33–45; Sherkat, Darren E., and Christopher G. Ellison. 2007. "Structuring the Religion-Environment Connection: Identifying Religious Influences on Environmental Concern and Activism." *Journal for the Scientific Study of Religion* 46(1):71–85; and Truelove, Heather Barnes, and Jeff Joireman. 2009. "Understanding the Relationship Between Christian Orthodoxy and Environmentalism: The Mediating Role of Perceived Environmental Consequences." *Environment and Behavior* 41(6):806–820.

7. Djupe and Hunt 2009.

8. See Taylor, Bron. 2009. *Dark Green Religion: Nature, Spirituality, and the Planetary Future.* Berkeley: University of California Press.

9. Atkin, Emily. 2014. "Group Representing Half a Billion Christians Says It Will No Longer Support Fossil Fuels." *Think Progress*, July 11. Retrieved September 11, 2014, http://thinkprogress.org/climate/2014/07/11/3459111/wcc-christians-divests/.

10. See Holy See. 2015. *Encyclical Letter Laudato Si' of the Holy Father Francis on Care for Our Common Home.* Libreria Editrice Vaticana.

11. All surveys are limited in their ability to measure behaviors. A survey can ask about behaviors, like how often a person attends religious services. Ultimately, though, the survey can only measure what the person says about his or her behavior, not the actual behavior itself. For instance, people tend to overestimate their religious service attendance. See, for example, Hadaway, C. Kirk, Penny Long Marler, and Mark Chaves. 1993. "What the Polls Don't Show: A Closer Look at U.S. Church Attendance." *American Sociological Review* 58(6): 741–752.

12. Forty Evangelicals, seventeen mainline Protestants, six Catholics, ten Reform, and two Orthodox Jews discussed stewardship.

13. Low SES Evangelical Church Houston Int2, conducted June 22, 2011.

14. High SES Reform Jewish Synagogue Houston Int2, conducted June 20, 2013.

15. Low SES Catholic Church Chicago Int6, conducted October 6, 2013.

16. Payton and Moody 2004.

17. For a further discussion of this theme, see Peifer, Jared, Elaine Howard Ecklund, and Cara Fullerton. 2014. "How Evangelicals from Two Churches in the American Southwest Frame Their Relationship with the Environment." *Review of Religious Research* 56(1):373–397.

18. Mid-Low SES Catholic Church Chicago Int5, conducted October 4, 2012.

19. High SES Mainline Church Houston Int16, conducted June 20, 2012.

20. Mid/Mid-High SES Sunni Muslim Mosque Houston Int14, conducted October 17, 2013,

21. Mid/Mid-High SES Sunni Muslim Mosque Houston Int15, conducted October 29, 2013.

22. Mid SES Orthodox Jewish Synagogue Houston Int5, conducted October 17, 2013.

23. Troster, Lawrence. 2008. "Tikkun Olam and Environmental Restoration: A Jewish Eco-Theology of Redemption." *Jewish Educational News* 28(2):1–6.

24. High SES Reform Jewish Synagogue Houston Int14, conducted September 3, 2013.

25. High SES Reform Jewish Synagogue Chicago Int18, conducted July 17, 2013.

26. High SES Evangelical Church Houston Int6, conducted July 23, 2012.

27. Mid-High SES Orthodox Jewish Synagogue Chicago Int2, conducted July 15, 2013.

28. Mid-High/High SES Evangelical Church Houston Int9, conducted July 29, 2011.

29. Mid-High/High SES Evangelical Church Houston Int4, conducted June 22, 2011.

30. Ibid.

31. Low/Mid-Low SES Evangelical Church Houston Int3, conducted August 22, 2013.

32. Low/Mid-Low SES Evangelical Church Houston Int11, conducted November 21, 2013.

33. Conversely, the environmental deprivation thesis suggests direct exposure to environmental pollution might lead to greater environmental concern of the not-in-my-backyard variety (see Mohai and Bryant 1998).

34. Low SES African American Evangelical Church Houston Int19, conducted August 11, 2011.

35. High SES Evangelical Church Houston Int18, conducted November 4, 2012.

36. Mid-High/High SES Evangelical Church Houston Int4, conducted June 22, 2011.

37. Mid SES Orthodox Jewish Synagogue Houston Int7, conducted October 20, 2013.

38. Hayhoe, Katharine, and Andrew Farley. 2009. *A Climate for Change: Global Warming Facts for Faith Based Decisions*. New York: Hachette.

39. High SES Evangelical Church Houston Int6, conducted July 23, 2012.

40. McCright, Aaron M., and Riley E. Dunlap. 2011. "The Politicization of Climate Change and Polarization in the American Public's Views of Global Warming, 2001–2010." *Sociological Quarterly* 52:155–194; Brulle, Robert J., Jason Carmichael, and J. Craig Jenkins. 2012. "Shifting Public Opinion on Climate Change: An Empirical Assessment of Factors Influencing Concern Over Climate Change in the U.S., 2002-2010." *Climatic Change* 114(2): 169–188.

41. Hayhoe, Katharine. 2015. "Climate, Politics and Religion-My Opinion." Retrieved June 5, 2015, http://katharinehayhoe.com/wp2016/2015/06/05/climate-politics-and-religion/.

42. See Peifer, Ecklund, and Fullerton 2014.

43. See Wikipedia. "Carbon Credit." Retrieved August 30, 2016, https://en.wikipedia.org/wiki/Carbon_credit.

44. Mid-High/High SES Catholic Church Houston Int14, conducted November 20, 2013.

45. Low/Mid-Low SES Evangelical Church Houston Int1, conducted August 15, 2013.

46. High SES Evangelical Church Houston Int7, conducted July 24, 2012.

47. Other research, such as Evans and Feng 2013, found that political ideology completely explains away the initial religion effect for climate-change attitudes in their analysis of General Social Survey data. The question that they examined, though, is potentially measuring a different concept than individuals' actual climate-change view. The question they used asked respondents, "The first issue is global warming. Global warming means a trend toward warmer temperatures throughout the world, with more extreme weather in many places and changes in food production that could affect our way of life. Some people believe that the burning of gasoline and other fossil fuels causes global warming. Others say that global warming has purely natural causes. . . . How well do the following groups understand the causes of global warming? Environmental Scientists." Note how this question does not directly ask the respondent's view on climate change, but instead asks about their perception of environmental scientists' competency. This may not get at actual acceptance of a particular view. As a parallel, an individual might think that biologists are generally competent while also rejecting their claims about evolution. See Evans, John H., and Justin Feng. 2013. "Conservative Protestantism and Skepticism of Scientists Studying Climate Change." *Climate Change* 121(4):595–608. Also see Ecklund, Elaine Howard, Christopher P. Scheitle, Jared Peifer, and Daniel Bolger. 2016. "Examining Links Between Religion, Evolution Views, and Climate Change Skepticism." *Environment and Behavior*. doi: 10.1177/0013916516674246.

48. Low/Mid-Low SES Evangelical Church Houston Int4, conducted August 30, 2013.

49. High SES Evangelical Church Houston Int24, conducted June 27, 2013.

50. Mid SES Orthodox Jewish Synagogue Houston Int6, conducted October 18, 2013.

51. National Association of Evangelicals. 2015. "Caring for God's Creation: A Call to Action." Retrieved August 30, 2016, http://nae.net/caring-for-gods-creation/.

52. Ibid.

53. See White, Robert S., ed. 2009. *Creation in Crisis: Christian Perspectives on Sustainability.* London: Society for Promoting Christian Knowledge.

54. Low SES Catholic Church Houston Int6, conducted October 6, 2013.

55. High SES Evangelical Church Houston Int13, conducted August 31, 2012.

56. Our more advanced analyses of our statistical data support this conclusion.

57. Vaidyanathan, Brandon, Simranjit Khalsa, and Elaine Howard Ecklund. N.d. "Naturally Ambivalent: Religion's Role in Shaping Environmental Action," unpublished manuscript.

58. Hayhoe and Farley 2009.

CHAPTER 7

Religious People Are Against
Scientific Technology

R abbi Aaron[1] leads us through the office suite that functions as the school he heads. The school has only four classrooms and is sparsely decorated with handmade art on the wall, paintings of ancient-looking synagogues that were made by the students. An Orthodox Jew, Rabbi Aaron's dress is plain; he wears a white button-up long-sleeved shirt, slacks, leather shoes, and a yarmulke, which sits insecurely slanted on his head. His thinning hair and wrinkles communicate life experience.

Rabbi Aaron tells us he doesn't think very much about issues of religion and science, and his responses to the questions we ask about evolution, climate change, and other hot-button science and faith issues are fairly passive. It is not until the topic of technology comes up that Rabbi Aaron becomes animated. He tells us he is scared of the increasing pace of online technology, and he wants the members of his synagogue to hold back and to hold back their children. As he sees it,

> We have major problems with social media. . . . I've done articles on non-Jewish people who write about how they've almost destroyed their lives because of Twitter. Facebook—the dangers of Facebook. And it's a scary thing how teenagers really don't understand what they're doing very often. . . . In the congregation, I speak strongly that kids should not have Facebook accounts. . . . [Parents] should be monitoring their [children's] computer use and their phone use and all of those things. In our day and time, it sounds authoritarian and czarist, but there are way too many casualties out there not to do it.

"So that's the war we're waging these days," Rabbi Aaron says to conclude our discussion of online technology. "More dangerous than dinosaurs [and evolution]."

MYTH: RELIGIOUS PEOPLE DISLIKE TECHNOLOGY

Several years ago, *Time* magazine ran an article discussing how a growing number of churches were using Twitter, highlighting that religious leaders were integrating social networking into their services.[2] At a time when social media was spreading pretty much everywhere, why the focus on churches? Was it particularly surprising or newsworthy that religious individuals and organizations were using the technology?

There seems to be a widespread sense among the public that religious groups are luddites, the last to accept any type of new technology. Although scholars often make a distinction between "technology" and "science," this distinction is fuzzy and porous in the public's mind,[3] and many of the same assumptions of epistemological conflict (tensions over ways of knowing) between religion and science are transferred to religion and technology. Moreover, there have been recent studies, like one published in 2014 by Allen B. Downey, a computer scientist at Olin College of Engineering, that show religious affiliation has decreased in the past several decades as Internet usage has increased. According to Downey, "It is easy to imagine at least two ways Internet use could contribute to disaffiliation. For people living in homogeneous communities, the Internet provides opportunities to find information about people of other religions (and none), and to interact with them personally. Also, for people with religious doubt, the Internet provides access to people in similar circumstances all over the world."[4] Downey believes the effect of Internet use on religious affiliation has been greater than the effect of education. "In the 2010 U.S. population," he writes, "Internet use could account for 5.1 million people with no religious affiliation, or 20% of the observed decrease in affiliation relative to the 1980s. Increases in college graduation between the 1980s and 2000s could account for an additional 5% of the decrease."

Yet the General Social Survey shows that 30% of those who attend religious services more than once a week report using the Internet for more than just email, compared with 36% of those who attend religious services less than once a year.[5] Even before we account for other social and demographic differences between these two groups, that's not a huge gap. The same data show that 22% of those who frequently attend religious services report having a smart phone, compared with 23% of those who rarely attend religious services.[6]

There is not much research that examines the relationship between religion and online technology, however. Heidi Campbell, a scholar of religion and communication who is one of the only people to systematically study the topic, writes, "In the last several decades we have seen significant changes take place in the ways communication technology is influencing how people practice religion."[7] She says, "There is a need for scholarship which looks carefully at religious communities as technology users who perform as active participants in the meaning-making processes surrounding technology."[8]

Our own data, from in-depth conversations with congregants, show that religious Americans are quite conflicted about the role of social media, like Twitter and Facebook, in their lives. We found that religious people accept communication technologies that facilitate evangelism, facilitate global networking with those of the same faith, and are used to help people of faith grow in faith (for example, doing a Bible study online or sending out Bible verses to church members on Twitter).

Danger of Thin Relationships

Both old and young religious Americans are concerned that social media and other communication technologies are reducing the depth of the interpersonal relationships, which are the cornerstone of faith communities. For example, a 24-year-old evangelical Christian,[9] who serves as a youth minister for a Houston congregation, told us about the kids he works with:

> A lot of my kids—all social media has really done . . . is give them access to their friends more often. [But] *I don't think necessarily it has increased the value of those interactions or anything.* . . . I've run into this Internet culture of memes. I've met three or four kids in the year that I've been here where that's their way of thinking—like they communicate in Internet language and memes, and they'd rather send me a funny picture than to actually give me a response. I've known a couple of kids where I'm just like: Parents, just shut off their Internet. We need to get them out for a little bit because they have no other way of interacting.

While social media has made it easier to interact with others quickly and frequently, some individuals in faith communities worry that online technologies are hazardous to the deep relationships that religious communities are built on and that humans need. In the words of a Rabbi at a Reform Jewish Synagogue in Houston,[10] "In an age where we're always connected, studies show that we're more disconnected now than we've ever been."

Expanding the Community

Other religious individuals praised the capacity of social media to allow us to talk more frequently with the people in our network and to share faith with people around the world. A 55-year-old senior pastor of a largely black congregation[11] told us he first had a largely negative impression of social media. "I was in my ignorance of it," he said. "You know, because people will get in on Facebook, holding up bottles of beer, sitting in hot tubs, and doing all kinds of crazy stuff, and so that's pretty much what I thought of the usage of it." Now, five years later, he sees the way social media can enhance church ministry:

> On a Sunday morning, there are people who are sending [out] my [sermon] while I'm preaching it. And I have more people tell me about my message before I get into the office here on Monday.... There was a time when if you saw some-one looking at a phone in the middle of the sermon you would say, "Get off of that! Put your electronic device away," and now we tell them [instead] to *adjust* [emphasis his] their electronic devices for worship.... We went from saying turn them off to adjust them for worship because the Bible is on their [phones] ... and then they can tweet or text relative to the message and what's going on, so that's good. And it's ... helped me to understand the power of social media for good and not just for the popular social.

"Because you have such a younger, broader audience now, and that's how a lot of younger people [relate]," said one evangelical man, approving the use of social media. "And you have to be able to reach people, and that is one of the avenues of reaching young people, you know. It's not like, 'Oh, come to church'; we can come to you. You can just look up at your own computer, and we can be right there." As an evangelical man in Houston explained,[12] "There's never been an opportunity like today, where we can get the message out all over the planet."

A number of religious individuals discussed how social media technologies help connect, strengthen, and sustain faith communities. Another member of a largely black church in Chicago,[13] for example, highlighted how social media can help the Christians he attends church with stay connected to their faith and to one another, saying,

> It allows people to communicate with each other quickly.... It allows people to sort of network and meet and just do things more effectively and more informed.
>   Interviewer: *So if you can, tell me how do you see these technologies in relation to your faith?*
>   Oh I think it strengthens the faith. I think just being able to tell your stories, praise God, or share stories with one another. If I can't make it to Bible class or if I want to see someone, hear someone's sermon, it's right there. It makes it a little more convenient, and we need to do whatever we can to keep one another uplifted—[and within the community] informing and keeping us connected. Letting us know about different events.

It was not just evangelical Christians, with a focus on sharing the gospel, who talked about the potential benefits of social media. Many of the individuals we spoke with from other traditions too stressed the positive aspects of these technologies. "We will have to listen and engage technology and social media and the debates of our times in a living, thriving, Reform Judaism," a Reform Rabbi told us. "And the only area where I sometimes have to correct people is to say: It's not 'Reformed Judaism', it's 'Reform'; it's a verb. So we're constantly meeting the needs of our time."

In short, the Amish do not represent all religious Americans. In fact, throughout our discussion, Rabbi Aaron looks at the computer on his desk, and his smart phone goes off several times. It's also important to remember that many of the concerns described above about weakening social relationships or dangerous behaviors by teens are not particularly religious in nature. Indeed, these are concerns that are expressed by religious and nonreligious Americans alike. There are particular technologies, however, for which religion *is* a distinct factor in shaping attitudes. Biomedical technologies, specifically those related to "human enhancement," tend to intersect directly with faith and can cause tension with religious groups. In other words, people of faith have *theological* concerns about these technologies.

THE PROBLEM TECHNOLOGIES

In our in-depth conversations with religious Americans, we also asked them about biomedical technologies. We focused on three in particular: reproductive genetic technologies (RGTs), in vitro fertilization (IVF), and human embryonic stem-cell (hESC) research. These technologies touch upon the two questions we have found to be central to shaping how religious individuals view scientific issues: the role of God and the sacredness of humans. In other words, these technologies have theological implications.

REALITY: RELIGIOUS PEOPLE HAVE CONCERNS ABOUT SOME TECHNOLOGIES MORE THAN OTHERS

Reproductive Genetic Technologies

RGTs encompass a range of techniques related to the genetic screening, selection, and treatment of embryos. Some RGTs are meant to identify and treat a disease in an embryo. Other RGTs are meant to select or create specific characteristics in an otherwise healthy embryo (for perceived enhancement purposes). These selection-focused technologies bring to mind science fiction like *Brave New World* and *Gattaca*. Some RGT interventions are possible today, while some are only theoretically possible in the future—but both actual and predicted uses have led to public debate. These include testing a fetus in utero to see if it has a disease (possible today), choosing the sex of a child by screening embryos and then only implanting those with the desired gender (possible today), and genetically modifying an embryo to ensure it does not have a disease or that it has a higher IQ or certain eye color (mainly a possibility only in the future). A 2016 survey by the Pew Research Center revealed that "the more religious people said they were, the less likely they were to want genetic alterations of babies or technologies to enhance adults. The differences were especially pronounced between evangelical Protestants and people who said they were atheists or agnostics."[14]

Our survey results show that support for RGTs depends greatly on whether the technology is aimed at treating a disease in an embryo (disease-focused) or selecting preferred characteristics in healthy embryos (selection-focused). Overall, almost two-thirds of US adults say that *selection-focused* RGTs are morally wrong, but only 12.8% of US adults view *disease-focused* RGTs as morally wrong. There are differences across religious groups, as seen in table 7.1. The religiously unaffiliated and adherents of non-Western faith traditions are the least likely to object to either type of RGT. Evangelicals are significantly more likely than the general population to oppose both selection-focused and disease-focused RGTs. These gaps remain even when we adjust for other differences between the groups. It is worth pointing out, however, that a large majority of evangelicals do not see a moral problem with disease-focused RGTs, and the majority of Americans overall, including more than half of the religiously unaffiliated, actually *do* object to selection-focused RGTs. In the big picture, then, religious and nonreligious Americans share many similarities in their attitudes toward these two categories of RGTs.

In Vitro Fertilization

While the use of RGTs *may* lead to the decision to destroy an embryo (e.g., if a screening determines that the embryo has a disease or unwanted characteristic), IVF, which is more widely utilized, nearly always leads to the destruction of embryos. During IVF, a woman's eggs are retrieved from her ovaries and, once outside the body, fertilized by sperm in a laboratory setting. Once the eggs are fertilized, an embryo is placed in the woman's uterus. Although widely claimed as the most effective form of assisted reproductive technology, IVF raises moral

TABLE 7.1 Percentage Saying Morally Wrong in Most Cases or Always

	All Respondents (a)	Evangelical Protestants (b)	Mainline Protestants	Catholics	Jews	Non-Western Religions	Atheists, Agnostic, Unaffiliated
Morally wrong: "Use of reproductive technologies to identify diseases in utero." Unadjusted	12.8%	19.4%[a]	11.8%[b]	14.6%[ab]	8.0%[b]	4.7%[ab]	3.3%[ab]
Adjusted	11.9%	16.8%[a]	11.4%[b]	13.9%[ab]	10.0%	4.9%[b]	3.7%[ab]
Morally wrong: "Using genetic engineering, that is, changing a person's DNA or genes, to create a baby that is smarter, stronger, or better looking." Unadjusted	64.2%	71.9%[a]	67.3%[ab]	64.5%[b]	62.1%[b]	49.9%[ab]	50.2%[ab]
Adjusted	65.0%	71.1%[a]	68.1%[a]	65.9%[b]	59.5%[b]	57.1%[b]	51.9%[ab]

a = Difference between percentage and percentage for all other US adults is statistically significant (p < .05).

b = Difference between percentage and percentage for evangelical Protestants is statistically significant (p < .05).

Source: Religious Understandings of Science, 2014. Adjusted percentages account for any influence from differences in education, political ideology, income, sex, age, region of residence, marital status, and race between the religious groups.

issues for some individuals, namely because the procedure can be done with or without a woman's own eggs or man's own sperm; under some conditions, IVF may involve eggs or sperm from a known or anonymous donor. In other cases, a surrogate might be used, when the biological mother's egg or biological father's sperm (or some combination of donor egg or donor sperm) is utilized and then the embryo is placed in another woman who carries the fetus to term.[15] IVF also generally results in more embryos than can be used, and there is moral controversy over what to do with the leftover embryos. In 2015, a *New York Times* article reported that there may be as many as one million frozen embryos in the United States, left over from couples who didn't use all the embryos they created through IVF.[16] These embryos must be stored in liquid nitrogen at a cost of $300 to $1,200 per year, until the couple decides what to do with them. If they don't want to have more children or pay to keep the embryos frozen, the options are to thaw and dispose of the embryos; donate them for research, which also means the embryos will eventually be destroyed; or donate them to another couple facing infertility. According to data from the Society for Assisted Reproduction Technology, more and more couples are choosing to donate their unused embryos to other couples, who haven't been able to conceive. In 2013, 1,084 IVF transfers used donated embryos, "nearly double the 596 transfers in 2009."[17]

IVF not only raises thorny ethical questions but also has an impact on how religious individuals think about creating a family. Many believe the process of conceiving should be "natural" and that children are God-given. As one woman from a largely black church[18] told us of IVF, "It just seems unnatural to me. That's where I am with that. And I think I am relatively liberal and relatively like, 'let us engage the sacred in science,' and I know it's going on, but I just don't know that I could promote [IVF]. And I don't know that I have any deep spiritual reason behind that except that it does not feel natural to me."

According to the sociologist Penny Edgell,[19] family and religion are deeply linked institutions, and this sense was echoed among the individuals we talked with about how faith influences their views of IVF. According to a Rabbi from a Reform Jewish synagogue in Houston,[20] "The life of being Jewish is very much grounded in families and having children. So there is a sense of wanting that, I think, for most people, if not all." The Rabbi explained that this focus of the faith can be difficult for members of his synagogue who are not parents "not by choice." He told us, "People get married later in life. . . . And biologically sometimes it just doesn't happen for some individuals. It's a tough thing because, like I said, this is very much family tradition. We have our holidays and it's about the kids and celebrating around a big family table."

When we surveyed Americans about IVF, we found some moral ambiguity, but also general support. Among all Americans, only 13% think IVF is in most cases or always morally wrong. When we compare the religious groups, we find that evangelicals (at 18%) and Catholics (at 15%) are the religious groups most likely to find IVF morally objectionable. A minority of mainline Protestants (11%), Jews (6%), and members of non-Western religions (8%) also find IVF morally objectionable.

We also asked those who took our survey their feelings on human cloning (mainly not a current possibility), an issue related to assisted reproduction. According to the National Human Genome Research Institute, "Cloning describes a number of different processes that can be used to produce genetically identical copies of a biological entity. The copied material, which has the same genetic makeup as the original, is referred to as a clone."[21] When we asked our survey respondents whether "creating a baby that is a clone of another person" is morally objectionable, we found that about 67% of Americans oppose human cloning. Among evangelicals, the proportion rises to 75%, and 69% of both mainline Protestants and Catholics, and 65% for Jews, oppose human cloning. Among atheists and agnostics, 52% find human cloning objectionable.

Human Embryonic Stem-Cell Research

Human embryonic stem-cell research *inherently* involves preventing an embryo from developing—and, thus, this research has been controversial among Americans since human embryonic stem cells were initially used for scientific purposes in 1998.[22] Human embryonic stem cells are unique because they are able to differentiate or change into all of the specialized cells in the human body.[23] They are used to test drugs, and they have the potential to treat a number of health problems and diseases, including cancer, heart disease, Parkinson's, and Alzheimer's. Human embryonic stem-cell researchers argue that hESC research has greater potential to yield disease cures than nonembryonic stem-cell research.[24]

For many religious believers, the ethical dilemma over hESC research seems to center on whether the benefits to humanity that could result from the research outweigh destroying potential human life.[25] As seen in table 7.2, when we asked whether "destroying human embryos" is morally acceptable "if doing so helps scientists find cures for disease," 47.2% of our survey respondents said that destroying human embryos is always or mostly "morally wrong." Again, we found significant differences across religious traditions. Almost two-thirds (about 66%) of evangelicals believe that destroying human embryos in the context of trying to cure diseases is morally wrong. This compares with 50% of Catholics, 46% of mainline Protestants, 32% of adherents of non-Western religions, 28% of Jews, and 20% of the religiously unaffiliated.

As we also see in table 7.2, there is much less objection across all religious groups to stem-cell research that does not involve human embryos. Only 14.2% of US adults describe such research as morally wrong. Evangelicals

TABLE 7.2 Percentage Saying Morally Wrong in Most Cases or Always

	All Respondents (a)	Evangelical Protestants (b)	Mainline Protestants	Catholics	Jews	Non-Western Religions	Atheists, Agnostic, Unaffiliated
Morally wrong: "Destroying human embryos if doing so helps scientists find cures for diseases."							
Unadjusted	47.2%	65.7%[a]	45.7%[b]	50.2%[ab]	28.4%[ab]	31.7%[ab]	20.1%[ab]
Adjusted	46.8%	61.7%[a]	45.9%[b]	49.9%[ab]	31.1%[a]	35.1%[b]	23.1%[ab]
Morally wrong: "Medical research that uses stem cells from sources that do NOT involve human embryos."							
Unadjusted	14.2%	20.6%[a]	13.3%[b]	15.3%[b]	7.8%[b]	12.4%[b]	4.1%[ab]
Adjusted	12.6%	17.2%[a]	11.8%[b]	13.5%[b]	10.1%	15.5%	4.5%[ab]

a = Difference between percentage and percentage for all other US adults is statistically significant (p < .05).

b = Difference between percentage and percentage for evangelical Protestants is statistically significant (p < .05).

Source: Religious Understandings of Science, 2014. Adjusted percentages account for any influence from differences in education, political ideology, income, sex, age, region of residence, marital status, and race between the religious groups.

are still significantly more likely than the general population to object to the research, while the religiously unaffiliated are significantly less likely to object. All the other religious groups do not statistically differ from the overall population.

In our conversations with religious Americans, we explored how they approach the ethical issues related to RGTs, IVF, and hESC research. We looked at how they reason about these technologies and how their religious beliefs influence their perceptions and stances.

REALITY: RELIGIOUS INDIVIDUALS ARE TORN BETWEEN CONFLICTING INTERESTS

"Wow. That's harder than evolution," says Lana,[26] a young Muslim student from Houston, when we begin to discuss RGTs. When we meet, she is friendly and open to talking about her beliefs. Religion is very important to her, and she makes a point to read at least one surah, or chapter, from the Quran every day. "Islam isn't just a religion," she says. "Your everyday life is Islam. Everything you do." She tells us,

> My parents were actually told I was going to have Down syndrome before they had me.... Their doctor suggested an abortion, and my mom and my dad ... they were like, I don't know, because Islam ... has to be weighed.... So they asked around, and they asked if that's something we can do, and I think they asked a scholar and he said, "Don't have an abortion." Thank God, or else I would not be here right now.

While Lana is aware that RGTs have the potential to help many people, she worries that parents will misuse the screening technology, choosing to "abandon this one and go to the next one." She tells us, "My only fear is that people will start aborting their children because they [find out something like they] have a 70% chance of getting cancer." She is not opposed to the use of IVF, however. As she says, "What's the problem? You're literally doing the same thing [as occurs inside the body] but outside of the body and then putting it back in the body."

A psychologist in her mid-30s, Rebecca[27] is a high-level researcher who works in a hospital. She carries herself with an air of reserved thoughtfulness and tilts her head to the side when asked more serious questions. She chooses her words slowly and carefully; precision seems very important to her. Her Christian faith, she says, affects "all aspects" of her life:

From the way I spend money, to my work, to my relationships, to my leisure activities, to how I feel about myself, how I feel about other people, the type of person I want to be. . . . Everything. I don't separate any issues of my life. It's very integrated or holistic [with my faith].

When asked about hESC research, Rebecca says,

I think if the work is conducted in an ethical manner and with the purpose to benefit human life, I think it is OK. I am anti-abortion. I believe in the sanctity of life a hundred percent. I believe . . . life begins at conception. However, if there's a situation where people do come into contact with embryonic stem cells then there might be redemption if they are used for the greater knowledge and the greater good as a result.

When discussing RGTs, IVF, and hESC research, many religious believers, like Rebecca and Lana, express competing theological values and interests. They want to honor God's role as creator; protect human sacredness; view families as natural and God-given; and alleviate human suffering, both from disease and the pain of infertility. Given the priority religious individuals put on alleviating suffering and honoring the place of humans in God's creation, how do they value the potential benefits of RGTs, IVF, and hESC research when weighed against concerns about protecting the sanctity of human life?

How these different values and interests are weighted in judging the morality of a particular technology is guided by different factors. Shaped primarily by religious texts and authorities, individuals from more conservative religious traditions tend to favor protecting human sacredness and honoring *God's unique role as creator*. These religious individuals tend to oppose RGTs, IVF, and hESC research, as they see them all as "playing God" or devaluing the sacredness of human life. Individuals from more liberal religious traditions tend to place more emphasis on the role of *humans as cocreators*, who can work alongside God to intervene and alleviate human suffering.

Some Religious People Don't Want Humans to "Play God"

In our in-depth discussions with people of faith, we found that their views on RGTs, IVF, and hESC research are generally divided according to the religious narrative they employ to describe God's nature and involvement with the world.[28] Scholars might call these religious narratives schemas, or complex interpretive frameworks, that come to bear on evaluation of these technologies, as either motivation for or post hoc justifications of moral assessments.[29]

Broadly, what we call the creator theology narrative focuses on God's role as master creator and maintains firmly established boundaries and a clear hierarchy between God's role and the human role. Thus, technologies that appear to intervene at the beginning of human life and influence the direction of that life are seen as morally and theologically wrong because they place humans in a God-like creator role (i.e., "playing God"). Alternatively, what we call the cocreator theology narrative attributes to God an interest in improving human life *but* acknowledges that, in some cases, God uses human assistance and intervention to alleviate human suffering. This narrative places God and humans together in a creative role—and leads to different moral evaluations of certain biomedical technologies.

The creator theology narrative was quite common across the monotheistic religious traditions we examined. Christians, Jews, and Muslims—especially those from more conservative theological streams within their faith traditions— invoked this narrative when they discussed their opposition to selection-focused RGTs (i.e., "designer babies"), focusing their opposition on the sin of "playing God" or altering God's intentional plan. They worry that people will use RGTs to select or prefer embryos with certain genetic characteristics, usurping God's creative and potentially redemptive powers. They also worry that manipulating human genetics is a form of "creation" that places humans on the same plane as God. For example, one man[30] from an evangelical congregation in Houston[31] said when discussing selection-focused RGTs,

> I referenced the Tower of Babel a little bit earlier and people tried to build a tower so high that they could get to God, that they could be equal with God. . . . And I think when we start playing God with human genetics, we are doing the same thing. We're putting ourselves equal with God, so . . . I think that would be sinful.

Similarly, a leader in a mainline Protestant church[32] told us—in a fairly colorful way—with regard to selection-focused RGTs that he thinks

> the idea of human beings fucking around with our genomes to create—to basically really completely and totally make ourselves God—that scares me a little. I think that is a really dangerous road [we are] going down, in part because of the theological implications. It's a pretty extraordinary form of idolatry.

Individuals who belong to more conservative religious traditions were more likely to extend the creator theology narrative to oppose disease-focused RGTs as well. These believers have a particular understanding of God's purposive creation. In their view, God has a plan for all of human life, and humans should not alter this plan through their tinkering. As a young evangelical man who works in the medical field[33] bluntly told us, "I believe God is in control, and that he's taking care of everything and [if] this child has a disease, then that's what God wants for this child." "I definitely don't think that they should abort the child or anything like that," a young Muslim woman[34] said when asked about the use of disease-focused RGTs. "If God is going to give it to you, he's giving it to you."

This kind of reasoning—that God is in control and humans should not tamper with his sovereignty—also came up when religious individuals discussed opposition to IVF. When we asked about IVF, we found that evangelicals and Catholics often used the view of "God as creator" or, in its negative form, humans "playing God" to justify opposition to the technology. (The Catholic Church officially opposes IVF, while some evangelical leaders are more accepting of the technology.) One evangelical woman[35] said that her "personal opinion is that it's not the right thing to do. [Those who use IVF] are treading on places that can get very dangerous—the word dangerous may not be right—but it could become disastrous. . . . I believe people that cannot have children need to resolve the fact that they do not. And they need to find children they can adopt, or they can love the children they encounter in life. That's probably what is meant for them to do."

After a long pause to consider his response to a question about IVF, a Catholic man[36] explained, "I would be opposed to it because there is plenty of option without using the best egg . . . there are a lot of orphans right now who need a good home. . . . I am totally against it, as is Catholicism. . . . I mean, I feel sorry for these people who cannot conceive because of health reasons and things, but again, that is the way we were designed by God." Another Catholic[37] we spoke with told us, "[IVF] is kind of like the human embryonic stem-cell question. It is almost the same answer. You know, I understand that there are people that emotionally are going through things and they really want to have a child, and I understand that. And it's not that I would deny them a child at all. It's the fact that the way that they do it crosses a line. And you are killing other children just to see if one will take."

Muslims who had a negative response to IVF also utilized the rationale of God as creator and the perspective that overstepping God's control or "playing God" would be dangerous. For example, one young Muslim,[38] when reflecting on IVF, said, "For those who are very adamant about it, well, it's their choice . . . and if you want to, then fine. It's just dancing close to the edge of playing God for me." And another Muslim woman[39] added, "I guess conducting research in order to regrow a limb or something, in my opinion that's OK . . . I think it's OK, I mean as long as you're not trying to defeat God himself. You're not doing that for the purpose of trying to be God, [with IVF you are] creating a human out of nothing."

Religious Americans Want to Honor the Sacredness of Human Life

"Technology's fine," an evangelical in his early 30s[40] told us when asked about RGTs. "Is the next question do I think it's right or wrong for a person to abort a fetus if it has a disease?" In addition to concerns about interfering with God's role as creator, many religious Americans we interviewed raised concerns about how RGTs, IVF, and hESC research might violate what they see as the inherent sacredness of human life. In particular, they expressed concerns about abortions resulting from the use of RGTs or the destruction of embryos in hESC research. The position that a religious group takes on abortion is frequently cited as determining the moral framework used in thinking about RGTs and hESC research, in particular. This is especially the case among evangelicals and Catholics, whose opposition to abortion has been well documented.[41]

The sacredness of human life frequently came up in our discussions about hESC research. We encountered religious individuals who feel that protecting embryos takes precedence over potential cures that could save human lives, and they frequently referred to biblical teachings or ideas about the nature of God in explaining their views. Most evangelical Christians drew on religious authority, particularly regarding beginning-of-life questions. A 50-year-old evangelical man[42] said, for example,

> I don't consider myself extremely knowledgeable, but . . . according to the Bible, human life is sacred. And I believe, based on my study of the Bible, that human life begins at conception. So any time after conception, if you're engaging in a practice that could lead to the destruction of human life, given that definition, I think that's a problem.

Catholics who said they oppose hESC research frequently connected their concern with protecting human embryos to the Catholic Church's teachings and God's authoritative role as creator. "I am against—well, the Church is against—embryonic stem cell research. . . . You have to destroy it—all these stem cells—and you destroy life," a Catholic social worker[43] said in our interview. "So I'm against it. I'm against it."

It is interesting to note that some religious individuals utilized scientific language in expressing their theological belief in the sanctity of life. An evangelical studying to be a dentist,[44] for example, told us,

> People often cite [the passage of Scripture] that God formed us in the womb, and He knew us from the very beginning. . . . The sperm and the egg come together,

the genetic code is set. . . . To extract that, and from thence prohibit life to continue unto its fullness, [*four-second pause*] is not a good idea. Now I don't know too deeply into it, but I do understand that there are other methods in which you gather stem cells that in no way has that same inhibition of life.

A Catholic medical student[45] explained,

I think people can say whatever they want to about, "Oh, yeah, it's not a living person." Yet, I'm of the opinion when you create a unique set of chromosomes, that person should be able to fend for himself or herself.

A number of religious individuals, however, made inaccurate scientific claims in defending their belief in the sanctity of human life. For example, many scientists argue that human embryonic stem cells hold greater advantages than human adult stem cells for a wide variety of therapies because of the unique abilities that human embryonic stem cells have, including the capacity to become any cell type in the body; yet a Catholic homemaker from Houston[46] said, "There have been significant studies which show that embryonic stem cells and adult stem cells in certain conditions work very similarly, almost—there's no difference," and adult stem cells "have exactly the same characteristics as embryonic stem cells and they're more stable." An evangelical who actually works in health management[47] told us that "very few people who actually do the research believe that embryonic stem cells have as much promise as adult stem cells." Another evangelical stated her belief that, "in the majority of cases, adult stem cells can serve the same purpose as embryonic stem cells and you don't have to kill anybody to get it."

Other religious individuals wrongly cited that human embryonic stem cells come mainly from abortions (when, in reality, they come from embryos left over from fertility treatments).[48] Lana,[49] whom we met earlier, told us, "If you're taking [stem cells] from aborted kids, we don't believe in abortion, so that would be an issue." One Reform Jewish woman said she was worried that women would purposefully become pregnant and then have abortions to produce embryos for research. Surprisingly, several highly educated respondents with doctorate degrees shared this concern.

Religious People Want to Alleviate Suffering

In his work, the sociologist John H. Evans[50] found that how religious individuals feel about RGTs is shaped in part by their feelings about suffering.[51] Although most of the evangelical and fundamentalist Christians in his sample supported using RGTs to reduce suffering, many individuals in these groups also saw potential value in suffering. These individuals did not think embryos that might have a disorder or disease should necessarily be destroyed, based on the belief that suffering may have pedagogical value for the person suffering.[52] The philosopher Bill Doolin and the communications expert Judy Motion too have found that some Christians believe suffering and disability are "part of the human experience" and—because people with disabilities can greatly enrich the lives of those around them—they would not want to see society devalue imperfection. Nonreligious and politically liberal religious individuals, Evans[53] found, think differently about suffering: They largely view suffering as something to stop as quickly as possible, providing a strong rationale for supporting the use of RGTs toward that end.

While our interviews showed many religious individuals oppose RGTs, IVF, and hESC research because they think the use of these technologies allows humans to usurp God's role as creator or dishonor the sacredness of human life, we also found religious believers who are strongly in favor of these technologies, basing their support on the potential these technologies hold to treat diseases and alleviate human suffering.

As we saw earlier, some religious believers worry disease-focused RGTs will lead to abortions—and they thus express opposition to the technologies, drawing on a creator theology that highlights God's role as master creator and the sanctity of human life. Interestingly, many of these same individuals quickly switched to a cocreator theology to express support for disease-focused RGTs that might allow interventions before birth to treat a disease. A youth group leader from an evangelical church in Houston,[54] for example, emphasized God's sovereignty and plan for creation, asserting that abortion is unacceptable because "all human life is precious. And this is who God has knit together and put in her womb." Then, without prompting, he switched to a cocreator theology to explain that when he and his wife discovered that their child might have Trisomy 18, a chromosomal disorder that in most cases leads to death shortly after birth, he would have utilized disease-focused RGTs if they could have prevented the condition. To justify this position, he claimed, "If God's giving me the power and the ability and the know-how to do it, I'd do it."

A woman who attends a largely black congregation in Houston and works as a nursing assistant[55] expressed her support for certain disease-focused RGTs in this way:

> I would think for having amniocentesis, finding out sickness or illness or whatever, I think the Good Lord would want you to know that because the enemy attacks newborns. It attacks you before you become colored to the world. It seems

like He starts to attack newborns earlier and earlier now. . . . So I feel that they have research that finds illnesses and sicknesses or corrective surgery that could be done while the baby is still in the womb, I think that's fantastic.

The cocreator theology narrative was most evident among members of mainline Protestant congregations. Rather than emphasizing God's sovereignty, as many evangelicals do, mainline Protestants tend to talk about a God who has "given" humans "physical responsibilities"—or, in other words, a role as cocreators. One mainline Protestant man who works at a zoo[56] expressed concern when first asked to consider disease-focused RGTs because "I think knowing something like that in an early stage where I couldn't do anything about it will just [*chuckle*] make it easier to doubt and be afraid." Yet he adjusted his response when asked to consider disease-focused RGTs that allow for human intervention, saying,

If I could do something, then sure, yes, I would want to know . . . you start swinging to the other extreme and just make it all about God's ability to heal and deliver [*he knocks at the table*].

Most mainline Protestants and Reform Jews we spoke with support disease-focused RGTs as a way to avoid suffering, *even if* they result in abortion. They also feel that potential cures that would help others are more important than protecting embryos, which, in their view, do not have human moral status. As a Reform Jewish woman[57] explained,

Well, it's an embryo until it's a fetus. So even science knows there's different stages. There's a zygote, first it's just a fertilized egg, it's a sperm and an egg. . . . But it's called that for a reason. I could see people wanting to call a fetus a baby. But an embryo? To me, if it's not viable—you know what that means? Able to live outside of the womb—[*five-second pause*] yeah, not a human being.

Some religious individuals also used cocreator theology and the alleviation of suffering to express support for hESC research. A college student who attends a largely black church in Chicago, for example, explained how he sees conducting hESC research as utilizing gifts that God gave humans:[58]

Here again, it's possible! God has given us all of these things and it comes a time, when we have all of these diseases or whatnot, and if God has given the person the knowledge to where he can perform such a procedure, I believe it's OK.

When discussing hESC research, Reform Jews were the most likely to invoke a mandate to help others based on their religious tradition or texts, and they often ground their support in traditional Jewish teachings. This comment from a Reform Jewish man in Chicago[59] was typical:

> There are certain basic moral principles in Judaism. . . . [O]ne of the ones that has always kind of stuck with me is basically any . . . religious law . . . can be suspended to . . . save a life for some bigger purpose. There are all these rules and you need to follow them, but when it comes down to it . . . no rule is perfect and there is always a reason to break a rule. And I feel like stem-cell research fits into that—in that there might be some obscure rules that you're violating . . . but the potential benefits of it to so many people are so massive. It's hard to say that all those people should potentially be denied a better life because of some rule.

Among both Reform and Orthodox Jews, it was common to reference religious tradition or texts in talking about hESC research, even when they said they were not sure what to believe about the research and would "leave that up to the Rabbis."[60]

We also encountered religious individuals who employed a cocreator theology framework to explain their support for IVF, highlighting the idea that God gave us science so that we could work with God to alleviate suffering and enhance the common good. "When you show me that man can actually create a person with a sperm and the egg and all of that, then I will start listening more to the people who say, 'Oh, you know you are not supposed to do that,' but I don't think that you have that fact with IVF," said a woman[61] from a largely African American evangelical church in Houston when talking about IVF, which she distinguishes from cloning. "I do not think that [IVF] in any way goes against the fact that God created the egg and the sperm. . . . He just made people smarter to where they can harvest them and freeze 'em, and use 'em. No, I do not have a problem with that!"

As might come as little surprise, many religious individuals we spoke with ultimately relied on their personal feelings and experiences when evaluating RGTs, IVF, or hESC research based on the potential to alleviate human suffering. In general, personally knowing people who have struggled with infertility issues was particularly important in forming a positive response to IVF. Even then, evangelicals and Catholics, as well as some Muslims, still struggled with whether and for how long IVF should be pursued. While we found Catholics in general were slightly more likely to have problems with IVF on the grounds of Church teachings, we also talked with many Catholics who knew and understood the

Church's position but held a different view, in part based on IVF's ability to help couples struggling with infertility. "I am all for it," one Catholic[62] said about IVF. "See, again, that is where my conflict is. It is like—so obviously . . . over time opinions have changed. The old traditional way of thinking: Then you do not do this in religion, you do not do that in religion. . . . But even now, the Pope is reconsidering all his thoughts because he has to—he has to come to realize that it is a modern world, and you have to develop new ideas or you are going to lose people that have come to believe in your religion. Yeah. Obviously in vitro is a great thing for somebody who cannot conceive."

When asked about hESC research, an evangelical woman in Houston[63] told us, "I'm partial to that because, as I said earlier, my mom had Alzheimer's, and stem cells were one of the ways that they believe—that research is looking at. They've actually got it in the test tube right now as a cure for Alzheimer's. . . . So . . . I'm passionate about that. I like the idea that there's a possibility that there is a cure that will come from that. So I don't think it's a bad thing if it's going to help us to find a cure."

LESSONS

Aldous Huxley's 1932 dystopian novel, *A Brave New World*, still seems to give voice to our greatest fears, especially the fears of some people of faith. Huxley tells the story of Miranda, who was raised for most of her life on an isolated island. When Miranda sees other people for the first time, she is overcome with excitement, but what she is actually observing is the worst of humanity, where people's life outcomes are determined by genetic selection. A very different time period than now, commentators think Huxley's novel was birthed from the tumultuous period of the early 20th century, where people were victims of the mass production of the Industrial Revolution that made cars, telephones, and radios available and cheap throughout the developing world. Yet Huxley uses the setting and characters in his science fiction novel to express widely held opinions, to encourage his readers to ponder the possibilities of losing individual identity or of hurting others in the fast-paced world of the future. For some of those we talked with, opposition to enhancement RGTs (what some call "designer babies") links them to *Brave New World*; they connect this secular touchstone to humans "trying to be our own Gods." For them, though, being our own God connects us to the dangers that may arise from that role: humans selecting one another's characteristics in the most discriminatory and harmful manner possible.

What have we learned that might empower both scientists and people of faith to contribute to and lead more productive and substantive dialogue between the science community and the faith community about RGTs, IVF, and hESC research? It is important to point out that many religious individuals do not seem to fully understand what RGTs, IVF, or hESC research involves or what the technologies really are. We believe that support for these technologies that have the potential to improve and save lives can be increased if scientists help religious people understand the basics of these technologies, emphasize the potential human benefits of the technologies, and fully engage with religious people's perceived implications of the technologies. Scientists need to—at the same time—recognize that often scientific development of technologies proceeds more quickly than moral reflection on those technologies. At the same time, reflective religious people and thoughtful theologians, in particular, have the potential to act as "moral brakes" against unfettered technological development and use without reflection on the implications.

Start Talking About Biomedical Technologies in Religious Communities

Across the religious traditions we studied, we found that RGTs, IVF, and hESC research are rarely, if ever, actually discussed in congregational contexts. When asked what he thinks about IVF, for example, a 22-year-old evangelical man[64] told the interviewer to "ask me in about four years when I am married and getting ready to have kids. . . . I have never thought about it to be honest." IVF is not "the sort of thing that is discussed at my church," he said.

"I know it's being talked about in the public. . . . But, as with so many issues, sometimes the average pastor doesn't know how to talk about it," a Catholic[65] priest explained. "So now the science is getting so complicated that sometimes you have to refer people. . . . We are not equipped to talk on everything scientific on the same level." This priest goes on further to explain that faith leaders who are many years beyond their seminary training are especially ill equipped to talk about the relevance of Church teachings to new reproductive technologies: "I am also twenty-six years out. Even more than that if you count my seminary days."

Then how can religious communities and congregations have informed and constructive conversations about biomedical technologies and their related moral issues?

Empower Scientists in Congregations to Explain Technologies

We think the first step is for congregations to sponsor discussions and lectures where scientists talk about biomedical technologies and the applications and implications of their research. Among the 23 congregations we studied, such events are rare.

These scientists can explain the basics of new biomedical technologies. They can help religious individuals fully grasp what RGTs are and the differences between disease-focused and selection-focused RGTs. For example, they can help religious individuals understand what hESC research involves and how scientists obtain human embryonic stem cells for research. They can ensure that religious individuals know what IVF is and how it works.

We believe it is especially important to invite scientists from the faith tradition of the congregation. These scientists are well equipped to connect their research to religious perspectives and concerns, such as the sacredness of life and the notion of suffering. Moreover, they are best positioned to share with congregants how religious beliefs can be reconciled with the practices, impacts, and implications of new biomedical technologies.

Focus on Common Goals and Make It Personal

Scientists who hope to increase religious support for biomedical technologies would do well to focus on how the technologies can be used to support the tenets and ideals of faith communities, specifically their potential to alleviate human suffering. Among the religious individuals we spoke with who support disease-focused RGTs, IVF, and hESC research, we found an emphasis on the potential of these technologies to prevent suffering or help those suffering from diseases or other health conditions.

Research suggests that scientists can make the health benefits of these technologies more salient by making them personal. In the small social science literature on hESC research, for example, there are clues that personal context and social ties matter a great deal when people think about this issue and the potential benefits of the research. For instance, a science communication and health policy researcher, Nick Dragojlovic, examined voting intentions on a 2004 California ballot initiative (Proposition 71) that would allow state funding for hESC research. Looking at county-level data and preelection surveys, he found moral opposition to the hESC research initiative was lower in counties with higher levels of elderly people and people suffering from chronic diseases.[66] Specifically, he found that "while the typical born-again Protestant in California was more likely to indicate an intention to vote against the initiative than voters espousing other religious beliefs, this cleavage disappeared in counties with greater proportions of elderly residents and of people suffering from chronic diseases like diabetes or heart disease. My interpretation of this result is that many voters who were predisposed to oppose Proposition 71 on moral grounds were nevertheless persuaded to support the initiative when the potential benefits of future stem cell therapies—namely, the reduction in the suffering of those afflicted by chronic diseases—was made salient to them."[67] While this is only a small study, it suggests that personal experience or personal potential benefit from hESC research might predispose a person to approve of the research. And although science itself often does not (and many think should not) provide space for moral reflection on the development and use of these technologies, thoughtful faith communities could provide such spaces.

NOTES

1. Mid SES Orthodox Jewish Synagogue Houston Intl, conducted August 21, 2013.

2. Rochman, Bonnie. 2009. "Twittering in Church, with the Pastor's O.K." *Time*, May 3. Retrieved March 24, 2015, http://content.time.com/time/magazine/article/0,9171,1900265,00.html.

3. As Georgine M. Pion and Mark W. Lipsey note, in their review of public opinion data, "Science and technology run together in an undifferentiated concept dominated by images of everyday medicine, industry, and household appliances . . . the core notion of basic scientific research hardly figures in the conception at all" (1981, p. 314). "Public Attitudes Toward Science and Technology: What Have the Surveys Told Us?" *Public Opinion Quarterly* 45(3):303–316.

4. Downey, Allen B. 2014. "Religious Affiliation, Education, and Internet Use." Retrieved March 24, 2015, http://arxiv.org/abs/1403.5534.

5. Association of Religion Data Archives. 2012. "General Social Survey 2012 Cross-Section and Panel Combined—Instructional Dataset." Retrieved March 24, 2015, http://thearda.com/Archive/Files/Analysis/GSS12ED/GSS12ED_Var316_1.asp.

6. Ibid.

7. Campbell, Heidi A., ed. 2013. *Digital Religion: Understanding Religious Practice in New Media Worlds.* New York: Routledge.

8. Campbell, Heidi A. 2010. *When Religion Meets New Media.* New York: Routledge.

9. Low/Mid-Low SES Evangelical Church Houston Int3, conducted August 22, 2013.

10. High SES Reform Jewish Synagogue Houston Int11, conducted August 8, 2013.

11. Mid-Low SES Evangelical Church Chicago Int4, conducted July 18, 2013.

12. Low/Mid-Low SES Evangelical Church Houston Int6, conducted September 7, 2013.

13. Mid-Low SES Evangelical Church Chicago Int2, conducted July 17, 2013.

14. See Funk, Cary, Brian Kennedy, and Elizabeth Podrebarac Sciupac. 2016. "U.S. Public Wary of Biomedical Technologies to 'Enhance' Human Abilities." Retrieved July 27, 2016, http://www.pewinternet.org/2016/07/26/u-s-public-wary-of-biomedical-technologies-to-enhance-human-abilities/.

15. For more information about the technical aspects of IVF, see http://www.mayoclinic.org/tests-procedures/in-vitro-fertilization/home/ovc-20206838, accessed November 3, 2016.

16. Lewin, Tamar. 2015. "Industry's Growth Leads to Leftover Embryos, and Painful Choices." *New York Times*, June 17.

17. See http://uk.businessinsider.com/what-happens-to-frozen-human-embryos-left-over-from-ivf-2015-6?r=US&IR=T, accessed November 3, 2016.

18. Mid-High/High SES Evangelical Church Houston Int14, conducted September 27, 2013.

19. Edgell, Penny. 2005. *Religion and Family in a Changing Society*. Princeton, NJ: Princeton University Press.

20. High SES Reform Jewish Synagogue Houston Int11, conducted August 8, 2013.

21. National Human Genome Research Institute. 2016. "Cloning." Retrieved November 10, 2016, https://www.genome.gov/25020028/cloning-fact-sheet/.

22. Mitra, R. 2001. "Science and Reason vs. Unreason." *Economic and Political Weekly* 36(43):4055–4056.

23. Matthews, Kirstin. 2009. "Stem Cell Research: A Science and Policy Overview." Retrieved August 13, 2014, http://bakerinstitute.org/media/files/Research/4a146856/stemcell-intro-0208.pdf.

24. National Institute of Health. 2011. "What Are the Similarities and Differences Between Embryonic and Adult Stem Cells?" Retrieved August 7, 2014, http://stemcells.nih.gov/info/basics/pages/basics5.aspx.

25. Devolder, Katrien. 2009. "To Be, or Not to Be?" *EMBO Reports* 10(12):1285–1287.

26. Mid/Mid-High SES Sunni Muslim Mosque Houston Int7, conducted October 4, 2013.

27. High SES Mainline Church Houston Int25, conducted June 21, 2013.

28. With relationship to RGTs, see, in particular, Ecklund, Elaine Howard, Jared Peifer, Virginia White, and Esther Chan. "Moral Schema and Intuition: How Religious Laypeople Evaluate Human Reproductive Genetic Technologies." *Sociological Forum* 32(2):277–297.

29. See D'Andrade, Roy G. 1991. "The Identification of Schemas in Naturalistic Data." Pp. 279–301 in *Person Schemas and Maladaptive Interpersonal Behavior*

Patterns, edited by M. Horowitz. Chicago: University of Chicago Press. And see also DiMaggio, Paul. 1997. "Culture and Cognition." *Annual Review of Sociology* 23:263–287.

30. Mid-High/High SES Evangelical Church Houston Int5, conducted July 5, 2011.

31. See Wikipedia. "Tower of Babel." Retrieved July 27, 2016, https://en.wikipedia.org/wiki/Tower_of_Babel.

32. High SES Mainline Church Houston Int12, conducted March 16, 2012.

33. High SES Evangelical Church Chicago Int8, conducted July 20, 2013.

34. Mid/Mid-High SES Sunni Muslim Mosque Houston Int5, conducted September 27, 2013.

35. Low/Mid-Low SES Evangelical Church Houston Int10, conducted November 13, 2013.

36. Mid-High/High SES Catholic Church Houston Int5, conducted October 2, 2013.

37. Mid-High/High SES Catholic Church Houston Int8, conducted October 16, 2013.

38. Mid/Mid-High SES Sunni Muslim Mosque Houston Int13, conducted October 10, 2013.

39. Mid/Mid-High SES Sunni Muslim Mosque Houston Int5, conducted September 27, 2013.

40. Mid-High/High SES Evangelical Church Houston Int9, conducted July 29, 2011.

41. Evans, John H. 2002. "Polarization in Abortion Attitudes in U.S. Religious Traditions, 1972–1998." *Sociological Forum* 17(3):397–422. See also Evans, John H., and Kathy Hudson. 2007. "Religion and Reproductive Genetics: Beyond Views of Embryonic Life?" *Journal for the Scientific Study of Religion* 46(4):565–581; Susumu, Shimazono. 2011. "The Ethical Issues of Biotechnology: Religious Culture and the Value of Life." *Current Sociology* 59(2):160–172.

42. Mid-High/High SES Evangelical Church Houston Int14, conducted December 2, 2011.

43. Mid-High/High SES Catholic Church Houston Int14, conducted November 20, 2013.

44. Mid-High/High SES Evangelical Church Houston Int11, conducted October 6, 2011.

45. Mid-High/High SES Catholic Church Houston Int6, conducted October 9, 2013.

46. Mid-High/High SES Catholic Church Houston Int9, conducted November 1, 2013.

47. High SES Evangelical Church Chicago Int6, conducted July 19, 2013.

48. National Institute of Health. 2015. "Stem Cell Basics." Retrieved July 26, 2016, http://stemcells.nih.gov/info/basics/pages/basics3.aspx.

49. Mid/Mid-High SES Sunni Muslim Mosque Houston Int7, conducted October 4, 2013.

50. J. Evans 2006.

51. Campbell, Courtney S. 1995. "The Ordeal and Meaning of Suffering." *Sunstone* 18(3):37–43.

52. See Doolin, Bill, and Judy Motion. 2010. "Christian Lay Understandings of Preimplantation Genetic Diagnosis." *Public Understanding of Science* 19:669–685.

53. J. Evans 2006.

54. Mid-High/High SES Evangelical Church Houston Int15, conducted December 10, 2011.

55. Low SES Evangelical Church Houston Int18, conducted August 10, 2011.

56. High SES Mainline Church Houston Int14, conducted June 9, 2012.

57. High SES Reform Jewish Synagogue Chicago Int10, conducted June 21, 2012.

58. Mid-Low SES Evangelical Church Chicago Int7, conducted July 21, 2013.

59. High SES Reform Jewish Synagogue Chicago Int4, conducted June 19, 2012.

60. Mid SES Orthodox Jewish Synagogue Houston Int8, conducted October 20, 2013.

61. Mid-High/High SES Evangelical Church Houston Int15, conducted October 2, 2013.

62. Mid-High/High SES Catholic Church Houston Int13, conducted November 17, 2013.

63. Low SES Evangelical Church Houston Int2, conducted June 22, 2011.

64. High SES Evangelical Church Chicago Int11, conducted September 24, 2013.

65. Mid-High/High SES Catholic Church Houston Int16, conducted February 11, 2014.

66. Dragojlovic, Nick. 2014. "Voting for Stem Cells: How Local Conditions Tempered Moral Opposition to Proposition 71." *Science and Public Policy* 41:359–369.

67. See, for example, Dragojlovic, Nick. 2014. "How Meaningful Are Public Attitudes Towards Stem Cell Research?" *Oxford University Press's Academic Insights for the Thinking World*, January 17.

CHAPTER 8

Beyond Myths, Toward Realities

In these chapters, we have heard the voices of religious Americans from different faith traditions. We have looked at the survey statistics and listened to the interviews. We have dispelled myths and uncovered realities.

After five years of research, here is what we know: Religious Americans of all types are interested in and appreciate science. They are open to accepting new narratives concerning the origin and development of life on earth. They are not inherently hostile to environmentalism or technological progress. They care about protecting the Earth and helping others. Yet they also care deeply about maintaining an active role for God in the world and—at least for the Christians, Jews, and Muslims we talked with—protecting the idea that humans are created in the image of God and thus hold a special place in creation. Can scientists use these insights to better connect with religious communities to promote the importance and value of science? We believe they can. Can religious people— even those who in the recent past have had the most conflict with science—be convinced to show greater support for science? We believe they can.

We have pushed scholars to move in new directions. We have added to the scholarship of theologians, historians, and philosophers[1] by advancing knowledge of what contemporary people from different religious groups really think about scientists and science and how they see the relationship between science and religion. Discussions of what religious people in the United States think about science have tended to focus on evangelical Christians, whether implicitly or explicitly, and to some extent this is true of what we present in this book. But we have also provided new insights into how American Muslims and Jews view science. In so doing, we show that Muslims and Jews do not see inherent conflict between their faith and science. Instead, they often share a desire to distance themselves from the conflict narrative by distancing themselves from anti-science views they perceive as typical of mainstream conservative Christians. That said, like Christians, both Muslims and Jews do identify certain specific areas of conflict between science and religion, based on their schemas of God and humans.

OUR MESSAGE TO TWO WOMEN (AND THE SCIENTISTS THEY FEAR)

Our journey through what religious people think about science was also a personal one. As we finished writing this book, we remembered two women we met many years ago, whose stories first motivated us to wonder what people of faith think about science. The first was the woman who told Elaine she would not want her children to go to Cornell University because she feared interacting with scientists would lead to a loss of faith. The second was the college student Chris met on a plane, who loved her biology coursework but was hesitant to pursue graduate school because she feared how her faith and views on evolution would be received in such a setting. What might we say to these women now?

Being a Scientist Does Not Mean Being Against God

We have seen throughout the preceding chapters that most, if not all, of the apparent tensions or conflicts between religion and science for religious people can be tied to concerns about what a particular scientific issue means for the perceived role of God in the world or the perceived sacredness of humanity. These concerns might manifest themselves as technical debates about scientific facts. Individuals might question the fossil record, make a distinction between microevolution and macroevolution, or simply state that they "don't buy" the science. This is a ruse. What they are *really* concerned about is what evolution *means* for their sense of who God is and the place of humans in the world. This is why many religious believers are willing to accept guided or theistic evolution— a human origin story that proposes a timeline of millions of years (rather than a young earth) but maintains a role for God in the process.

Given our research, we might tell the college student Chris met on the plane that if she is indeed a "true believer" in young-earth creationism, she will most likely have a difficult time pursuing an advanced education and career in the biological sciences. The facts of evolution are what they are. But there is certainly room to perceive a sense of meaning, purpose, and even a role for God while working in the scientific enterprise. We would tell the woman who feared her child pursuing education at Cornell that we found many scientists whose belief in God and the sacredness of humanity have actually motivated them to pursue scientific training to the fullest extent. Such faith-based narratives of meaning should not cause a problem for studies and a career in science.

Scientists Need to Listen to the Concerns of Religious Believers

When it comes to those areas in which great tension does exist between religion and science, it will help scientists to understand the true source of those tensions and to approach these tensions with a desire to *understand* the point of view held by people of faith, even if scientists would generally not agree with that point of view. In a recent article for the *Guardian*, the journalist Richard Grant argues that science communicators need to take the time to listen to their audience because "most people simply want to know that someone is listening, that someone is taking their worries seriously; that someone cares for them. It's more about who we are and our relationships than about what is right or true."[2]

Religious Believers and Scientists Need to Meet Face-to-Face

The fears of the two women we spoke to were shaped by their perception of scientists as some abstract, alien group of individuals whose interests and concerns are entirely distinct from their own. We would now be able to tell them research shows this assumption is false. Many people who are working in science are actually religious. Although religion is rare among scientists who teach at elite universities, there is little evidence that irreligiosity among university scientists has anything to do specifically with being a scientist. And as we saw in chapter 4, scientists working *outside of universities* are about as likely to be religious as other Americans with similar levels of education.

We wish that these women had had the chance to meet some of the scientists we have, those who are also committed to a faith tradition. On this five-year journey, we have come to think that religious scientists have the *most* potential to be effective bridge builders between scientific and religious communities because they are often open to discussing religious and spiritual ideas and are already trusted by members of their religious communities. Some of these scientists even believe that religion can meaningfully intersect with their research. Within their faith communities, religious scientists can act as ambassadors for science, helping to dispel the stereotype that all scientists are atheists or antireligion. Religious scientists are the best evidence that religious people *can* be scientists and that scientific training does not have to lead to a loss of faith. Segregation between religious and scientific communities only feeds into the anxieties and suspicions expressed by the two women we met.

DIALOGUE THAT BRINGS CHANGE

Based on what we have learned about how people from different faith traditions view science, we have become even more convinced that what we need is a sincere dialogue between scientists and people of faith. While many religious people are interested in science, they are also deeply suspicious of scientists. To reach people of faith, scientists need a more accurate understanding of what people of faith think about science, as well as why they think about certain concepts, theories, and technologies the way they do. They need to have a presence in religious communities, where they can engage religious believers and begin to build trust. We hope our findings here might be the first step toward this kind of dialogue by helping scientists better understand how those from different faith traditions view scientific research and the beliefs that inform their perspective.

Potential Pitfalls

As they approach a new dialogue, religious individuals and scientists must be aware of some potential pitfalls. In our survey data and conversations with religious believers, we found that there are some faith frameworks of meaning that impede or contradict science, science education, or science policy. For instance, one reading of the creator-theology framework suggests that a God who is always in control means humans have very little agency to alter the fate of humanity; this perspective might understandably frustrate scientists working to rectify climate change or alleviate suffering using disease-focused reproductive genetic technologies (RGTs). Rather than simply being frustrated, however, it is important that scientists try to identify and understand the motivations behind these religious frameworks (even if the ultimate goal is to change thinking). For example, when many religious believers think about RGTs, they feel tension between a desire to end suffering and a desire to protect human embryos. Recognizing the different facets of religious thinking on such topics could help scientists direct their efforts and their interpretive frames or schemas toward those narratives that are "mutually beneficial."

At the same time, we would encourage all scientists to refrain from making theological claims—and to highlight, when relevant, that their work does not make theological assertions. Explaining the world in terms of natural forces is not the same as saying that the natural world is all that there is and all that is important. Scientific theories do not say anything about supernatural forces, which by definition are beyond the laws of nature. Science has limitations, and religious individuals want to see that scientists believe this, and will not try to utilize science to make arguments about things outside the scope of science or take science beyond its intended purpose (what the philosopher Gregory Peterson calls "disciplinary imperialism").[3] Although it may seem like an unorthodox assertion, we also think that, under certain circumstances and in certain contexts (like when they are talking to fellow parishioners or giving a public talk in a faith community, or even when a student asks a question about faith and science in a private office discussion), scientists should be more vocal and transparent about their personal faith beliefs and the ways in which they see wonder, awe, and beauty in the natural world.

Models of Dialogue

Where do we see this kind of dialogue happening? As we traveled around the country talking with scientists and people of faith, certain efforts stood out. Two years ago, Elaine had the chance to be part of an invitation-only event held by BioLogos,[4] an organization that sponsors dialogues and invites Christians to see the harmony between science and biblical faith. Some of the most famous pastors and scientists in the nation were present, and because the conference was off the record, they felt free to share their true views and concerns. A number of scientists and pastors said they learned from the other group, and their opinions were changed during the course of this event. "We want to dispel misconceptions that Christians have about science and scientists, by giving faith leaders the opportunity to talk with—and worship alongside—scientists with deep Christian faith," says Deborah Haarsma, the president of BioLogos and a scientist, about what motivates her organization. "We have found that building relationships leads to reduced suspicion and more positive engagement."

We also found a model of dialogue in the Jewish community. While most Jews see little conflict between religion and science, many do not see the full range of potential for collaboration between the two. The Scientists in Synagogues effort "offers Jews opportunities to explore the most interesting and pressing questions surrounding Judaism and science, and to share how some of the most thoughtful Jewish scientists integrate their Judaism and their scientific work."[5] As the project director Rabbi, Geoffrey A. Mitelman, told us, "The challenge in the Jewish community isn't to embrace science. The challenge is getting Jews excited about Judaism. Too often, Jews compartmentalize their Jewish perspective and their love for science. But by bringing both science and religion into the conversation about topics such as environmentalism, the power of awe and mystery, or how technology is changing our lives, we can better integrate those two realms."

The Who and Where of Dialogue

Where do we start this dialogue? The results of our research indicate that—at least in the United States—we need to focus our dialogue efforts on evangelicals. Most surveys estimate that evangelicals represent somewhere between 20% and 40% of the US population.[6] Because of their numbers and their power in certain societal institutions, evangelicals tend to drive public and political opinion and discussion on issues of science and faith. Yet there are fewer evangelical Protestants in academic science than in other kinds of occupations, which is perhaps why evangelical Protestants are much more likely than other groups to view scientists as hostile to religion. They are also much more likely to view the religion and science relationship as one of conflict, and they are twice as likely as members of the general population and other religious groups to turn to a pastor or other church leader when they have a question about science. For this reason, it is crucial for scientists to be in dialogue with evangelical Christians, particularly evangelical leaders. What these leaders think about science—and the resources they have to help them speak about challenging scientific issues— is likely to have an impact on the ways their followers engage with science.

We hope to see religious leaders—and evangelical Christian leaders, in particular—emerge as supporters of scientific advancement and as drivers of change in the perception of science among their faith communities. Our survey data show that congregants ask their religious leaders questions about the implications of science and they trust their responses. Thus, it is up to these faith leaders to create an atmosphere in which their congregants can feel comfortable discussing difficult issues related to faith and science. A young Catholic medical student we talked with recalled his personal struggle dealing with his support for evolution in a congregation where the priest is a creationist. He felt that he had to suppress his views in his church and worried that his evolutionary perspective "could wreck everything" that other congregants believed. Where could he go, then, to critically think about and discuss how his faith might be compatible with science?

We suggest religious leaders openly acknowledge the concerns of their congregants when it comes to the relationship between religion and science and that they actively promote discussions about science and faith, particularly among young people. Many religious individuals look to their religious leaders not only to help them engage with and understand scientific ideas, but also to help them maintain a sense of meaning and purpose in the face of scientific theories and technologies. For many people of faith, religious leaders are their authorities on matters of moral reflection related to new scientific discoveries. As a member of an evangelical church told us at the end of our conversation, "Science really can't answer the question of 'why?' or 'for what purpose?' or 'to what end?'"

Pursue Common Interests

To our surprise, we found that there are many shared interests and a great potential for shared efforts between scientific and religious communities on important issues. Religious people express a significant amount of interest in and appreciation of science. This is especially the case when science is perceived to tap into the concerns Christians, Jews, and Muslims almost uniformly have about ending suffering and improving the well-being of humanity. There is, then, opportunity for scientists to draw on these narratives of meaning, using them to find common ground with religious individuals on issues related to science education and policy.

We are not suggesting that scientists use religious language or ideals cynically or superficially, but that they engage with them sincerely in an attempt to build on common interests and understandings. Can evolution be explained so that it doesn't totally eliminate the role of God, at least in the mind of the person that it is being explained to? Can religious ideals be used to build support for environmentalism? Can medical technologies be presented so that their potential to alleviate suffering is highlighted? If scientists can better understand and speak to the real, specific concerns of religious individuals—and perhaps even show how science can coexist with religious concepts and ideals—they have a better shot at building bridges and advancing science in the process.

In an effort we have just started, we are trying to bring scientific and religious communities together around a common area of concern—minority representation in science. We find that African Americans and Latinos, who are traditionally underrepresented in science, are overrepresented in conservative Christian communities.[7] Our goal is to uncover where African American and Latino communities see conflict between religion and science, as well as the conditions under which religious communities might encourage young people to go into science. We have just begun to explore how churches (as the civic organization in which the majority of black and Latino Americans, in particular, are involved) might increase minority representation in science, technology, engineering, and mathematics (STEM) fields. Pastors in these churches suggested that, for black and Latino youth, the opportunity to see someone of their skin color and their faith tradition in STEM would be incredibly significant. As one Latino pastor[8] put it, "I do think . . . it is helpful to have somebody of your own skin color [in science] because . . . to see one of your own would give an inspiration." Similarly, an African American pastor[9] explained, "Science still for a lot of African Americans is a no-trespassing zone." Increasing socioeconomic and racial diversity in science is a little-explored area where we believe scientific and religious communities can begin to work together for a common goal.

If we were to talk again today with the two women we met so many years ago, we would encourage them to keep talking with scientists, keep thinking about the relationship between science and religion, and keep an open mind. If scientists and people of faith are to begin to have more informed, meaningful, and productive relationships, scientists need to better understand how religious people really view science and scientists, and religious individuals need to better understand science and scientists (including how they view religion). Both groups need to move beyond the myths and stereotypes. The reality is that they need to listen to one another, learn from each other, and work together if they are to achieve their best and highest goals.

NOTES

1. See, in particular, Lindberg, David C., and Ronald L. Numbers, eds. 1986. *God and Nature: Historical Essays on the Encounter Between Christianity and Science.* Berkeley: University of California Press.

2. See Grant, Richard P. 2016. "Why Scientists Are Losing the Fight to Communicate Science to the Public." *Guardian*, August 23.

3. For an excellent article on this topic, which utilizes the concept of disciplinary imperialism, see Peterson, Gregory R. 2003. "Demarcation and the Scientistic Fallacy." *Zygon: Journal of Religion and Science* 38:751–761.

4. See www.biologos.org, accessed October 3, 2016.

5. See http://sinaiandsynapses.org/scientists-in-synapses/; this effort is part of the broader Sinai and Synapses effort.

6. See Hackett, Conrad, and D. Michael Lindsay. 2008. "Measuring Evangelicalism: Consequences of Different Operationalization Strategies." *Journal for the Scientific Study of Religion* 47(3):499–514.

7. See, in particular, Korver-Glenn, Elizabeth, Esther Chan, and Elaine Howard Ecklund. 2015. "Perceptions of Science Education Among African American and White Evangelicals: A Texas Case Study." *Review of Religious Research* 57(1):131–148.

8. Lat23: Latino, Pastor, Male.

9. AfAm41: African American, Pastor, Male.

In the Field for Religious Understandings of Science

The data for *Religion vs. Science* come from the Religious Understandings of Science (RUS) study, a broad study of how religiously involved Americans perceive science, how Americans employed or educated in scientific professions perceive religion, and how the entire general US population thinks about the religion and science interface. The RUS study is a mixed-methods effort comprising participant observation, document analysis, qualitative semistructured interviews, and a nationally representative general population survey. Alongside the RUS study throughout the book, we also cite other surveys, as well as other researchers' work on science and religion.

QUALITATIVE DATA OVERVIEW

We began with qualitative observational and interview data, which were collected over a four-year period in twenty-three congregations between 2010 and 2014. In total, qualitative data consist of 248 congregational observations and 319 interviews in two cities, Chicago and Houston. These research sites include evangelical, mainline, and Catholic churches, as well as Orthodox and Reform Jewish Synagogues and Sunni Muslim mosques.

It is important to note that the congregations and religious organizations that we used as research sites within these two cities were not selected for representativeness or through random selection. Instead, sites were selected for diversity of characteristics theorized to affect the religion and science interface. These features include theological stance, tradition identification, congregation size and location, and congregational demographics. Sites that were leader organizations—through their large membership and presence—in each city were specifically targeted on the assumption that their congregants' and religious leaders' attitudes might have an impact on the religion and science relationship within the city and nationally. After obtaining permission from congregational leaders to study their congregations, researchers selected events and services to attend based on the information on the organizations' websites; attendance at these events helped researchers find interview respondents. Qualitative data were collected by Ecklund and a team of trained undergraduate, graduate, and postdoctoral researchers. We utilized a purposive qualitative sampling approach, by selecting respondents with various levels of involvement in the congregation as well as with representative demographic characteristics.

Religious Case Selection

This is the first study of its kind to feature in-depth interviews with such a wide array of religious people regarding their attitudes toward science, including groups that are not often represented in such studies, such as African American Protestants, Orthodox Jews, and Muslims. We focused the qualitative data collection primarily on evangelical Christians, but we also studied Catholics (both Latino as well as primarily white congregations) as well Muslims and Jews. And we considered the ethnic and racial classification of congregations. For example, researchers highlight how science and religion have cooperated in ways that were harmful to black Americans.[1] For example, we know that scientific and theological discourse both contributed to pseudo-scientific experiments, such as the US eugenics movements and the pseudo-medical clinical trials of Tuskegee.[2] And black Americans remain one of the most overrepresented racial groups in Christian religious traditions that seem to have tension with some forms of science, which some scholars link to an underrepresentation of African Americans in science careers.[3]

We also wanted to focus specifically on non-Christian religious traditions. While most of the recent modern debate about religion and science has put evangelical Christians at the fore, increasing numbers of Muslims are also becoming involved in these debates, and Islam in America is gaining prominence. Most Muslims in the United States are Sunni, with South Asians and Arabs among the two largest ethnic groups.[4] Because they fare better than average on income and education, South Asian Muslims have established their own mosques and associations in greater numbers than other ethnic subgroups.[5] Hence, most of our interview sample of Muslims is South Asian. Our sampling strategy did not permit inclusion of Shiite Muslims, who represent 11% of American Muslims.[6] We also studied Jews (both Reform and Orthodox). Judaism is a religious tradition that is important to science in recent American history.[7] While "Jewish" may refer to both religious and ethnic identity, by sampling within synagogues we have sought the perspectives of practicing religious Jews, while recognizing the diversity within this community.

Table A.1 provides an overview of the qualitative data collection.

TABLE A.1 Overview of Qualitative Data

	Total (N)	Christian (N)	Jewish (N)	Muslim (N)	Houston (N)	Chicago (N)
Semistructured interviews	319	227	64	28	206	113
Organization observations	248	185	34	29	221	29
Archival materials	273					

Selection of Research Cities and Religious Organizations

Houston and Chicago were chosen due to their population size and potential prominence in the broader American context of religion and science. Houston is a southwestern city; it is home to the world's largest medical center and three major universities. Consequently, it provides an interesting setting to examine themes related to science education and religion. Chicago is a Midwestern city. It is home to many universities and two major medical centers, housing schools of theology and Bible institutes, as well as a religiously diverse population. Unlike Houston, it is not typically considered a Bible Belt city.

Research sites vary along axes relevant to sociological considerations of religion and science, including socioeconomic status, racial composition, religious tradition, theological perspectives (conservative to progressive), geographic location (urban or suburban), and age of congregants. The socioeconomic status (SES) of the research sites ranges from very low to very high. SES is approximated using a three-part composite consideration. We utilized the 2010 US Census to ascertain the median and mean incomes for the zip code of the research as well as the percentage of the workforce occupied in that zip code in management, business, science, or the arts. We also determined SES through evaluations of the congregants' signs of SES, including dress, modes of transportation, building quality, and congregational operating budget. Finally, we used postinterview evaluation of each respondent's education level.

Interviews

A total of 319 interviews were completed for the RUS study between May 2011 and January 2014. More than two-thirds (N = 227) of these interviews were completed with Christians; 64 interviews were completed with Jewish respondents and 28 interviews with Muslim respondents. *To facilitate the central project focus on evangelicals, nearly half the interviews (N = 143) were completed with evangelical respondents.*

Respondents were recruited for the study in the following ways: Researchers attended religious services to personally meet and invite congregation members to participate in the study. Additionally, researchers utilized a modified snowball approach, meaning that some of those we interviewed were recommended by existing respondents or suggested by congregational leadership. Finally, at some research sites, respondents volunteered for participation through an open invitation provided by congregational leadership.

These methods resulted in a diverse group of interview respondents, which we think reflects the demographics of each congregation. Respondents were of various ages and ethnic backgrounds. The average respondent age is 48 years. Just over half (55%) of the sample is male, while the remaining 45% is female. Almost 60% of the sample is white (59%), 16% black, 13% Hispanic, and 11% Asian or other ethnicity. One-fifth of those who participated in an interview were employed in science-related occupations, and 15% were religious leaders. Nearly three-quarters (74%) had at least a bachelor's degree.

Interviews lasted between 26 minutes and two and a half hours with an average length of one hour and six minutes, and median length of one hour and two minutes. All interviews were conducted in English or Spanish; Spanish-language interviews were fully transcribed in Spanish and translated to English prior to analysis. Interviews were completed in person or over the phone, although 80% of interviews were completed in person.

Interview Guides

Two semistructured interview guides were utilized in this study: one for congregation leaders and another for congregation members (as well as Spanish-language guides for Spanish-language interviews—all respondents from primarily Latino congregations were offered an option of a Spanish-language interview and were able to opt to complete the interview in Spanish or English). The guides were semistructured in order to allow a focused exploration of themes of particular interest to the broader RUS study, while simultaneously allowing the interviewer to structure the interview around each respondent's unique answers and insights. This allows previous insights gained through engagement with the literature or from previous interviews on science and faith to be closely examined as well as to provide space for new themes or theoretical insights to arise.[8]

Both guides hinge on the relationship between faith and science and opinions on science topics and faith history. The leader's guide includes institutional
information regarding the congregation's leadership structure, history, and phi-
losophy. The complete interview guide is included as Appendix B.

Interview Analysis

All interviews were recorded with informed consent from the respondent (Rice
University–Protocol 11-188E). And respondents received information about the
study before participation. Respondents from primarily Latino congregations
were offered the option of completing the interviews in Spanish. The interviews
were independently transcribed, edited, and systematically coded by a team of
researchers for themes related to the central research questions. We did not test
specific hypotheses but used a modified inductive approach to analyze the interviews.[9] Specifically, each interview was thematically coded for how respondents
discussed their attitudes related to the different scientific issues we discuss in the
book. In this process, researchers looked for differences in both explanations of
as well as nonverbal utterances in response to an issue, such as laughter.

The growing literature on moral intuition tends to be skeptical of qualitative
interviews. The sociologist Stephen Vaisey states, "Because interview methods engage with discursive consciousness alone, they cannot rule out the possibility that deeply internalized moral attractions and repulsions (grounded
in schematic associations acquired through cultural experience rather than in
conscious beliefs), are patterned in motivationally important ways."[10] Contrary
to this view, our attention to producing detailed transcriptions of interviews,
attentive to laughter and other nonverbal data, or measuring the extent to which
respondents pause after a question, enables us to advance the scholarship in
this area. And we maintain that the narratives respondents use are important
because narratives, as well as even attempts at creating narratives, reveal discursive and nondiscursive practices that individuals use to actively produce social
and psychological realities in conversation with the interviewer.[11]

QUANTITATIVE METHODS

Subsequently, these data inform a general population survey of 10,241
Americans. While the interview and observational data inform the survey, the
interview respondents were not selected directly from the sample of survey
respondents. The survey sample consists of general population adults (ages 18

TABLE A.2 Interview Respondent Demographics by Religious Tradition

		Age	Age Category				Gender		Race				Employment		Education
	N	Average (Years)	<30 %	31–50 %	51–70 %	71+ %	Male %	Female %	White %	Black %	Hispanic %	Other %	Science Occupation %	Religious Leader %	> Bachelor's Degree %
Christian															
Evangelical	143	48	27	24	38	10	56	44	54	35	8	3	18	17	74
Mainline	38	50	11	34	45	11	55	45	97	—	—	3	32	13	89
Catholic	46	47	9	48	41	2	57	43	24	—	63	13	9	15	54
Latino Catholic	30	49	7	43	47	3	63	37	20	—	77	3	—	20	30
African American	50	52	16	22	50	12	38	62	4	96	—	—	12	18	58
Jewish															
Reform	40	56	5	33	58	5	55	45	98	—	3	—	30	13	98
Orthodox	24	53	8	33	54	4	54	46	96	—	—	4	21	13	92
Muslim	28	27	(20)	4	4	—	54	46	7	4	4	86	25	14	42
Total	319	48	22	30	41	7	55	45	59	16	13	12	21	15	74

and older and both English- and Spanish-speaking participants), and an over-sample of adults in science occupations (computer and mathematics; architecture and engineering; life, physical, and social sciences; medical doctors). The sample was identified using GfK's KnowledgePanel; approximately 95% of the sample consists of general public adults, while the remaining 5% consists of an oversample of individuals in science occupations. Potential respondents were contacted via email using the standard GfK email introduction. Respondents were asked by GfK to log in to a password-protected website and asked to complete the survey. Surveys were self-administered and accessible any time of day for a designated period. Participants could complete a password-protected survey only once. To encourage survey completion, potential respondents received up to five email reminders prior to the survey end date.

Survey Overview

The KnowledgePanel is a probability-based online nonvolunteer access panel. Panel members are recruited using a statistically valid sampling method with a published sample frame of residential addresses that covers approximately 97% of US households. Sampled non-Internet households, when recruited, are provided a netbook computer and free Internet service so they may also participate as online panel members. The KnowledgePanel consists of about 50,000 adult members (ages 18 and older) and includes persons living in cell-phone-only households.

The survey produced 10,241 total valid respondents from 16,746 invited panelists in the United States. Because we included an oversample of 341 individuals employed in science-related fields (individuals who are likely different than the general population), we utilize a poststratification weight that adjusts for this oversample and nonresponse patterns based on population benchmarks from the October 2012 Current Population Survey.[12] Survey responses were made anonymous by GfK prior to sending results to the Rice University team. Table A.3 compares some of the demographics of the RUS respondents to the US adult population. As shown in this table, the RUS respondents are quite similar to the population of adults in the United States, although slightly older and more educated.

Survey Instrument

The survey instrument includes both questions original to the RUS and others replicated from general population surveys that include, but are not limited to, the General Social Survey, Baylor Religion Survey, Pew Research Center surveys, and others. Skip patterns were applied to certain questions within the survey instrument. The instrument took an average of 24 minutes to complete. The full survey instrument is in Appendix C.

TABLE A.3 Demographics of Survey Respondents

	US Adult Population	RUS Respondents— Unweighted	RUS Respondents— Weighted
Sex			
Male	48.3%	50.8%	47.9%
Female	51.7%	49.2%	52.1%
Mean age	44.87	49.96	47.10
Educational attainment			
Less than HS diploma	17.6%	8.4%	12.7%
HS diploma	28.5%	27.9%	29.1%
Some college	27.1%	28.6%	28.9%
Bachelor's degree or higher	26.7%	35.1%	29.2%
Region			
Northeast	18.3%	17.9%	18.2%
Midwest	21.4%	23.6%	21.6%
South	37.0%	35.0%	36.9%
West	23.3%	23.4%	23.3%

Pilot Survey

A pretest was fielded between November 19, 2013, and November 20, 2013, by GfK KnowledgePanel® via a web survey. A total of 36 surveys were completed out of the 83 invited to participate. Survey participants were invited to participate in the survey by receiving the following email:

Dear,

Thanks for being an integral part of KnowledgePanel! We are asking for your participation in a confidential, twenty-minute web survey designed by researchers at Rice University (Houston, TX). The purpose of this study is to explore how Americans perceive the relationship between religion and science, as well as their opinions about important issues like medicine, technology and education.

The survey data is being collected by KnowledgePanel on behalf of Rice University. We emphasize that this is academic research and all information you provide is protected by law and will be kept strictly confidential by both the project research teams at KnowledgePanel and Rice University. For more information about this study, please contact Professor Ecklund directly, ehe@rice.edu. To confirm the legitimacy of this research, you may contact Rice University's Institutional Review Board, irb-io@rice.edu, and identify this study as #11-188X.

Thank you in advance for your participation.

Elaine Howard Ecklund, Primary Investigator
Herbert S. Autrey Chair in Social Sciences, Rice University
&
KnowledgePanel Support Team
www.knowledgepanel.com

An additional privacy statement was included.

The pilot phase ran from December 3, 2013, through December 16, 2013. Data from the pretest informed revisions of the survey instrument, specifically focused on amending low-response questions, revising response categories, and other minor changes. The pilot also tested the effectiveness of preincentives and prenotifications in increasing response rate. In Ecklund's previous studies with academic scientists[13] she found that mailed prenotification letters with cash incentives increased response rates. Since this survey, however, utilized a preexisting survey panel we tested the effectiveness of this method on a general population. To do so, the pilot sample (N = 600) was split into three groups (N = 200). The first group received a prenotification letter including a dollar preincentive. The second received an email prenotification with a dollar preincentive. The third received no prenotification or preincentive. In contrast to Ecklund's previous studies, the pilot data revealed panelists responded at the highest rate without prenotification or preincentive (a procedure most closely mirroring GfK's common method) (see table A.4). Consequently, the main survey was fielded without prenotification or preincentive.

TABLE A.4 Preincentive and Prenotification Results

	Frequency	Percentage	Valid Percentage	Cumulative Percentage
Letter prenotification + preincentive	197	32.6	32.6	32.6
Email prenotification + preincentive	202	33.4	33.4	66
No prenotification	205	34	34.0	100
Total	605	100	100	

Main Survey

The main survey ran from December 27, 2013, to January 13, 2014, and garnered 10,241 responses. Of the responses, 9,798 represented a random sample of the general US English- and Spanish-speaking adult population. Three hundred and forty-one of these respondents represented an intentional oversampling of panel members whose occupations were in one of several targeted sectors that the researchers identified as potentially including higher proportions of individuals that might be considered scientists. These occupational sectors were as follows:

1. Computer and Mathematics
2. Architecture and Engineering
3. Life, Physical, and Social Sciences
4. Medical Doctor (such as physician, surgeon, dentist, veterinarian)
5. Other Health-Care Practitioner
6. Health Technologist
7. Health-Care Support

For the purpose of comparison and analysis, the oversample was drawn to increase the number of respondents from these science-related occupational sectors. Because the individuals in this science oversample are likely not representative of the general population, sampling weights are applied in the analyses so that these cases do not adversely influence the accuracy of population estimates.

Completion and Response Rates

The 62.7% completion rate results from dividing the total surveys completed by the total N invited and qualified to take the survey from the existing GfK panel.[14] Taking into account stages of recruitment into the panel and the completion of a panel profile, the cumulative response rate for the RUS survey was 5.6%.[15] See Chang and Krosnick[16] for extensive discussion of response rates with panel surveys.

Survey Analysis

Several decisions had to be made concerning the analysis of the survey data and the presentation of those analyses in the preceding chapters. One of the key decisions concerned which religious groups we would examine and how those groups would be defined. This is particularly the case with Protestants. Given the implicit or explicit focus on evangelicals in many of the discussions concerning religion and science issues, it was clearly important to identify evangelical Protestants. There are different strategies for doing this, however.[17] A common strategy is to subdivide Protestants based on the denomination that an individual identifies with or the kind of religious organization an individual attends.[18] The potential downside to this method is that some denominations are fairly heterogeneous. For example, there are some United Methodist Church individuals or congregations that are fairly conservative or evangelical, but this denomination is typically classified as a mainline or a liberal-moderate denomination in surveys. Given this issue, we decided to define evangelicals more on an identity rather than denominational affiliation basis. The first religious identity question on the survey asked respondents, "Religiously, do you consider yourself to be Protestant, Catholic, Jewish, Mormon, Muslim, not religious, or something else? If more than one, click the one that best describes you:

1. Protestant
2. Catholic
3. Just a Christian
4. Jewish
5. Mormon
6. Muslim
7. Eastern Orthodox
8. Buddhist
9. Hindu
10. Sikh
11. Baha'i
12. Jain
13. Not religious
14. Agnostic
15. Atheist
16. Something else

Table A.5 shows the distribution of responses to this question in the RUS survey compared to the 2012 General Social Survey (GSS). The GSS only offers five responses (Protestant, Catholic, Jewish, Other, None) on its initial religious preference question, so we have to combine some of the RUS categories when making comparisons. As would be expected, given that both are probability samples of US adults, the distributions of religious traditions are quite similar. The main difference is that there is a slightly lower percentage of religiously unaffiliated individuals in the RUS (14.95% when combining the not religious, atheist, and agnostic categories) compared to the GSS (19.95%) and a slightly lower percentage of individuals in the Protestant category in the GSS (45.94%)

TABLE A.5 Initial Religious Preference Question of RUS Survey Respondents Compared to Initial Religious Preference Question of 2012 GSS Survey Respondents

	RUS	2012 GSS
Protestant	27.58%	45.94
Just a Christian	22.58%	("Protestant")
Catholic	23.59%	23.65%
Jewish	1.91%	1.88%
Mormon	1.72%	
Muslim	0.32%	
Eastern Orthodox	0.33%	
Buddhist	1.10%	8.87%
Hindu	0.70%	("Other")
Sikh	0.08%	
Baha'i	0.04%	
Jain	0.01%	
Something else	5.08%	
Not religious	6.89%	
Agnostic	4.00%	19.95%
Atheist	4.06%	("None")

compared to the RUS (50.16). These differences are likely related to each other. That is, it is likely that some of the individuals who might pick "None" when they are only given the five GSS response options were instead tempted to choose "Just a Christian" in the broader range of categories on the RUS survey.

As seen in table A.5, there are two religious categories in the RUS data that we do not present in the preceding chapters. The first is for "Mormons" and the second is for the "something else" category. We do not present the results for Mormons as they were not a focus of the project and we did not conduct any interviews or observations among Mormon congregations. We do not present the "something else" category simply because it is such a heterogeneous category that it is difficult, if not impossible, to make any conclusions from it.

Later in the survey we asked respondents whether they identify with a variety of religious terms. Specifically, this question asked, "How well do the following terms describe your religious identity?"

a) Bible-believing
b) Evangelical
c) Mainline Christian
d) Spiritual
e) Fundamentalist
f) Seeker
g) Theologically conservative
h) Theologically liberal
i) Pentecostal
j) Charismatic
k) Born-again
l) Mystic
m) Contemplative
n) Religious Right
o) Religious Left

For each of the above identities, the respondents could say that the identity describes them (1) not at all, (2) not very well, (3) somewhat well, or (4) very well. To define evangelicals, we identified individuals who chose either the "Protestant" or "just a Christian" response to the first question and who said that the term "evangelical" describes their religious identity "very well" or "somewhat well." Those that selected the "Protestant" or "just a Christian" responses but said that the "evangelical" term does not describe them well or at all were classified as Mainline Protestant.

In table A.6 we examine how our self-identification classification compares to a classification based on RUS survey respondents' denominational affiliation. We see that 71% of individuals who identify as evangelical are also in evangelical denominations. Another 17% are in denominations that are typically classified as mainline Protestant, while 9.3% are in historically black Protestant denominations. Another 2% didn't provide enough information about their denomination to classify them in a tradition. Looking at the individuals we categorize as mainline Protestant, we see that 34% are in denominations often classified as evangelical, while 39% are in denominations classified as mainline Protestant. We also see that individuals we classified as mainline Protestant were less likely to have provided enough information about a denominational affiliation to clearly classify them based on that information.

You will note that when we are reporting survey results we often refer to members of "non-Western traditions." This is by no means ideal. We recognize that there are vast differences between Muslims, Hindus, Sikhs, Jains, and other

TABLE A.6 Comparing Protestant Respondents' Religious Tradition Based on Self-Identification and Denominational Affiliation

Based on denominational affiliation	Based on Self-Identification Classification Used in Book (See Text)	
	Evangelical Protestant	Mainline Protestant
Evangelical Protestant	71.01%	34.17%
Mainline Protestant	17.20%	39.12%
Black Protestant	9.30%	10.01%
Other\unknown	2.49%	16.70%
	100%	100%

groups in this category. We combine these groups because there are too few individuals in our data belonging to these groups to analyze them individually. We use the shorthand of "non-Western" simply as a stylistic device to avoid repeatedly listing all of the individual groups included in this category. This label is not sufficient given its Western-centrist connotation. An alternative label might be "non-Judeo Christian," but that also could be seen as problematic.

A second decision we needed to make concerning the analysis and presentation of the survey data concerned whether and to what extent we should statistically control for other factors beyond religion that might differ between individuals. Such factors include variables like sex, age, education, and race. For some purposes, a raw or unadjusted percentage is meaningful and important. For example, if you are planning outreach to religious groups concerning a science-related issue, all you might want to know is what group is most in need of the outreach. This might just require knowing which group expresses a particular view, regardless of whether it is really the group's religious tradition or other factors that drive the view. For other purposes, we often want to know if religion is *really* causing a difference between individuals or whether it just so happens that individuals belonging to this particular religious group have, say, a higher or lower educational attainment. Because both sets of statistics might be useful, we present both unadjusted or "raw" percentages and also the "adjusted" or percentages after statistically eliminating the effects of several other demographic and social variables. These variables include individuals' education, political ideology, income, sex, age, region of residence, marital status, and race. The adjusted percentages allow us to see what the differences between the religious groups would be if the religious groups were identical to each other on these demographic and social variables.

Main Sample Interview Guide

Interview Guide for Religious Understandings of Science Study

QUESTIONS ON RELIGIOUS IDENTITY, BELIEF, OR PRACTICE

1) Why don't you start by telling me a little bit about the work you do? (*Here we are trying to get a sense of what they do day-to-day for their work but also the name of their actual occupation so you should ask this directly if it is not volunteered*)
2) About how long have you been attending this [church/synagogue/mosque/ student group] and what sort of activities are you involved in?
3) Thinking more broadly, how does religion or spirituality affect your life these days? [*If the respondent seems confused by this question, then ask, "How is your life different because of your religious commitment, if at all?*] For example, what kind of activities do you participate in outside of the congregation as a part of your faith?
4) And how about prayer—to what extent is prayer relevant to your religious experience? [*If yes*] Could you tell me a little bit about the kinds of things you pray for? [*If yes*] If you or a family member were ill, how would you see prayer relating to that experience? Would you or your congregation pray for them? Why? [*If yes*] How do you think about "unanswered prayers" for healing?

EXPERIENCES WITH SCIENTISTS AND
OPINIONS OF SCIENCE

5) We are going to transition now to asking a few questions about your experiences with science. To start, could you give me your working definition of science, just a sentence or two of what you understand science to be? [*It is important here to make sure that we do not make the respondent feel badly for how much they know or do not know about science*]

6) When you think about science what kinds of images come to mind? [*Probe: Is this person an atheist?*]

7) Would you expect there to be any differences between a religious scientist and a nonreligious scientist? Why or why not?

8) To what extent do you think that scientists have particular biases? [*If they are biased*]—what are some of those biases? And why do you think scientists have them?

THOUGHTS ON SCIENCE AND FAITH INTERFACE

I am interested in how you see the relationship between your faith tradition and science.

9) Some say there is a "conflict between science and religion." How would you personally respond to such a statement? [*If they think there is a conflict*] What are the areas of conflict that you see? [*If they do not think there is a conflict*] What are some issues that other people typically perceive as conflicts between science and religion?

10) Thinking back to your primary and secondary education, do you recall any teachers bringing up religion in a science class? If so, how did you feel about the way it was discussed?

11) Do you ever feel like you have to choose between what [*your Holy Book or for Catholic respondents the Church teachings*] says and what science says? [*If yes*] Why do you feel like you have to choose? [*Probe for an example of conflict*] [*If no*] Can you tell me about your view of why there is no conflict in these understandings?

12) I know that some religious people have sacred texts like the [*say name of text of tradition*], which include descriptions of various miracles. Do you believe that miracles occurred in the past as they are described in the [*insert name of Holy Book*]? How do you think science might relate to these miracles?

13) Has there been a shift in how you view the relationship between religion and science? [Can you remember a time in your life when you felt differently than you do now about the relationship between religion and science?] [*If yes*]: What was the nature of this shift and what prompted it? [*If no*]: Can you imagine anything that might cause you to have a different perspective?

SPECIFIC SCIENTIFIC ISSUES

Now I'd like to think about some specific scientific issues.

14) How about we start with evolution. How does evolution relate to your personal beliefs about the development of life on Earth? Do you think that it offers the best explanation for life on Earth? Why or why not?

15) How do you think evolution relates to your faith tradition? Can it be compatible with the teachings of [the Bible/Torah/Koran]? [*If yes*] How is it compatible? [*If no*] In what ways does it conflict and why is this an important point of conflict?

16) What about the teaching of creationism or intelligent design in schools? Do you think that either or both should be taught alongside evolution, in place of it, or not at all? Why?

17) What kind of effect, if any, do you think science education might have on a child's developing faith? Is this effect positive or negative?

18) Thinking about a different topic now. How about embryonic stem-cell research? Some people say that scientists should be able to conduct medical research using stem cells from human embryos. Where do you stand on this issue?

19) How do you feel about in vitro fertilization, or IVF, for parents who are unable to conceive? How do you think IVF relates to your religious beliefs?

20) How do you feel about reproductive technologies that can tell a "to-be" parent about qualities of their unborn child such as whether the unborn child has a disease? [*Potentially change wording for some traditions.*]

21) How do you feel about reproductive technologies that would allow a parent to select qualities for their child such as gender, hair, or eye color? How do you feel about parents making those choices?

22) Another topic we are interested in is social media. How do you see social media technologies in relation to your faith? For example, what kind of role do these technologies have on the sense of community within your congregation?

23) How about the environment. What does your faith tradition say about the environment? For example, the kind of responsibilities [Christians/Jews/Muslims] have to care for the earth?

24) Does this affect how you live? To what extent does this perspective on the environment influence the kinds of things you buy?

25) What do you think about climate change? Do you think it is occurring? Why or why not? How does your faith play into your thoughts on climate change, if at all?

26) Research in neuroscience suggests that certain parts of the brain are associated with spiritual experiences and can even explain why some people are more religious than others. What do you think about that? [*Alt. wording:* Do you think it's possible that if your brain were wired differently, you would have different religious beliefs? Could people be biologically disposed to be religious?]

27) Can you imagine any type of scientific evidence or discovery that might cause you to question your faith?

SCIENCE IN RELIGIOUS ORGANIZATION

28) To what extent do the leaders in your religious organization talk about science or the relationship of science to the teachings of your faith tradition?

29) Do you ever feel like you have to choose between what your leaders say and how you understand your religious text?

30) Have you ever heard science talked about informally at your congregation [*If yes*] What types of things have you heard discussed?

31) Are there any other issues related to science and faith that I didn't mention that you think are important?

DEMOGRAPHICS

For the sake of bookkeeping, there are some questions I would like to ask you to help me situate you among other individuals I have talked with:

32) How old are you?

33) How would you describe yourself racially or ethnically?

34) Are you currently married or in a long-term committed relationship? [*Discern which one.*] What is the ethnicity or race of your partner?

35) Do you have any children?
36) [*If yes*] How many?
37) What gender are they?
38) What are their ages?
39) What level of schooling have you been through?
40) What is your occupation?
41) [*If married or partnered*] What is your spouse's occupation?
42) What are your parents' occupations?
43) You currently live where?

[For Latino Respondents Not Born in the United States]

44) What is your country of origin?
45) How many years have you lived in the United States?

Survey Instrument

FINAL PROGRAMMED MAIN SURVEY ENGLISH QUESTIONNAIRE

Religious Understandings of Science

Thank you for your interest in our survey. We would like to find out your opinions about a wide range of issues affecting society today.

DEGREE: Highest degree earned

DEGREE. What is the highest degree that you have earned?

No high school diploma 1
GED 2
High school diploma... 3
Vocational/technical diploma 4
Associate's degree 5
Bachelor's degree 6
Master's degree 7
Doctorate degree 8
MD\DVM\DDS\JD 9
Other 10

AREA: Primary area of study

[ASK IF DEGREE>5]
AREA. Which of the following best represents your major or primary area of study for your highest degree?

AGRICULTURE 1
ARTS (e.g., Fine Art, Theater) 2
BIOLOGICAL SCIENCES (e.g., Biology, Environmental Science) 3

SCIOCCUP: Working in scientific occupation

SCIOCCUP. Would you say that your current occupation is science-related?

Yes 1
No 2

SCIOCCUP2: Working in scientific occupation

[ASK IF SCIOCCUP = YES]
SCIOCCUP2. Do you work at a college or university?

Yes 1
No 2

SCIOCCUP3: Working in scientific occupation

[ASK IF SCIOCCUP = YES AND SCIOCCUP2 = 1(YES) OR 2(NO)]
SCIOCCUP3. And what is your occupation?

Specify: [TEXTBOX]
[TERMINATE IF XSCIENCE = 2 AND (SCIOCCUP = NO OR SCIOCCUP
   REFUSED]

SCIMAG: Consumption of popular science literature

SCIMAG. In the last month have you read in print or online any science-focused
magazines, such as *National Geographic, Discover, Smithsonian, Popular Science,*
or *Scientific American*?

Yes 1
No 2

SCINEWS: Interest in science news

SCINEWS. If you saw a headline on a newspaper or website about a new scientific discovery, how likely are you to read the full story?

Very likely 1
Somewhat likely 2
Not very likely 3
Not at all likely 4

QUEST_*: Answering questions about science

QUEST. If you had a question about science, how likely would you be to consult the following sources?

(QUEST_PHD) A book written by a PhD scientist
(QUEST_WEB) A general Internet source, such as Wikipedia
(QUEST_SCI) A scientific magazine, such as *National Geographic, Discover, Smithsonian, Popular Science,* or *Scientific American*
(QUEST_OCC) A person working in a scientific occupation
(QUEST_TEA) A teacher at a local school or college
(QUEST_FRI) A friend or family member
(QUEST_TXT) A religious text
(QUEST_LDR) A religious leader
(QUEST_CON) Other people at your religious congregation

1) Very likely
2) Somewhat likely
3) Not very likely
4) Not at all likely

SCIVIEW_*: Views on science

SCIVIEW. How much do you agree or disagree with the following statements?

(SCIVIEW_1) Overall, modern science does more harm than good.
(SCIVIEW_2) Because of science and technology, there will be more opportunities for the next generation.

(SCIVIEW_3) Given enough time, science will be able to provide a natural explanation for everything.

(SCIVIEW_4) Science makes our way of life change too fast.

(SCIVIEW_5) Scientists should be open to considering miracles in their theories and explanations.

(SCIVIEW_6) Scientific research is valuable even when it doesn't provide immediate tangible benefits like new medicines or technologies.

(SCIVIEW_7) Science can only truly explain what can be seen and touched.

1) Strongly agree
2) Agree
3) Neither agree nor disagree
4) Disagree
5) Strongly disagree

SCIFRNDS: Science occupations among closest friends

SCIFRNDS. Think about your five closest friends. How many would you say work in science-related occupations?

1) None of them
2) One or two of them
3) Three or four of them
4) All of them

RELFRND_*: Religious affiliation of closest friends

PROGRAMMING NOTE: FOR RELFRND, ADD CHECK SO THAT "ALL OF THEM" CAN ONLY BE SELECTED FOR ONE RELIGION. IF "ALL OF THEM" IS SELECTED, ALL OTHER CHOICES SHOULD BE "NONE OF THEM." IF NEEDED, PROMPT WITH "ALL OF THEM" CANNOT BE SELECTED IN COMBINATION WITH ANY OTHER RESPONSE. PLEASE CHECK AND ADJUST YOUR ANSWERS.

RELFRND. Thinking about those same closest five friends, how many would you say are. . .

(RELFRND_1) Evangelical Christians
(RELFRND_2) Catholics

(RELFRND_3) Jews

(RELFRND_4) Muslims

(RELFRND_5) Buddhists

(RELFRND_6) Hindus

(RELFRND_7) Atheists

(RELFRND_8) Mainline Protestants

1) None of them

2) One or two of them

3) Three or four of them

4) All of them

LOGIC: RANDOMLY ASSIGN HALF OF XSCIENCE = 1 RESPONDENTS TO GROUP = 1 OR GROUP = 2 WITH

EQUAL PROBABILITY OF BEING ASSIGNED TO EITHER ONE.

Group1 1

Group2 2

DAWKINS: Familiar with Dawkins

[IF GROUP = 1]

DAWKINS. Have you heard of a scientist named Dr. Richard Dawkins?

Yes 1

No 2

[IF DAWKINS = NO]

[RANDOMLY SELECT 1/10 PEOPLE FROM GROUP 1 WHO HAVE DAWKINS = NO AND SHOW THE DAWKINS DESCRIPTION BELOW]

Dr. Richard Dawkins is an evolutionary biologist and emeritus fellow at Oxford University. Dr. Dawkins is also an outspoken atheist who has said that the existence of God and miracles is "very improbable" and that religion and science are in conflict with each other.

LOGIC: ASSIGN RESPONDENTS BASED ON THEIR RESPONSE TO QDAWKINS. IF QDAWKINS = NO ASSIGN TO DOV_DAWKINS = 1 (ONLY IF DESCRIPTION IS SHOWN OTHERWISE ASSIGN TO DOV_DAWKINS = 2); IF

QDAWKINS = YES ASSIGN TO DOV_DAWKINS = 2.

dawkins description shown 1

no dawkins description shown 2

COLLINS: Familiar with Collins

[IF GROUP = 2]

COLLINS. Have you heard of a scientist named Dr. Francis Collins?

Yes 1

No 2

[IF COLLINS = NO]

[RANDOMLY SELECT 1/10 PEOPLE FROM GROUP 2 WHO HAVE
COLLINS = NO AND SHOW THE COLLINS DESCRIPTION BELOW]

Dr. Francis Collins is a geneticist who has directed the Human Genome
Project and the National Institutes of Health. Dr. Collins is also an outspoken
Christian who has said that God is capable of performing miracles and that reli-
gion and science are "entirely compatible."

LOGIC: ASSIGN RESPONDENTS BASED ON THEIR RESPONSE TO
QCOLLINS. IF QCOLLINS = NO ASSIGN TO DOV_COLLINS = 1 (ONLY IF
DESCRIPTION IS SHOWN OTHERWISE ASSIGN TO DOV_COLLINS = 2);
IF QCOLLINS = YES ASSIGN TO DOV_COLLINS = 2.

collins description shown 1

no collins description shown 2

[PROGRAMMER NOTE: THE REMAINING QUESTIONS ARE ASKED OF
ALL RESPONDENTS]

RELSCI: Stance on science-religion relationship

[RANDOMIZE AND RECORD ORDER OF ITEMS 1–4 IN RELSCI]

RELSCI. Which of the following BEST represents your view. "For me personally, my understanding of science and religion can be described as a
relationship of. . ."

conflict. . .I consider myself to be on the side of religion 1

conflict. . .I consider myself to be on the side of science 2

independence. . .they refer to different aspects of reality 3

collaboration. . .each can be used to help support the other 4

SCIVIEW_*

SCIVIEW_1. How much do you agree or disagree with the following statements?

(SCIVIEW_8) Most scientists are hostile to religion.

(SCIVIEW_9) We trust too much in science and not enough in religious faith.

(SCIVIEW_10) The quality of science and mathematics education in American schools is inadequate.

(SCIVIEW_11) Scientists should be allowed to do research that causes pain and injury to animals like dogs and chimpanzees if it produces new information about human health problems.

(SCIVIEW_12) Most religious people are hostile to science.

1) Strongly agree
2) Agree
3) Neither agree nor disagree
4) Disagree
5) Strongly disagree

SCIOCC_*: Assessment of scientific nature of occupations

SCIOCC. How scientific do you view each of the following occupations?

(SCIOCC_1) Biologist
(SCIOCC_2) Engineer
(SCIOCC_3) Plumber
(SCIOCC_4) Anthropologist
(SCIOCC_5) TV weather forecaster
(SCIOCC_6) High school chemistry teacher
(SCIOCC_7) Psychologist
(SCIOCC_8) Physician/doctor
(SCIOCC_9) Pastor, minister, or clergyperson
(SCIOCC_10) Electrician
(SCIOCC_11) Sociologist
(SCIOCC_12) Physicist
(SCIOCC_13) Nurse

1) Very scientific
2) Somewhat scientific
3) A little scientific
4) Not at all scientific

SCIMORAL_*: Views on morality of technologies

[RANDOMIZE AND RECORD ORDER OF ITEMS SCIMORAL1 THROUGH SCIMORAL10]

SCIMORAL. How morally acceptable do you personally believe each of the following is?

(SCIMORAL_1) Destroying human embryos if doing so helps scientists find cures for diseases.

(SCIMORAL_2) Creating a baby that is a clone of another person.

(SCIMORAL_3) Using genetic engineering, that is, changing a person's DNA or genes, to create a baby that is smarter, stronger, or better looking.

(SCIMORAL_4) Medical research that uses stem cells from sources that do NOT involve human embryos.

(SCIMORAL_5) Use of reproductive technologies to identify diseases in utero.

(SCIMORAL_6) Euthanasia or physician-assisted suicide.

(SCIMORAL_7) Using in vitro fertilization.

(SCIMORAL_8) Having an abortion for any reason.

(SCIMORAL_9) Having an abortion if the mother's life is in danger.

(SCIMORAL_10) Having an abortion if there is a strong chance of serious defect in the baby.

1) Always morally acceptable
2) Morally acceptable in most cases, with exceptions
3) Not a moral issue
4) Morally wrong in most cases, with exceptions
5) Always morally wrong
6) I am not aware of the issue

SCIPRIO: Views on priorities of scientists

SCIPRIO. Scientists working in universities are involved in many different activities. How important do you think each of the following should be for a scientist in a university?

(SCIPRIO1) Teaching students

(SCIPRIO2) Pursuing patents for technologies that can then be sold to companies

(SCIPRIO3) Publishing research findings in academic journals read by other scientists

(SCIPRIO4) Speaking to and writing for the general public to help them understand science

1) Very important
2) Somewhat important

3) Not very important

4) Not important at all

RELPERSON

RELPERSON. To what extent do you consider yourself a religious person? Are you very religious, moderately religious, slightly religious, or not religious at all?

Very religious 1

Moderately religious 2

Slightly religious 3

Not religious at all 4

RELIG: Religious affiliation

RELIG. Religiously, do you consider yourself to be Protestant, Catholic, Jewish, Mormon, Muslim, not religious, or something else? If more than one, click the one that best describes you:

Protestant 1

Catholic 2

Just a Christian 3

Jewish 4

Mormon 5

Muslim 6

Eastern Orthodox 7

Buddhist 8

Hindu 9

Sikh 10

Baha'i 11

Jain 12

Not religious/none 13

Agnostic 14

Atheist 15

Something else 16

RELIG2: Religious denomination

[ASK IF RELIG = 1, 3 OR 16]

RELIG2. What specific religious denomination or tradition do you consider yourself to be? (If you consider yourself to be more than one, answer for the one you attend most.)

1. Adventist
2. Anabaptist
3. Anglican
4. Assemblies of God (Assembly of God)
5. Association of Unity Churches
6. Baptist
7. Bible Church/Believing
8. Brethren
9. Charismatic
10. Christian or just Christian
11. Christian and Missionary Alliance (CMA)
12. Christian Science (Christian Scientist)
13. Church of Christ (Churches of Christ)
14. Church of God
15. Church of England
16. Church of the Nazarene
17. Calvary Chapel
18. Congregationalist
19. Disciples of Christ
20. Episcopalian
21. Evangelical
22. Evangelical Covenant Church
23. Evangelical United Brethren
24. Evangelical Free Church
25. Four Square
26. Free Methodist Church
27. Friends
28. Fundamentalist
29. Holiness
30. Independent
31. Interdenominational Protestant
32. Jehovah's Witness
33. Just Protestant
34. Lutheran
35. Mennonite
36. Methodist
37. Missionary Church
38. Moravian

39. Nazarene
40. Native American
41. Nondenominational Protestant
42. Pagan
43. Pentecostal
44. Presbyterian
45. Quaker
46. Reformed
47. Salvation Army
48. Unitarian-Universalist
49. United Church of Christ (UCC)
50. Unity Church
51. Vineyard Fellowship
52. Wesleyan Church
53. Wiccan
54. Willow Creek Association church
55. Other [Specify] [TEXTBOX]

RELIG3: Anabaptist

[ASK IF RELIG2 = 2]
RELIG3. What kind of Anabaptist church is that?

Amish 1
Brethren 2
Brethren in Christ 3
Church of the Brethren 4
Evangelical Friends Alliance 5
Friends 6
General Conference of Mennonite Church 7
Just Anabaptist 8
Mennonite 9
Mennonite Brethren 10
Moravian 11
Quaker 12
Other Anabaptist 13

RELIG4: Baptist

[ASK IF RELIG2 = 6]
RELIG4. With which Baptist group is your church associated?

American Baptist Association 1

American Baptist Churches in the USA (American Baptist Churches USA) ....
....2

Baptist Bible Fellowship 3

Baptist Brethren 4

Baptist General Conference 5

Baptist Missionary Association 6

Charismatic Baptist 7

Conservative Baptist Association of America.. 8

Free Will Baptist 9

Fundamentalist Baptist (no denominational ties) 10

General Association of Regular Baptists (GARB) 11

General Baptist 12

Independent Baptist 13

Just Baptist 14

Missionary Baptist 15

National Baptist Convention of America, or USA, Inc. 16

National Missionary Baptist Convention of America 17

North American Baptist Conference 18

Northern Baptist 19

Primitive Baptist 20

Progressive National Baptist Convention, Inc. 21

Reformed Baptist 22

Southern Baptist (Convention) 23

United Baptist 24

United Free Will Baptist 25

Other Baptist 26

RELIG5: Methodist

[ASK IF RELIG2 = 36]

RELIG5. With which Methodist group is your church associated?

African Methodist Episcopal (AME) 1

African Methodist Episcopal (AME) Zion 2

Christian Methodist Episcopal (CEM) 3

Free Methodist (Free Methodist Church) 4

Just Methodist 5

United Methodist/United Methodist Church 6

Wesleyan Methodist 7

Other Methodist 8

RELIG6: Presbyterian

[ASK IF RELIG2 = 44]
RELIG6. With which Presbyterian group is your church associated?

Associate Reformed Presbyterian 1
Bible Presbyterian Church 2
Cumberland Presbyterian 3
Evangelical Presbyterian Church (EPC) 4
Just Presbyterian 5
Orthodox Presbyterian Church (OPC) 6
Presbyterian Church in America (PCA) 7
Presbyterian Church in the USA (PCUSA) 8
Reformed Presbyterian Churches of North America 9
Other Presbyterian 10

RELIG7: Lutheran

[ASK IF RELIG2 = 34]
RELIG7. With which Lutheran group is your church associated?

American Lutheran Church 1
Evangelical Lutheran Church in America 2
Free Lutheran 3
Lutheran Brethren 4
Lutheran Church in America 5
Just Lutheran 6
Missouri synod 7
Wisconsin synod 8
Other Lutheran 9

RELIG8: Reformed

[ASK IF RELIG2 = 46]
RELIG8. With which Reformed group is your church associated?

Christian Reformed Church (CRC) 1
Dutch Reformed 2
Just Reformed 3
Reformed Church in America (RCA) 4
Other Reformed 5

RELIG9: Congregational

[ASK IF RELIG2 = 18]
RELIG9. With which Congregational group is your church associated?

Congregational Bible Church 1
Conservative Congregational Christian 2
Congregational Christian Churches 3
Just Congregational 4
United Church of Christ (UCC) 5
Other Congregational 6

RELIG10: Christian church

[ASK IF RELIG2 = 10]
RELIG10. When you say you are "Christian or just Christian," does that mean the church you attend is associated with the Christian Church—Disciples of Christ, some other Christian group, or is the church you attend just Christian?

Christian Church—Disciples of Christ 1
Just Christian 2
Other Christian group 3

RELIG11: Church of Christ

[ASK IF RELIG2 = 13]
RELIG11. With which Church of Christ is your church associated?

Church (Churches) of Christ 1
Church of God in Christ 2
United Church of Christ (UCC) 3
Just Church of Christ 4
Other Church of Christ group 5

RELIG12: Church of God

[ASK IF RELIG2 = 14]
RELIG12. With which Church of God group is your church associated?

Church of God, General Conference 1
Church of God, Holiness 2

Church of God in Christ 3
Church of God of Anderson, Indiana 4
Church of God of Cleveland, Tennessee 5
Church of God of Huntsville, Alabama 6
Church of God of Prophecy 7
Church of God of the Apostolic Faith 8
Just Church of God 9
Pentecostal Church of God 10
Worldwide Church of God 11
Other Church of God 12

RELIG13: Pentecostal

[ASK IF RELIG2 = 43]
RELIG13. With which Pentecostal group is your church associated?

Apostolic Pentecostal 1
Assemblies of God (Assembly of God) 2
Church of God, General Conference 3
Church of God, Holiness 4
Church of God in Christ 5
Church of God in Christ, International 6
Church of God of Anderson, Indiana 7
Church of God of Cleveland, Tennessee 8
Church of God of Huntsville, Alabama 9
Church of God of Prophecy 10
Church of God of the Apostolic Faith 11
Four Square Gospel 12
Full Gospel 13
Just Pentecostal 14
Pentecostal Church of God 15
Pentecostal Holiness Church 16
Spanish Pentecostal 17
United Pentecostal Church International 18
Other Pentecostal 19

RELIG14: Jewish

[ASK IF RELIG = 4]
RELIG14. With which Jewish group is your synagogue or temple associated?

Conservative Judaism 1

Haredi Judaism 2

Hasidic Judaism 3

Humanistic Judaism 4

Jewish Renewal 5

Modern Orthodox 6

Reconstructionist Judaism 7

Reform Judaism 8

Other Jewish [Specify] [TEXTBOX] 9

RELIG15: Muslim

[ASK IF RELIG = 6]

RELIG15. With which branch of Islam are you associated?

Ahmaddiya 1

Nation of Islam 2

Shi'a 3

Sufi 4

Sunni 5

Other Muslim [Specify] [TEXTBOX] 6

ATTEND: Religious service attendance

ATTEND. How often do you attend religious services?

Never 1

Less than once a year 2

About once or twice a year 3

Several times a year 4

About once a month 5

Two to three times a month 6

Nearly every week 7

Every week 8

Several times a week 9

RELIGKID: Religious affiliation

RELIGKID. In what religion were you raised? Were you raised Protestant, Catholic, Jewish, Mormon, Muslim, not religious, or something else? If more than one, click the one that best describes you:

Protestant 1
Catholic 2
Just a Christian 3
Jewish 4
Mormon 5
Muslim 6
Eastern Orthodox 7
Buddhist 8
Hindu 9
Sikh 10
Baha'i 11
Jain 12
Not religious/none 13
Agnostic 14
Atheist 15
Something else 16

RELIGKID2: Religious denomination

[ASK IF RELIGKID = 1, 3, OR 16]
RELIGKID2. In what specific religious denomination or tradition were you raised? (If you were raised in more than one, answer for the one you attended most.)

1. Adventist
2. Anabaptist
3. Anglican
4. Assemblies of God (Assembly of God)
5. Association of Unity Churches
6. Baptist
7. Bible Church/Believing
8. Brethren
9. Charismatic
10. Christian or just Christian
11. Christian and Missionary Alliance (CMA)
12. Christian Science (Christian Scientist)
13. Church of Christ (Churches of Christ)
14. Church of God
15. Church of England

16. Church of the Nazarene
17. Calvary Chapel
18. Congregationalist
19. Disciples of Christ
20. Episcopalian
21. Evangelical
22. Evangelical Covenant Church
23. Evangelical United Brethren
24. Evangelical Free Church
25. Four Square
26. Free Methodist Church
27. Friends
28. Fundamentalist
29. Holiness
30. Independent
31. Interdenominational Protestant
32. Jehovah's Witness
33. Just Protestant
34. Lutheran
35. Mennonite
36. Methodist
37. Missionary Church
38. Moravian
39. Nazarene
40. Native American
41. Nondenominational Protestant
42. Pagan
43. Pentecostal
44. Presbyterian
45. Quaker
46. Reformed
47. Salvation Army
48. Unitarian-Universalist
49. United Church of Christ (UCC)
50. Unity Church
51. Vineyard Fellowship
52. Wesleyan Church
53. Wiccan
54. Willow Creek Association Church
55. Other [Specify] [TEXTBOX]

RELIGKID3: Anabaptist

[ASK IF RELIGKID2 = 2]

RELIGKID3. With which Anabaptist group was the church in which you were raised associated?

Amish 1
Brethren 2
Brethren in Christ 3
Church of the Brethren 4
Evangelical Friends Alliance 5
Friends 6
General Conference of Mennonite Church 7
Just Anabaptist 8
Mennonite 9
Mennonite Brethren 10
Moravian 11
Quaker 12
Other Anabaptist 13

RELIGKID4: Baptist

[ASK IF RELIKIDG2 = 6]

RELIGKID4. With which Baptist group was the church in which you were raised associated?

American Baptist Association 1
American Baptist Churches in the USA (American Baptist Churches USA)
.... 2
Baptist Bible Fellowship 3
Baptist Brethren 4
Baptist General Conference 5
Baptist Missionary Association 6
Charismatic Baptist 7
Conservative Baptist Association of America..................................... 8
Free Will Baptist 9
Fundamentalist Baptist (no denominational ties) 10
General Association of Regular Baptists (GARB) 11
General Baptist 12
Independent Baptist 13
Just Baptist 14

RELIGKID5: Methodist

[ASK IF RELIGKID2 = 36]
RELIGKID5. With which Methodist group was the church in which you were
raised associated?

African Methodist Episcopal (AME) 1
African Methodist Episcopal (AME) Zion 2
Christian Methodist Episcopal (CEM) 3
Free Methodist (Free Methodist Church) 4
Just Methodist 5
United Methodist/United Methodist Church 6
Wesleyan Methodist 7
Other Methodist 8

RELIGKID6: Presbyterian

[ASK IF RELIGKID2 = 44]
RELIGKID6. With which Presbyterian group was the church in which you were
raised associated?

Associate Reformed Presbyterian 1
Bible Presbyterian Church 2
Cumberland Presbyterian 3
Evangelical Presbyterian Church (EPC) 4
Just Presbyterian 5
Orthodox Presbyterian Church (OPC) 6

Presbyterian Church in America (PCA) 7

Presbyterian Church in the USA (PCUSA) 8

Reformed Presbyterian Churches of North America 9

Other Presbyterian 10

RELIGKID7: Lutheran

[ASK IF RELIGKID2 = 34]

RELIGKID7. With which Lutheran group was the church in which you were raised associated?

American Lutheran Church 1

Evangelical Lutheran Church in America 2

Free Lutheran 3

Lutheran Brethren 4

Lutheran Church in America 5

Just Lutheran 6

Missouri synod 7

Wisconsin synod 8

Other Lutheran 9

RELIGKID8: Reformed

[ASK IF RELIGKID2 = 46]

RELIGKID8. With which Reformed group was the church in which you were raised associated?

Christian Reformed Church (CRC) 1

Dutch Reformed 2

Just Reformed 3

Reformed Church in America (RCA) 4

Other Reformed 5

RELIGKID9: Congregational

[ASK IF RELIGKID2 = 18]

RELIGKID9. With which Congregational group was the church in which you were raised associated?

Congregational Bible Church 1

Conservative Congregational Christian 2

Congregational Christian Churches 3

Just Congregational 4

United Church of Christ (UCC) 5

Other Congregational 6

RELIGKID10: Christian church

[ASK IF RELIGKID2 = 10]

RELIGKID10. When you say you were raised as a "Christian or just a Christian," do you that mean that your church was associated with the Christian Church—Disciples of Christ, some other Christian group, or was the church you attended just Christian?

Christian Church—Disciples of Christ 1

Just Christian 2

Other Christian group 3

RELIGKID11: Church of Christ

[ASK IF RELIGKID2 = 13]

RELIGKID11. With which Church of Christ was your church associated?

Church (Churches) of Christ 1

Church of God in Christ 2

United Church of Christ (UCC) 3

Just Church of Christ 4

Other Church of Christ group 5

RELIGKID12: Church of God

[ASK IF RELIGKID2 = 14]

RELIGKID12. With which Church of God group was your church associated?

Church of God, General Conference 1

Church of God, Holiness 2

Church of God in Christ 3

Church of God of Anderson, Indiana 4

Church of God of Cleveland, Tennessee 5

Church of God of Huntsville, Alabama 6

RELIGKID13: Pentecostal

[ASK IF RELIGKID2 = 43]
RELIGKID13. With which Pentecostal group was your church associated?

Apostolic Pentecostal 1
Assemblies of God (Assembly of God) 2
Church of God, General Conference 3
Church of God, Holiness 4
Church of God in Christ 5
Church of God in Christ, International 6
Church of God of Anderson, Indiana 7
Church of God of Cleveland, Tennessee 8
Church of God of Huntsville, Alabama 9
Church of God of Prophecy 10
Church of God of the Apostolic Faith 11
Four Square Gospel 12
Full Gospel 13
Just Pentecostal 14
Pentecostal Church of God 15
Pentecostal Holiness Church 16
Spanish Pentecostal 17
United Pentecostal Church International 18
Other Pentecostal 19

RELIGKID14: Jewish

[ASK IF RELIGKID = 4]
RELIGKID14. With which Jewish group is your synagogue or temple associated?

Conservative Judaism 1
Haredi Judaism 2
Hasidic Judaism 3
Humanistic Judaism 4

Jewish Renewal 5

Modern Orthodox 6

Reconstructionist Judaism 7

Reform Judaism 8

Other Jewish [Specify] [TEXTBOX] 9

RELIGKID15: Muslim

[ASK IF RELIGKID = 6]

RELIG15. With which branch of Islam are you associated?

Ahmaddiya 1

Nation of Islam 2

Shi'a 3

Sufi 4

Sunni 5

Other Muslim [Specify] [TEXTBOX] 6

ATTENDKID: Religious service attendance in childhood

ATTENDKID. What about when you were around 11 or 12, how often did you attend religious services then?

Never 1

Less than once a year 2

About once or twice a year 3

Several times a year 4

About once a month 5

Two to three times a month 6

Nearly every week 7

Every week 8

Several times a week 9

SACBOOK: Frequency of reading religious texts

SACBOOK. Outside of attending religious services, about how often do you read the Bible, Koran, Torah, or other sacred book?

Never 1

Less than once a year 2

About once or twice a year 3
Several times a year 4
About once a month 5
Two to three times a month 6
Nearly every week 7
Every week 8
Several times a week 9

RELIGINTERP: Strictness of interpretation of religion

[ASK IF RELIG = 1, 2, 3, 4, 5, 6, 7, 8, 9, 10, 11, 12, OR 16]

    [RANDOMIZE AND RECORD ORDER OF ITEMS 1–2 IN RELIGINTERP]

    RELIGINTERP. As you read the statements below, please indicate whether the FIRST statement or the SECOND statement comes closer to your own views even if neither is exactly right:

    There is only ONE true way to interpret the teachings of my religion. 1

    There is MORE than one way to interpret the teachings of my religion. 2

TRADMOD: Adopting religion to modernity

[ASK IF RELPERSON = 1, 2, OR 3]

TRADMOD. Thinking about your religion, to what extent do you agree or disagree with each of the following statements?

    Strongly agree 1
    Agree 2
    Neither agree nor disagree 3
    Disagree 4
    Strongly disagree 5

    (TRADMOD_1) My church or denomination should preserve its traditional beliefs and practices.

    (TRADMOD_2) My church or denomination should adjust traditional beliefs and practices in light of new circumstances.

ID_*: Religious identification

ID. How well do the following terms describe your religious identity?

(ID_BIB) Bible-believing
(ID_EVAN) Evangelical
(ID_MAIN) Mainline Christian
(ID_SPIR) Spiritual
(ID_FUND) Fundamentalist
(ID_SEEK) Seeker
(ID_CON) Theologically conservative
(ID_LIB) Theologically liberal
(ID_PENT) Pentecostal
(ID_BORN) Born-again

1) Not at all
2) Not very well
3) Somewhat well
4) Very well

PRAY: Frequency of prayer

PRAY.: About how often do you pray?

Never 1
Less than once a year 2
About once or twice a year 3
Several times a year 4
About once a month 5
Two to three times a month... 6
Nearly every week 7
Every week 8
Several times a week 9
Once a day 10
Several times a day..11

BIBLE: Views about Bible

[IF RELIG = 1, 2, 3, 5, OR 7]
BIBLE. Which of these statements comes closest to describing your feelings about the Bible?

The Bible is the actual word of God and is to be taken literally, word for word.
.... 1
The Bible is the inspired word of God but not everything should be taken literally, word for word. 2

The Bible is an ancient book of fables, legends, history, and moral precepts recorded by man. 3

This does not apply to me. 4

RELINFL: Views on religion's influence on American life

RELINFL. At the present time, do you think religion as a whole is increasing its influence on American life or losing its influence?

Losing its influence 1

Increasing its influence 2

[IF RELINFL = REFUSED; PROMPT ONCE]

RELINFL_1. At the present time, do you think religion as a whole is increasing its influence on American life or losing its influence?

Losing its influence 1

Neither increasing nor decreasing its influence ....

.... 2

Increasing its influence 3

GOODBAD: Evaluation of changing influence of religion in America

[SP; SKIP IF RELINFL AND RELINFL_1 REFUSED]

GOODBAD. All in all, do you think the influence of religion [INSERT TEXT OF RESPONSE TO RELINFL OR RELINFL_1] on American life is a good thing or a bad thing?

Good thing 1

Bad thing 2

GOD: Beliefs about God

GOD. Which one statement comes closest to your personal beliefs about God?

I don't believe in God. 1

I don't know whether there is a God, and I don't believe there is any way to find out. 2

I don't believe in a personal God, but do believe in a Higher Power of some kind. 3

I find myself believing in God some of the time, but not at others. ....

.... 4

While I have doubts, I feel that I do believe in God. ....
.... 5
I know God really exists and I have no doubts about it. ....
.... 6

EXP_*: Religious experiences

EXP. Have you ever had any of the following experiences?

(EXP_MIR1) I witnessed a miraculous, physical healing.
(EXP_MIR2) I received a miraculous, physical healing.
(EXP_CALL) I felt called by God to do something.
(EXP_VOIC) I heard the voice of God speaking to me.
(EXP_ANG) I was protected from harm by a guardian angel.
(EXP_CONV) I had a religious conversion experience.
(EXP_UNIV) I felt one with the universe.
Yes. 1
No. 2

GOD_*: Belief's about God's involvement with the world

[ASK IF GOD = 2, 3, 4, 5, 6]
GOD_1. Based on your personal understanding, do you think God is . . .
(GOD_REM) Removed from the affairs of the world
(GOD_CON1) Concerned with the well-being of the world
(GOD_CON2) Concerned with my personal well-being
(GOD_INV1) Directly involved in the affairs of the world
(GOD_INV2) Directly involved in my affairs

1) Strongly agree
2) Agree
3) Neither agree nor disagree
4) Disagree
5) Strongly disagree

SHARE: Frequency of sharing faith with strangers

[ASK IF RELIG = 1, 2, 3, 4, 5, 6, 7, 8, 9, 10, 11, 12, OR 16]

SHARE. How often in the past month have you witnessed or shared your faith with strangers?

1) Not at all
2) One or two times
3) Three or four times
4) Five or more times

WORK2: Prevalence of religious references in workplace

WORK2. How often has the topic of religion come up at your place of work?

Very often 1
Sometimes 2
Rarely 3
Never 4

WORK3: Religious discrimination in workplace

WORK3. How often have you felt discriminated against at your place of work because of your religious beliefs?

Very often 1
Sometimes 2
Rarely 3
Never 4

RLG_EXCL: Religious exclusivity

RLGEXCL: Which of the following statements comes closest to your own views:

3) There is very little truth in any religion.
4) There are basic truths in many religions.
3) There is truth only in one religion.
4) Don't know

RELTALK: Frequency of talking about religion

RELTALK. In the past month, about how often have you talked with people of a different religion about your religious views, whatever they may be?

1) Not at all
2) One or two times
3) Three or four times
4) Five or more times

CONTRAD1: Approach to contradictions in religious text

[ASK IF RELIG = 1, 2, 3, 5, 7, OR 16]
CONTRAD1. If some scientific discovery appeared to contradict something in the Bible, would you be:

Much more likely to believe the Bible 1
Somewhat more likely to believe the Bible 2
Somewhat more likely to believe scientific findings 3
Much more likely to believe scientific findings 4
I don't have a religious text 5

RELTEXTSCI: Science found in religious text

[ASK IF RELPERSON = 1, 2, OR 3]
TELTEXTSCI. To what extent do you agree with the following statement: "Sometimes I have to choose between the teachings of my religious text and scientific findings"?

Strongly agree 1
Agree 2
Neither agree nor disagree 3
Disagree 4
Strongly disagree 5

ORIGINS_*: Views on human origins

ORIGINS. On the next two screens, we present six theories about the origin and development of the universe and life on Earth. How likely is it that each is true or false?

(ORIGINS_1) *Creationism*—God created the universe, the Earth, and all of life within the past 10,000 years.

(ORIGINS_2) *Recent Human Creation*—God created the universe and the Earth billions of years ago; plants and animals evolved over millions of years from earlier life forms, but God intervened to create humans within the past 10,000 years.

(ORIGINS_3) *God-guided Evolution*—God created the universe and the Earth billions of years ago; God started and has guided human evolution over millions of years.

(ORIGINS_4) *Intelligent Design*—The universe and Earth came into being billions of years ago, and humans evolved over millions of years according to the design of an Intelligent Force.

(ORIGINS_5) *God-initiated Evolution*—God created the universe and the Earth billions of years ago; but all life, including humans, evolved over millions of years from earlier life forms due to environmental pressures to adapt and without any guidance from God or an Intelligent Force.

(ORIGINS_6) *Natural Evolution*—The universe and Earth came into being billions of years ago; all life, including humans, evolved over millions of years from earlier life forms due to environmental pressures to adapt; there was no God or Intelligent Force involved in either the creation or evolution of life.

1) Definitely false
2) Probably false
3) Probably true
4) Definitely true
5) Not at all sure

CHILDOCC_*: Occupational preferences for children

CHILDOCC. How much would you recommend to a child of yours to enter the following occupations as an adult?

(CHILDOCC_1) Biologist
(CHILDOCC_2) Engineer
(CHILDOCC_3) Plumber
(CHILDOCC_4) Anthropologist
(CHILDOCC_5) TV weather forecaster
(CHILDOCC_6) High school chemistry teacher
(CHILDOCC_7) Psychologist
(CHILDOCC_8) Physician/doctor
(CHILDOCC_9) Pastor, minister, or clergyperson
(CHILDOCC_10) Electrician
(CHILDOCC_11) Sociologist
(CHILDOCC_12) Physicist
(CHILDOCC_13) Nurse

1) Would recommend strongly
2) Would recommend somewhat
3) Would not recommend at all

TEACHALT1: Views on teaching alternatives to evolution

TEACHALT1. Would you generally favor or oppose teaching creationism instead of evolution in public schools?

Strongly favor 1
Somewhat favor 2
Somewhat oppose 3
Strongly oppose 4

TEACHALT2: Views on teaching alternatives to evolution

TEACHALT2. Would you generally favor or oppose teaching creationism along with evolution in public schools?

Strongly favor 1
Somewhat favor 2
Somewhat oppose 3
Strongly oppose 4

TEACHALT3: Views on teaching alternatives to evolution

TEACHALT3. Would you generally favor or oppose teaching intelligent design instead of evolution in public schools?

Strongly favor 1
Somewhat favor 2
Somewhat oppose 3
Strongly oppose 4

TEACHALT4: Views on teaching alternatives to evolution

TEACHALT4. Would you generally favor or oppose teaching intelligent design along with evolution in public schools?

Strongly favor 1
Somewhat favor 2
Somewhat oppose 3
Strongly oppose 4

NEURO: Neuroscience and religion

NEURO. Differences in people's religiosity can be explained by the fact that their brains are wired differently.

Strongly agree 1
Agree 2
Neither agree nor disagree 3
Disagree 4
Strongly disagree 5

ENVSHOP: Purchasing and environment

ENVSHOP. I think about the effect on the environment when making shopping decisions.

Never 1
Rarely 2
Occasionally 3
Frequently 4

CLIMATE: Views on climate change

CLIMATE. Which of the following statements best represent your opinion about climate change?

The climate is changing and human actions are a significant cause of the change. 1
The climate is changing but human actions are only partly causing the change. 2
The climate is changing but not because of human actions. ....
.... 3
The climate is not changing. 4

INT_*: Interest in various issues

INT. Please tell me how interested you are in the following things:

(INT_FORP) Foreign policy
(INT_SCHO) Local school issues
(INT_ARTS) The arts
(INT_SCI) New scientific discoveries
(INT_ECON) Economic and business issues
(INT_MED) New medical discoveries
(INT_SPORT) Sports and outdoor recreation
(INT_SPACE) Space exploration
(INT_ENV) The environment
(INT_RELI) Religion

1) Very interested
2) Moderately interested
3) Not at all interested

PROB_*: Views on money spent on various problems

PROB. We are faced with many problems in this country, none of which can be solved easily or inexpensively. For each problem below, do you think we're spending too much money on it, too little money, or about the right amount?

(PROB_1) Space exploration program
(PROB_2) The military, armaments, and defense
(PROB_3) Improving the nation's education system
(PROB_4) Improving and protecting the environment
(PROB_5) Supporting scientific research
(PROB_6) Improving and protecting the nation's health

1) Too much
2) About the right amount
3) Too little

CONFID_*: Trust in institutions

CONFID. I am going to name some institutions in this country. As far as the people running these institutions are concerned, how much confidence do you have?

(CONFID_1) Corporations
(CONFID_2) Religious organizations and leaders

(CONFID_3) The press
(CONFID_4) Colleges and universities
(CONFID_5) The scientific community
(CONFID_6) US Congress
(CONFID_7) The military

1) A great deal
2) Some
3) Hardly any

IMPORT*: Importance of issues

There are many issues in society that produce debate. How important are the following debates to you?

(IMPORT1) Debates concerning guns
(IMPORT2) Debates concerning health care
(IMPORT3) Debates concerning the relationship between religion and science
(IMPORT4) Debates concerning abortion

Very important...1
Somewhat important 2
Not very important 3
Not at all important 4

KIDS: Number of children

How many children have you ever had?

Specify number: _____

POLVIEW: Political views

Would you describe your political views as extremely liberal, liberal, slightly liberal, moderate, slightly conservative, conservative, or extremely conservative?

1) Extremely liberal
2) Liberal
3) Slightly liberal
4) Moderate
5) Slightly conservative
6) Conservative
7) Extremely conservative

NOTES

1. See, for example, Graves, Joseph L. 2004. *The Race Myth: Why We Pretend Race Exists in America.* New York: Dutton; Omi, Michael, and Howard Winant. 1994. *Racial Formation in the United States: From the 1960s to the 1990s.* New York: Routledge. See also Pinn, Anthony B. 2003. *Terror and Triumph: The Nature of Black Religion.* Minneapolis, MN: Augsburg Fortress; West, Cornel. 2002 [1982]. *Prophesy Deliverance! An Afro-American Revolutionary Christianity.* Louisville, KY: Westminster John Knox Press.

2. See Corbie-Smith, G. 1999. "The Continuing Legacy of the Tuskegee Syphilis Study: Considerations for Clinical Investigation." *American Journal of the Medical Sciences* 317(1):5–8; Gamble, Vanessa. 1999. "Race and the New Genetics: A Historical Perspective." Pp. 163–186 in *The Implications of Genetics for Health Professionals*, edited by M. Hager. New York: Josiah Macy Jr. Foundation; Graves 2004; Morning, Ann. 2011. *The Nature of Race: How Scientists Think and Teach About Human Difference.* Berkeley: University of California Press; Paul, Diana. B. 1998. *Controlling Human Heredity: 1865 to the Present.* New York: Humanity Books.

3. See Ellison, Christopher G., and Marc A. Musick. 1995. "Conservative Protestantism and Public Opinion Towards Science." *Review of Religious Research* 36(3):245–262; Kosmin, Barry A., Ariela Keysar, and Nava Lerer. 1992. "Secular Education and the Religious Profile of Contemporary Black and White Americans." *Journal for the Scientific Study of Religion* 31(4):523–532. See also Granger and Price for a discussion of scholarly interpretations that the overrepresentation of black Americans in conservative Christian congregations *may* lead to underrepresentation in science careers. Granger, Maury D., and Gregory N. Price. 2007. "The Tree of Science and Original Sin: Do Christian Religious Beliefs Constrain the Supply of Scientists?" *Journal of Socio-Economics* 36:144–160.

4. See Schmidt, Garbi. 2004. *Islam in Urban America: Sunni Muslims in Chicago.* Philadelphia, PA: Temple University Press.

5. See Serhan, R. 2014. "Muslim Immigration to America." Pp. 29–46 in *The Oxford Handbook of American Islam*, edited by Y. Haddad and J. Smith. Oxford: Oxford University Press.

6. See Pew Research Center. 2015. "The Future of World Religions: Population Growth Projections, 2010–2050." Retrieved April 27, 2015, http://www.pewforum.org/2015/04/02/religious-projections-2010-2050/.

7. See Vaidyanathan, Brandon, David Johnson, Pamela Prickett, and Elaine Howard Ecklund. "Rejecting the Conflict Narrative: American Jewish and Muslim Views on Science and Religion." *Social Compass* 63(4):478–496.

8. Strauss, Anselm, and Juliet M. Corbin. 1990. *Basics of Qualitative Research: Grounded Theory Procedures and Techniques.* Thousand Oaks, CA: Sage.

9. See Rubin, Herbert J., and Irene S. Rubin. 2011. *Qualitative Interviewing: The Art of Hearing Data.* Thousand Oaks, CA: Sage.

10. See p. 1687 in Vaisey, Stephen. 2009. "Motivation and Justification: A Dual-Process Model of Culture in Action." *American Journal of Sociology* 114(6):1675–1715. See also Vaisey, Stephen. 2014. "Is Interviewing Compatible with the Dual-Process Model of Culture?" *American Journal of Cultural Sociology* 2:150–158. In addition, see Pugh, Allison J. 2013. "What Good Are Interviews for Thinking About Culture? Demystifying Interpretive Analysis." *American Journal of Cultural Sociology* 1:42–68. And see Vaisey 2014 for a response to Pugh.

11. See Davies, Bronwyn, and Rom Harre. 1990. "Positioning: The Discursive Production of Selves." *Journal for the Theory of Social Behaviour* 20(1):43–63.

12. The specific benchmarks are for gender, race and Hispanic ethnicity, education, household income, region, household Internet access, and household primary language.

13. See Ecklund, Elaine Howard. 2010. *Science vs. Religion: What Scientists Really Think*. New York: Oxford University Press; Ecklund, Elaine Howard, David R. Johnson, Christopher P. Scheitle, Kirstin R. W. Matthews, and Steven W. Lewis. 2016. "Religion Among Scientists in International Context: Methods and Initial Results from a New Cross-National Survey of Scientists." *Socius* 2:1–9.

14. See Chang, Linchiat, and Jon A. Krosnick. 2010. "Comparing Oral Interviewing with Self-Administered Computerized Questionnaires: An Experiment." *Public Opinion Quarterly* 74(1):154–167.

15. Callegaro, Mario, and Charles DiSogra. 2008. "Computing Response Metrics for Online Panels." *Public Opinion Quarterly* 72:1008–1032.

16. See Chang and Krosnick 2010.

17. See Hackett, Conrad, and D. Michael Lindsay. 2008. "Measuring Evangelicalism: Consequences of Different Operationalization Strategies." *Journal for the Scientific Study of Religion* 47(3):499–514.

18. See Steensland, Brian, Lynn D. Robinson, W. Bradford Wilcox, Jerry Z. Park, Mark D. Regnerus, and Robert D. Woodberry. 2000. "The Measure of American Religion: Toward Improving the State of the Art." *Social Forces* 79(1):291–318.

BIBLIOGRAPHY

Association of Religion Data Archives. 2012. "General Social Survey 2012 Cross-Section and Panel Combined—Instructional Dataset." Retrieved March 24, 2015. http://thearda.com/Archive/Files/Analysis/GSS12ED/GSS12ED_Var316_1.asp.

Atkin, Emily. 2014. "Group Representing Half a Billion Christians Says It Will No Longer Support Fossil Fuels." *Think Progress,* July 11. Retrieved September 11, 2014. http://thinkprogress.org/climate/2014/07/11/3459111/wcc-christians-divests/.

Bader, Christopher, and Paul Froese. 2005. "Images of God: The Effect of Personal Theologies on Moral Attitudes, Political Affiliation, and Religious Behavior." *Interdisciplinary Journal of Research on Religion* 1:1–24.

Baker, Joseph. 2012. "Public Perceptions of the Incompatibility Between 'Science and Religion.'" *Public Understanding of Science* 21(3):340–353.

Baker, Joseph. 2013. "Acceptance of Evolution and Support for Teaching Creationism in Public Schools: The Conditional Impact of Educational Attainment." *Journal for the Scientific Study of Religion* 52(1):216–228.

Barbour, Ian. 1971. *Issues in Science and Religion.* New York: HarperCollins College Division.

Barna Group. 2011. "Six Reasons Young Christians Leave Church." Retrieved March 24, 2015. https://www.barna.org/barna-update/teens-nextgen/528-six-reasons-young-christians-leave-church#.UyFvXI0x-2y.

Beliefnet. 2006. "God Is Not Threatened by Our Scientific Adventures." Retrieved September 25, 2016. http://www.beliefnet.com/News/Science-Religion/2006/08/God-Is-Not-Threatened-By-Our-Scientific-Adventures.aspx.

Berger, Peter. 1967. *The Sacred Canopy: Elements of a Sociological Theory of Religion.* Garden City, NY: Doubleday.

Berger, Peter L. 2008. "Secularization Falsified." *First Things.* Retrieved September 17, 2014. http://www.firstthings.com/article/2008/02/002-secularization-falsified.

Berkman, Michael, and Eric Plutzer. 2010. *Evolution, Creationism, and the Battle to Control America's Classrooms.* Cambridge: Cambridge University Press.

"Bill Nye Debates Ken Ham—HD (Official)." YouTube video, 2:45:32. Posted by "Answers in Genesis." February 4, 2014. http://www.youtube.com/watch?v=z6kgvh G3AkI&feature=youtube_gdata_player.

Biologos. Retrieved August 27, 2014. http://biologos.org/.

Bishop, Bill. 2008. *The Big Sort: Why the Clustering of Like-Minded America Is Tearing Us Apart.* Boston and New York: Mariner Books of Houghton Mifflin Harcourt.

Boss, Judith A. 1994. "First Trimester Prenatal Diagnosis: Earlier Is Not Necessarily Better." *Journal of Medical Ethics* 20(3):146–151.

Boyd, Heather H. 1999. "Christianity and the Environment in the American Public." *Journal for the Scientific Study of Religion* 38(1):36–44.

Brem, Sarah K., Michael Ranney, and Jennifer Schindel. 2003. "Perceived Consequences of Evolution: College Students Perceive Negative Personal and Social Impact in Evolutionary Theory." *Science Education* 87(2):181–206.

Brooke, John Hedley, and Ronald Numbers, eds. 2011. *Science and Religion Around the World*. New York: Oxford University Press.

Bruenig, Elizabeth. 2015. "Why Do Evangelicals Like James Inhofe Believe That Only God Can Cause Climate Change?" *New Republic*. Retrieved February 10, 2015. https://newrepublic.com/article/120889/evangelical-james-inhofe-says-only-god-can-cause-climate-change.

Brulle, Robert J., Jason Carmichael, and J. Craig Jenkins. 2012. "Shifting Public Opinion on Climate Change: An Empirical Assessment of Factors Influencing Concern over Climate Change in the U.S., 2002–2010." *Climatic Change* 114(2):169–188.

California Institute for Regenerative Medicine. 2011. "Myths and Misconceptions About Stem Cell Research." Retrieved October 2, 2014. http://www.cirm.ca.gov/our-progress/myths-and-misconceptions-about-stem-cell-research#2.

Callegaro, Mario, and Charles DiSogra. 2008. "Computing Response Metrics for Online Panels." *Public Opinion Quarterly* 72:1008–1032.

Campbell, Courtney S. 1995. "The Ordeal and Meaning of Suffering." *Sunstone* 18(3):37–43.

Campbell, Heidi A. 2010. *When Religion Meets New Media*. New York: Routledge.

Campbell, Heidi A., ed. 2013. *Digital Religion: Understanding Religious Practice in New Media Worlds*. New York: Routledge.

Carson, Rachel. 1962. *Silent Spring*. Boston: Houghton Mifflin.

Center for the Study of Science in Muslim Societies. Retrieved August 27, 2014. https://www.hampshire.edu/ssims/center-for-the-study-of-science-in-muslim-societies.

Chan, Esther, and Elaine Howard Ecklund. 2016. "Narrating and Navigating Authorities: Understandings of the Bible and Science Among Evangelical and Mainline Protestants." *Journal for the Scientific Study of Religion* 55(1):54–69.

Chang, Linchiat, and Jon A. Krosnick. 2010. "Comparing Oral Interviewing with Self-Administered Computerized Questionnaires: An Experiment." *Public Opinion Quarterly* 74(1):154–167.

Chaves, Mark. 1994. "Secularization as Declining Religious Authority." *Social Forces* 72(3):749–774.

Chaves, Mark. 2011. *American Religion: Contemporary Trends*. Princeton, NJ: Princeton University Press.

Collins, Francis S. 2007. *The Language of God: A Scientist Presents Evidence for Belief*. New York: Free Press.

Connor, Steve. 2015. "For the Love of God … Scientists in Uproar at £1m Religion Prize." *Independent*. Retrieved January 15, 2015. http://www.independent.co.uk/news/science/for-the-love-of-god-scientists-in-uproar-at-1631m-religion-prize-2264181.html.

Conrad, Peter. 1999. "Uses of Expertise: Sources, Quotes, and Voice in the Reporting of Genetics in the News." *Public Understanding of Science* 8(4):285–302.

Corbie-Smith, G. 1999. "The Continuing Legacy of the Tuskegee Syphilis Study: Considerations for Clinical Investigation." *American Journal of the Medical Sciences* 317(1):5–8.

Coyne, Jerry A. 2012. "Science, Religion, and Society: The Problem of Evolution in America." *Evolution* 66(8):2654–2663.

D'Andrade, Roy G. 1991. "The Identification of Schemas in Naturalistic Data." Pp. 279–301 in *Person Schemas and Maladaptive Interpersonal Behavior Patterns*, edited by M. Horowitz. Chicago: University of Chicago Press.

Davies, Bronwyn, and Rom Harre. 1990. "Positioning: The Discursive Production of Selves." *Journal for the Theory of Social Behaviour* 20(1):43–63.

Dawkins, Richard. 2006. *The God Delusion*. New York: Houghton Mifflin.

Dawkins, Richard. 2011. "Why There Almost Certainly Is No God." *Huffington Post,* May 25. Retrieved October 3, 2014. http://www.huffingtonpost.com/richard-dawkins/why-there-almost-certainl_b_32164.html.

De Dios Vial Correa, Juan. 2000. "Declaration on the Production of the Scientific and Therapeutic Use of Human Embryonic Stem Cells." *Pontifical Academy for Life*. Retrieved September 12, 2014. http://www.vatican.va/roman_curia/pontifical_academies/acdlife/documents/rc_pa_acdlife_doc_20000824_cellule-staminali_en.html.

Dembski, William A., and Jonathan Witt. 2010. *Intelligent Design Uncensored: An Easy-to-Understand Guide to the Controversy*. Downers Grove, IL: InterVarsity.

Dennett, Daniel C. 1996. *Darwin's Dangerous Idea: Evolution and the Meanings of Life*. New York: Simon and Schuster.

Derbyshire, John. 2008. "Science Equals Murder." *National Review,* April 30. Retrieved September 3, 2014. http://www.nationalreview.com/corner/162377/science-equals-murder-john-derbyshire.

Devolder, Katrien. 2009. "To Be, or Not to Be?" *EMBO Reports* 10(12):1285–1287.

Dickson, David. 2005. "The Case for a 'Deficit Model' of Science Communication." *SciDev.Net,* June 27. Retrieved October 3, 2014. http://www.scidev.net/global/.

Dietz, Thomas, Amy Dan, and Rachael Shwom. 2007. "Support for Climate Change Policy: Social Psychological and Social Structural Influences." *Rural Sociology* 72(2):185–214.

DiMaggio, Paul. 1997. "Culture and Cognition." *Annual Review of Sociology* 23:263–287.

Djupe, Paul A., and Patrick K. Hunt. 2009. "Beyond the Lynn White Thesis: Congregational Effects on Environmental Concern." *Journal for the Scientific Study of Religion* 48(4):670–686.

Doolin, Bill, and Judy Motion. 2010. "Christian Lay Understandings of Preimplantation Genetic Diagnosis." *Public Understanding of Science* 19:669–685.

Doran, Caroline Josephine. 2009. "The Role of Personal Values in Fair Trade Consumption." *Journal of Business Ethics* 84(4):549–563.

Downey, Allen B. 2014. "Religious Affiliation, Education, and Internet Use." Retrieved March 24, 2015. http://arxiv.org/abs/1403.5534.

Dragojlovic, Nick. 2014. "How Meaningful Are Public Attitudes Towards Stem Cell Research?" *Oxford University Press's Academic Insights for the Thinking World*, January 17.

Dragojlovic, Nick. 2014. "Voting for Stem Cells: How Local Conditions Tempered Moral Opposition to Proposition 71." *Science and Public Policy* 41:359–369.

Dunlap, Riley E., and Robert E. Jones. 2002. "Environmental Concern: Conceptual and Measurement Issues." Pp. 482–524 in *Handbook of Environment Sociology*, edited by Riley E. Dunlap and William Michelson. Westport, CT: Greenwood.

Durkheim, Emile. [1915] 1965. *The Elementary Forms of Religious Life*. New York: Free Press.

Ebreo, Angela, James Hershey, and Joanne Vining. 1999. "Reducing Solid Waste Linking Recycling to Environmentally Responsible Consumerism." *Environment and Behavior* 31(1):107–135.

Eckberg, D. L., and A. Nesterenko. 1984. "For and Against Evolution: Religion, Social Class, and the Symbolic Universe." *Social Science Journal* 22(1):1–18.

Eckberg, Douglas L., and T. Jean Blocker. 1996. "Christianity, Environmentalism, and the Theoretical Problem of Fundamentalism." *Journal for the Scientific Study of Religion* 35(4):343–355.

Ecklund, Elaine Howard. 2010. *Science vs. Religion: What Scientists Really Think*. New York: Oxford University Press.

Ecklund, Elaine Howard, David R. Johnson, Sarah Hamshari, Kirstin R. W. Matthews, and Steven W. Lewis. 2015. "A Global Lab: Religion Among Scientists in International Context." Conference report.

Ecklund, Elaine Howard, David R. Johnson, Christopher P. Scheitle, Kirstin R. W. Matthews, and Steven W. Lewis. 2016. "Religion Among Scientists in International Context: Methods and Initial Results from a New Cross-National Survey of Scientists." *Socius* 2:1–9.

Ecklund, Elaine Howard, and Elizabeth Long. 2011. "Scientists and Spirituality." *Sociology of Religion* 72(3):253–274.

Ecklund, Elaine Howard, Jared L. Peifer, Virginia White, and Esther Chan. "Moral Schema and Intuition: How Religious Laypeople Evaluate Human Reproductive Genetic Technologies." *Sociological Forum* 32(2):277–297.

Ecklund, Elaine Howard, and Christopher P. Scheitle. 2014. "Surveying Religious People About Science and Scientists." Presented at the annual meeting of American Association for the Advancement of Science, February 16, Chicago, IL.

Ecklund, Elaine Howard, Christopher P. Scheitle, Jared Peifer, and Dan Bolger. 2016. "Examining Links Between Religion, Evolution Views, and Climate Change Skepticism." *Environment and Behavior*. doi: 10.1177/0013916516674246.

Ecklund, Elaine Howard, and Jeff Smith. 2015. "Congregational Conversations." *Christian Century*, August 5, pp. 26–29.

Edgell, Penny. 2005. *Religion and Family in a Changing Society*. Princeton, NJ: Princeton University Press.

Editors, The. 2005. "Okay, We Give Up—We Feel So Ashamed." *Scientific American*, March 28. Retrieved September 27, 2014. http://www.scientificamerican.com/article/okay-we-give-up/.

Einstein, Albert. 1954. *Ideas and Opinions*. New York: Bonanza.

Ellingson, Stephen, Vernon A. Woodley, and Anthony Paik. 2012. "The Structure of Religious Environmentalism: Movement Organizations, Interorganizational Networks, and Collective Action." *Journal for the Scientific Study of Religion* 51(2):266–285.

Elliott, Kevin C. 2011. *Is a Little Pollution Good for You? Incorporating Societal Values in Environmental Research*. Oxford: Oxford University Press.

Ellison, Christopher G., and Marc A. Musick. 1995. "Conservative Protestantism and Public Opinion Towards Science." *Review of Religious Research* 36(3):245–262.

Emerson, Michael O. 1996. "Through Tinted Glasses: Religion, Worldviews and Abortion Attitudes." *Journal for the Scientific Study of Religion* 35(1):41–55.

Emerson, Michael O., and David Hartman. 2006. "The Rise of Religious Fundamentalism." *Annual Review of Sociology* 32:127–144.

Episcopal Church General Convention. 2004. "Support Human Embryonic Stem Cell Research." *Journal of the General Convention of the Episcopal Church* 613f.

Evans, John H. 2002. *Playing God? Human Genetic Engineering and the Rationalization of Public Bioethical Debate*. Chicago: University of Chicago Press.

Evans, John H. 2002. "Polarization in Abortion Attitudes in U.S. Religious Traditions, 1972–1998." *Sociological Forum* 17(3):397–422.

Evans, John H. 2006. "Religious Belief, Perceptions of Human Suffering and Support for Reproductive Genetic Technology." *Journal of Health Politics, Policy and Law* 31(6):1047–1074.

Evans, John H. 2010. *Contested Reproduction: Genetic Technologies, Religion, and Public Debate*. Chicago: University of Chicago Press.

Evans, John H. 2011. "Epistemological and Moral Conflict Between Religion and Science." *Journal for the Scientific Study of Religion* 50(4):707–727.

Evans, John H. 2016. *What Is a Human? What the Answers Mean for Human Rights*. New York: Oxford University Press.

Evans, John H., and Michael S. Evans. 2008. "Religion and Science: Beyond the Epistemological Conflict Narrative." *Annual Review of Sociology* 34:87–105.

Evans, John H., and Justin Feng. 2013. "Conservative Protestantism and Skepticism of Scientists Studying Climate Change." *Climate Change* 121(4):595–608.

Evans, John H., and Kathy Hudson. 2007. "Religion and Reproductive Genetics: Beyond Views of Embryonic Life?" *Journal for the Scientific Study of Religion* 46(4):565–581.

Evans, Michael S. 2012. "Who Wants a Deliberative Public Sphere?" *Sociological Forum* 27(4):872–895.

Evans, Michael S. 2016. *Seeking Good Debate: Religion, Science, and Conflict in American Public Life*. Berkeley: University of California Press.

Everhart, Donald, and Salman Hameed. 2013. "Muslims and Evolution: A Study of Pakistani Physicians in the United States." *Evolution: Education and Outreach* 6(1):2–8.

Faia, Michael A. 1976. "Secularization and Scholarship Among American Professors." *Sociological Analysis* 37(1):63–73.

Ferngren, Gary B. 2002. *Science and Religion: A Historical Introduction*. Baltimore, MD: Johns Hopkins University Press.

Finke, Roger, and Rodney Stark. 1998. "Religious Choice and Competition." *American Sociological Review* 63(5):761–766.

Finocchiaro, Maurice A. 2009. "Myth 8. That Galileo Was Imprisoned and Tortured for Advocating Copernicanism." Pp. 68–78 in *Galileo Goes to Jail and Other Myths About Science and Religion*, edited by Ronald Numbers. Cambridge, MA: Harvard University Press.

Finson, Kevin D. 2002. "Drawing a Scientist: What We Do and Do Not Know After Fifty Years of Drawings." *School Science and Mathematics* 102(7):335–345.

"Francis Collins." N.d. *Other Voices*. PBS. Retrieved October 3, 2014. http://www.pbs.org/wgbh/questionofgod/voices/collins.html.

"Francis S. Collins: By the Book." 2013. *New York Times*, July 25. Retrieved June 27, 2014. http://www.nytimes.com/2013/07/28/books/review/francis-s-collins-by-the-book.html?pagewanted=all.

Freeman, David. 2014. "New Survey Suggests Science and Religion Are Compatible, But Scientists Have Their Doubts." *Huffington Post*, March 17. Retrieved June 26, 2014. http://www.huffingtonpost.com/2014/03/17/science-religion-survey-compatible-scientists-doubt_n_4953194.html.

Froese, Paul, and Christopher Bader. 2010. *America's Four Gods: What We Say About God-and What That Says About Us*. Oxford: Oxford University Press.

Funk, Cary, and Becka A. Alper. 2015. "Perception of Conflict Between Science and Religion." Pew Research Center, October 22. Retrieved April 27, 2015. http://www.pewinternet.org/2015/10/22/perception-of-conflict-between-science-and-religion/.

Funk, Cary, Brian Kennedy, and Elizabeth Podrebarac Sciupac. 2016. "U.S. Public Wary of Biomedical Technologies to 'Enhance' Human Abilities." Pew Research Center. Retrieved July 27, 2016. http://www.pewinternet.org/2016/07/26/u-s-public-wary-of-biomedical-technologies-to-enhance-human-abilities/.

Gallup. "Evolution, Creationism, Intelligent Design." Retrieved September 28, 2016. http://www.gallup.com/poll/21814/Evolution-Creationism-Intelligent-Design.aspx.

Gallup, George Jr., and D. Michael Lindsay. 1999. *Surveying the Religious Landscape: Trends in U.S. Beliefs*. Harrisburg, PA: Morehouse.

Gamble, Vanessa. 1999. "Race and the New Genetics: A Historical Perspective." Pp. 163–186 in *The Implications of Genetics for Health Professionals*, edited by M. Hager. New York: Josiah Macy Jr. Foundation.

Garfield, E. 1978. "Scientists' Image in Movies and TV Programs." *Current Contexts* 10:5–12.

Gauchat, Gordon. 2012. "Politicization of Science in the Public Sphere: A Study of Public Trust in the United States, 1974 to 2010." *American Sociological Review* 77(2):167–187.

Giberson, Karl, and Mariano Artigas. 2006. *Oracles of Science: Celebrity Scientists Versus God and Religion*. Oxford: Oxford University Press.

Glaser, Barney G., and Anselm L. Strauss. 2009. *The Discovery of Grounded Theory: Strategies for Qualitative Research*. Piscataway, NJ: Transaction.

Goidel, Kirby, and Matthew Nisbet. 2006. "Exploring the Roots of Public Participation in the Controversy over Embryonic Stem Cell Research and Cloning." *Political Behavior* 28(2):175–192.

Gottweis, Herbert. 2010. "The Endless hESC Controversy in the United States: History, Context, and Prospects." *Cell Stem Cell* 7(5):555–558.

Gould, Stephen Jay. 1977. *Ever Since Darwin: Reflections in Natural History*. New York: W. W. Norton.

Gould, Stephen Jay. 1997. "Nonoverlapping Magisteria." *Natural History* 106:16–22.

Granger, Maury D., and Gregory N. Price. 2007. "The Tree of Science and Original Sin: Do Christian Religious Beliefs Constrain the Supply of Scientists?" *Journal of Socio-Economics* 36:144–160.

Grant, Richard P. 2016. "Why Scientists Are Losing the Fight to Communicate Science to the Public." *Guardian*, August 23.

Graves, Joseph L. 2004. *The Race Myth: Why We Pretend Race Exists in America*. New York: Dutton.

Greeley, Andrew. 1993. "Religion and Attitudes Toward the Environment." *Journal for the Scientific Study of Religion* 32(1):19–28.

Greenfieldboyce, Nell. 2011. "'Shrimp on a Treadmill': The Politics of 'Silly' Studies." National Public Radio. August 23.

Gross, Neil, and Solon Simmons. 2009. "The Religiosity of American College and University Professors." *Sociology of Religion* 70(2):101–129.

Guessoum, Nidhal. 2010. "Religious Literalism and Science-Related Issues in Contemporary Islam." *Zygon* 45(4):817–840.

Guhin, Jeffrey. 2016. "Why Worry About Evolution? Boundaries, Practices, and Moral Salience in Sunni and Evangelical High Schools." *Sociological Theory* 34(2):151–174.

Hackett, Conrad, and D. Michael Lindsay. 2008. "Measuring Evangelicalism: Consequences of Different Operationalization Strategies." *Journal for the Scientific Study of Religion* 47(3):499–514.

Hadaway, C. Kirk, and Penny Long Marler. 2005. "How Many Americans Attend Worship Each Week? An Alternative Approach to Measurement." *Journal for the Scientific Study of Religion* 44:307–322.

Hadaway, C. Kirk, Penny Long Marler, and Mark Chaves. 1993. "What the Polls Don't Show: A Closer Look at US Church Attendance." *American Sociological Review* 58(6):741–752.

Hand, Carl M., and Kent D. Van Liere. 1984. "Religion, Mastery-over-Nature, and Environmental Concern." *Social Forces* 63(2):555–570.

Harris, Gardiner. 2009. "For N.I.H. Chief, Issues of Identity and Culture." *New York Times*, October 5, pp D1.

Harris, Richard J., and Edgar W. Mills. 1985. "Religion, Values, and Attitudes Toward Abortion." *Journal for the Scientific Study of Religion* 24(2):137–154.

Harris, Sam. 2006. "Jewry's Big Question: Why Are Atheists So Angry?" *Huffington Post*. Retrieved January 15, 2015. http://www.huffingtonpost.com/sam-harris/jewcys-big-question-why-a_b_35180.html.

Harris, Sam. 2011. *The Moral Landscape: How Science Can Determine Human Values.* New York: Free Press.

Harris, Sam. 2011. "Science Must Destroy Religion." *Huffington Post*, May 25. Retrieved April 1, 2015. http://www.huffingtonpost.com/sam-harris/science-must-destroy-reli_b_13153.html.

Harris, Sam, Jonas T. Kaplan, Ashley Curiel, Susan Y. Bookheimer, Marco Iacoboni, and Mark S. Cohen. 2009. "The Neural Correlates of Religious and Nonreligious Belief." *PLoS ONE* 4(10):e7272.

Hayhoe, Katharine. 2015. "Climate, Politics and Religion—My Opinion." Retrieved June 5, 2015. http://katharinehayhoe.com/wp2016/2015/06/05/climate-politics-and-religion/.

Hayhoe, Katharine, and Andrew Farley. 2009. *A Climate for Change: Global Warming Facts for Faith-Based Decisions.* New York: Hachette.

Hill, Jonathan P. 2014. "The Recipe for Creationism." Retrieved September 20, 2016. http://biologos.org/blogs/archive/the-recipe-for-creationism.

Hill, Jonathan P. 2014. "Rejecting Evolution: The Role of Religion, Education, and Social Networks." *Journal for the Scientific Study of Religion* 53(3):575–594.

Hill, Jonathan P. 2014. "Rethinking the Origins Debate." *Christianity Today*, February 4.

Hitchens, Christopher. 2014. *Mortality*. Reprint edition. New York: Twelve.

Hoffmann, John P., and Sherrie Mills Johnson. 2005. "Attitudes Toward Abortion Among Religious Traditions in the United States: Change or Continuity?" *Sociology of Religion* 66(2):161–182.

Holy See, The. 2015. *Encyclical Letter Laudato Si' of the Holy Father Francis on Care for Our Common Home.* Libreria Editrice Vaticana.

Huxley, Aldous. 1932. *Brave New World.* London: Chatto and Windus.

Intergovernmental Panel on Climate Change. 2015. *Fifth Assessment Report.* Retrieved October 7, 2014. http://www.ipcc.ch/.

Jammer, Max. 2002. *Einstein and Religion: Physics and Theology.* Princeton, NJ: Princeton University Press.

Kanagy, Conrad L., and Hart M. Nelsen. 1995. "Religion and Environmental Concern: Challenging the Dominant Assumptions." *Review of Religious Research* 37(1):33–45.

Kanagy, Conrad L., and Fern K. Willits. 1993. "A 'Greening' of Religion? Some Evidence from a Pennsylvania Sample." *Social Science Quarterly* 74(3):674–683.

Kearns, Laurel. 1996. "Saving the Creation: Christian Environmentalism in the United States." *Sociology of Religion* 57(1):55–70.

Keister, Lisa. 2003. "Religion and Wealth: The Role of Religious Affiliation and Participation in Early Adult Asset Accumulation." *Social Forces* 82(1):173–205.

Kerr, Anne, Sarah Cunningham-Burley, and Amanda Amos. 1998. "Drawing the Line: An Analysis of Lay People's Discussions About the New Genetics." *Public Understanding of Science* 7(2):113–133.

Kincaid, Ellie. 2015. "An Increasingly Common Medical Procedure Is Raising Ethical Questions We're Not Prepared to Deal With." *Business Insider UK*, June 19.

Kingsolver, Barbara. 2012. *Flight Behavior*. New York: Harper.

Konisky, David M., Jeffrey Milyo, and Lilliard E. Richardson Jr. 2008. "Environmental Policy Attitudes: Issues, Geographical Scale, and Political Trust." *Social Science Quarterly* 89(5):1066–1085.

Korver-Glenn, Elizabeth, Esther Chan, and Elaine Howard Ecklund. 2015. "Perceptions of Science Education Among African American and White Evangelicals: A Texas Case Study." *Review of Religious Research* 57(1):131–148.

Kosmin, Barry A., Ariela Keysar, and Nava Lerer. 1992. "Secular Education and the Religious Profile of Contemporary Black and White Americans." *Journal for the Scientific Study of Religion* 31(4):523–532.

Krauss, Lawrence. 2010. "Faith and Foolishness: When Religious Beliefs Become Dangerous." *Scientific American*, August 1, p. 340.

Kruvand, Marjorie. 2012. "Dr. Soundbite: The Making of an Expert Source in Science and Medical Stories." *Science Communication* 34(5):566–591.

Lapidus, Ira M. 2014. *A History of Islamic Societies*, 3rd edition. New York: Cambridge University Press.

Leakey Foundation. N.d. "The Leakey Family." Retrieved September 28, 2016. https://leakeyfoundation.org/about/the-leakey-family/.

Lester, Lane, and James C. Hefley. 1998. *Human Cloning: Playing God or Scientific Progress?* Grand Rapids, MI: Fleming H. Revell.

Leuba, James H. 1934. "Religious Beliefs of American Scientists." *Harper's Magazine*, August.

Lewin, Tamar. 2015. "Industry's Growth Leads to Leftover Embryos, and Painful Choices." *New York Times*, June 17.

Lindberg, David C., and Ronald L. Numbers, eds. 1986. *God and Nature: Historical Essays on the Encounter Between Christianity and Science*. Berkeley: University of California Press.

Machamer, Peter, ed. 1998. *The Cambridge Companion to Galileo*. Cambridge: Cambridge University Press.

Marina, Peter. 2013. *Getting the Holy Ghost: Urban Ethnography in a Pentecostal Tongue-Speaking Church*. Lanham, MD: Lexington.

Masci, David. 2007. "How the Public Resolves Conflicts Between Faith and Science." Pew Research Center. Retrieved September 25, 2016. http://www.pewforum.org/2007/08/27/how-the-public-resolves-conflicts-between-faith-and-science/.

Matthews, Kirstin. 2009. "Stem Cell Research: A Science and Policy Overview." Rice University's Baker Institute for Public Policy. Retrieved August 13, 2014. http://bakerinstitute.org/media/files/Research/4a146856/stemcell-intro-0208.pdf.

Mayo Clinic. 2016. "In Vitro Fertilization (IVF): Overview." Retrieved November 3, 2016. http://www.mayoclinic.org/tests-procedures/in-vitro-fertilization/home/ovc-20206838.

Mazur, Allan. 2005. "Believers and Disbelievers in Evolution." *Politics and the Life Sciences* 23(2):55–61.

McCright, Aaron M., and Riley E. Dunlap. 2011. "The Politicization of Climate Change and Polarization in the American Public's Views of Global Warming, 2001–2010." *Sociological Quarterly* 52:155–194.

McGrath, Alister E. 2015. *Dawkins God: From the Selfish Gene to the God Delusion*. Chichester: Wiley-Blackwell.

McPherson, Miller, Lynn Smith-Lovin, and James M. Cook. 2001. "Birds of a Feather: Homophily in Social Networks." *Annual Review of Sociology* 27: 415–444.

Mead, Margaret, and Rhoda Metraux. 1957. "Image of the Scientist Among High-School Students: A Pilot Study." *Science* 126:384–390.

Mertig, Angela G., Riley E. Dunlap, and Denton E. Morrison. 2002. "The Environmental Movement in the United States." Pp. 448–481 in *Handbook of Environment Sociology*, edited by Riley E. Dunlap and William Michelson. Westport, CT: Greenwood.

Middleton, J. Richard. 2011. "Image of God." In *Dictionary of Scripture and Ethics*, edited by J. B. Green. Grand Rapids, MI: Baker Academic.

Miller, Jon D., Eugenie C. Scott, and Shinji Okamoto. 2006. "Public Acceptance of Evolution." *Science* 313(5788):765–766.

Mitra, R. 2001. "Science and Reason vs. Unreason." *Economic and Political Weekly* 36(43):4055–4056.

Mohai, Paul. 1990. "Black Environmentalism." *Social Science Quarterly* 71(4):744–765.

Mohai, Paul, and Bunyan Bryant. 1998. "Is There a 'Race' Effect on Concern for Environmental Quality?" *Public Opinion Quarterly* 62:475–505.

Mooney, Chris. 2013. "Why Climate Change Skeptics and Evolution Deniers Joined Forces." *Mother Jones*, November 27. Retrieved February 10, 2015. http://www.motherjones.com/blue-marble/2013/11/why-climate-change-skeptics-evolution-deniers-joined-forces.

Morning, Ann. 2011. *The Nature of Race: How Scientists Think and Teach About Human Difference*. Berkeley: University of California Press.

Munson, Ziad W. 2009. *The Making of Pro-life Activists: How Social Movement Mobilization Works*. Chicago: University of Chicago Press.

Napolitano, Carol L., and Oladele A. Ogunseitan. 1999. "Gender Differences in the Perception of Genetic Engineering Applied to Human Reproduction." *Social Indicators Research* 46(2):191–204.

National Academy of Science. 2008. "Compatibility of Science and Religion." Retrieved October 2, 2014. http://www.nas.edu/evolution/Compatibility.html.

National Association of Evangelicals. 2015. "Caring for God's Creation: A Call to Action." Retrieved August 30, 2016. http://nae.net/caring-for-gods-creation/.

National Center for Science Education. 2008. "Science and Religion, Methodology and Humanism." Retrieved September 25, 2016. https://ncse.com/religion/science-religion-methodology-humanism.

National Human Genome Research Institute. 2015. "All About the Human Genome Project (HGP)." October 1. Retrieved February 17, 2016. http://www.genome.gov/10001772.

National Human Genome Research Institute. 2016. "Cloning." Retrieved November 10, 2016. https://www.genome.gov/25020028/cloning-fact-sheet/.

National Institutes of Health. 2009. "Embryonic Stem Cell Research: A Decade of Debate from Bush to Obama." Retrieved August 7, 2014. http://www.ncbi.nlm.nih.gov/pmc/articles/PMC2744932/.

National Institutes of Health. 2010. "What Are Embryonic Stem Cells?" Retrieved August 7, 2014. http://stemcells.nih.gov/info/basics/pages/basics3.aspx.

National Institutes of Health. 2011. "What Are the Similarities and Differences Between Embryonic and Adult Stem Cells?" Retrieved August 7, 2014. http://stemcells.nih.gov/info/basics/pages/basics5.aspx.

National Institutes of Health. 2015. "Stem Cell Basics." Retrieved July 26, 2016. http://stemcells.nih.gov/info/basics/pages/basics3.aspx.

Nepstad, Sharon E., and Rhys H. Williams. 2007. "Religion in Rebellion, Resistance, and Social Movements." Pp. 419–437 in *The SAGE Handbook of the Sociology of Religion*, edited by J. A. D. Beckford. Los Angeles: Sage.

Nerlich, Brigitte, and David D. Clarke. 2003. "Anatomy of a Media Event: How Arguments Clashed in the 2001 Human Cloning Debate." *New Genetics and Society* 22(1):43–59.

Newport, Frank. 2012. "Americans, Including Catholics, Say Birth Control Is Morally Acceptable." Gallup. Retrieved October 3, 2014. http://www.gallup.com/poll/154799/Americans-Including-Catholics-Say-Birth-Control-Morally.aspx.

Nielsen, Michael E., Jennifer Williams, and Brandon Randolph-Seng. 2009. "Religious Orientation, Personality, and Attitudes About Human Stem Cell Research." *International Journal for the Psychology of Religion* 19(2):81–91.

Nisbet, Matthew C. 2004. "The Competition for Worldviews: Values, Information, and Public Support for Stem Cell Research." *International Journal of Public Opinion Research* 17(1):90–112.

Nisbet, Matthew C. 2004. "Trends: Public Opinion About Stem Cell Research and Human Cloning." *Public Opinion Quarterly* 68:131–154.

Noy, Shiri, and Timothy L. O'Brien. 2016. "Science, Religion, and Public Opinion in the United States." *Socius*. doi: 10.1177/2378023116651876.

Numbers, Ronald L. 2006. *The Creationists: From Scientific Creationism to Intelligent Design*. Cambridge, MA: Harvard University Press.

Numbers, Ronald, ed. 2009. *Galileo Goes to Jail and Other Myths About Science and Religion*. Cambridge, MA: Harvard University Press.

Oberlin, Kathleen (Casey). 2015. "Science Museums and Cultural Authority: The Case of the Creation Museum." *Cosmologics: A Magazine of Science, Religion, and Culture*, October 15.

Omi, Michael, and Howard Winant. 1994. *Racial Formation in the United States: From the 1960s to the 1990s*. New York: Routledge.

Oxford Annotated Bible Revised Standard Version. 1952. Oxford: Oxford University Pres. Retrieved September 12, 2014. http://archive.org/details/OxfordAnnotatedBibleRevisedStandardVersion-r.s.v.1952.

Pardo, Rafael, and Felix Calvo. 2008. "Attitudes Toward Embryo Research, Worldviews and the Moral Status of the Embryo Frame." *Science Communication* 30(1):8–47.

Paul, Diana. B. 1998. *Controlling Human Heredity: 1865 to the Present.* New York: Humanity Books.

Payton, Robert L., and Michael Moody. 2004. "Stewardship." Pp. 457–460 in *Philanthropy in America: A Comprehensive Historical Encyclopedia, Volume 3,* edited by Dwight F. Burlingame. Santa Barbara, CA: ABC-CLIO.

Peifer, Jared L. 2012. "Socially Responsible Investing and the Power to Do Good: Whose Dollars Are Being Heard?" *Research in the Sociology of Work* 23:103–129.

Peifer, Jared, Elaine Howard Ecklund, and Cara Fullerton. 2014. "How Evangelicals from Two Churches in the American Southwest Frame Their Relationship with the Environment." *Review of Religious Research* 56(1):373–397.

Peifer, Jared L., Simranjit Khalsa, and Elaine Howard Ecklund. 2016. "Political Conservatism, Religion, and Environmental Consumption in the United States." *Environmental Politics* 25(4):661–689.

Petersen, Larry R. 2001. "Religion, Plausibility Structures, and Education's Effect on Attitudes Toward Elective Abortion." *Journal for the Scientific Study of Religion* 40(2):187–203.

Peterson, Gregory R. 2003. "Demarcation and the Scientistic Fallacy." *Zygon: Journal of Religion and Science* 38:751–761.

Pew Research Center. 2008. "Americans Say They Like Diverse Communities; Election, Census Trends Suggest Otherwise." Retrieved November 25, 2016. http://www.pewsocialtrends.org/2008/12/02/americans-say-they-like-diverse-communities-election-census-trends-suggest-otherwise/.

Pew Research Center. 2013. "Abortion Viewed in Moral Terms." Retrieved August 26, 2014. http://www.pewforum.org/2013/08/15/abortion-viewed-in-moral-terms/.

Pew Research Center. 2013. "Public's Views on Human Evolution." Retrieved August 26, 2014. http://www.pewforum.org/files/2013/12/Evolution-12-30.pdf.

Pew Research Center. 2014. "Political Polarization in the American Public." Retrieved November 25, 2016. http://www.people-press.org/2014/06/12/political-polarization-in-the-american-public/.

Pew Research Center. 2015. "The Future of World Religions: Population Growth Projections, 2010–2050." Retrieved April 27, 2015. http://www.pewforum.org/2015/04/02/religious-projections-2010-2050/.

Pinn, Anthony B. 2003. *Terror and Triumph: The Nature of Black Religion.* Minneapolis, MN: Augsburg Fortress.

Pion, Georgine M., and Mark W. Lipsey. 1981. "Public Attitudes Toward Science and Technology: What Have the Surveys Told Us?" *Public Opinion Quarterly* 45(3):303–316.

Population Reference Bureau. "More U.S. Scientists and Engineers Are Foreign-Born." Retrieved July 22, 2016. http://www.prb.org/Publications/Articles/2011/usforeign-bornstem.aspx.

Pugh, Allison J. 2013. "What Good Are Interviews for Thinking About Culture? Demystifying Interpretive Analysis." *American Journal of Cultural Sociology* 1:42–68.

Rios, Kimberly, Zhen Hadassah Cheng, Rebecca R. Totton, and Azim F. Shariff. 2015. "Negative Stereotypes Cause Christians to Underperform in and Disidentify With Science." *Social Psychological and Personality Science* 6(8):959–967.

Robertson, John A. 1994. *Children of Choice: Freedom and the New Reproductive Technologies.* Princeton, NJ: Princeton University Press.

Rochman, Bonnie. 2009. "Twittering in Church, with the Pastor's O.K." *Time*, May 3. Retrieved March 24, 2015. http://content.time.com/time/magazine/article/0,9171,1900265,00.html.

Roos, J. Micah. 2014. "Measuring Science or Religion? A Measurement Analysis of the National Science Foundation Sponsored Science Literacy Scale 2006–2010." *Public Understanding of Science* 23(7):797–813.

Rubin, Herbert J., and Irene S. Rubin. 2011. *Qualitative Interviewing: The Art of Hearing Data.* Thousand Oaks, CA: Sage.

Sabra, A. I. 1996. "Situating Arabic Science: Locality Versus Essence." *Isis* 87(4):654–670.

Sacks, Jonathan. 2011. *The Great Partnership. Science, Religion and the Search for Meaning.* London: Hodder and Stoughton.

Sagan, Carl. 1994. *Pale Blue Dot: A Vision of the Human Future in Space.* New York: Random House.

Sagan, Carl. 1996. *The Demon-haunted World: Science as a Candle in the Dark.* New York: Ballantine.

Sargent, John F. Jr. 2014. "The U.S. Science and Engineering Workforce: Recent, Current, and Projected Employment, Wages, and Unemployment." *Congressional Research Service* R43061.

Scheitle, Christopher P. 2011. "Religious and Spiritual Change in College: Assessing the Effect of a Science Education." *Sociology of Education* 84(2):122–136.

Scheitle, Christopher P., and Elaine Howard Ecklund. 2015. "The Influence of Celebrity Scientists on the Public's View of Religion and Science: An Experimental Assessment." *Public Understanding of Science.* doi: 10.1177/0963662515588432.

Scheitle, Christopher P., and Elaine Howard Ecklund. 2016. "Recommending a Child Enter a STEM Career: The Role of Religion." *Journal of Career Development.* doi: 10.1177/0894845316646879.

Schenker, Joseph G. 2005. "Assisted Reproduction Practice: Religious Perspectives." *Reproductive BioMedicine Online* 10(3):310–319.

Schibeci, R. A. 1986. "Images of Science and Scientists and Science Education." *Science Education* 70(2):139–149.

Schmidt, Garbi. 2004. *Islam in Urban America: Sunni Muslims in Chicago.* Philadelphia, PA: Temple University Press.

Scott, Eugenie C. 2009. *Evolution vs. Creationism: An Introduction*. Westport, CT: Greenwood.

Serhan, R. 2014. "Muslim Immigration to America." Pp. 29–46 in *The Oxford Handbook of American Islam*, edited by Y. Haddad and J. Smith. Oxford: Oxford University Press.

Sewell, William H. Jr. 1992. "A Theory of Structure: Duality, Agency, and Transformation." *American Journal of Sociology* 98(1):1–29.

Shaiko, Ronald G. 1987. "Religion, Politics, and Environmental Concern: A Powerful Mix of Passions." *Social Science Quarterly* 68(2):244–262.

Sherkat, Darren E. 2011. "Religion and Scientific Literacy in the United States." *Social Science Quarterly* 92(5):1134–1150.

Sherkat, Darren E., and Christopher G. Ellison. 2007. "Structuring the Religion-Environment Connection: Identifying Religious Influences on Environmental Concern and Activism." *Journal for the Scientific Study of Religion* 46(1):71–85.

Shibley, Mark A., and Jonathon L. Wiggins. 1997. "The Greening of Mainline American Religion: A Sociological Analysis of the Environmental Ethics of the National Religious Partnership for the Environment." *Social Compass* 44:333–348.

Singer, Eleanor, Toni Antonucci, and John Van Hoewyk. 2004. "Racial and Ethnic Variations in Knowledge and Attitudes About Genetic Testing." *Genetic Testing* 8(1):31–43.

Singer, Eleanor, Amy Corning, and Mark Lamias. 1998. "Trends: Genetic Testing, Engineering, and Therapy: Awareness and Attitudes." *Public Opinion Quarterly* 62(4):633–664.

Smith, Christian, and Melina Lundquist Denton. 2005. *Soul Searching: The Religious and Spiritual Lives of American Teenagers*. New York: Oxford University Press.

Snow, C. P. 1964. *The Two Cultures*. Cambridge: Cambridge University Press.

Southern Baptist Convention. 1991. "Resolution on Human Embryonic and Stem Cell Research." Retried August 12, 2013. http://www.sbc.net/resolutions/amResolution.asp?ID=620.

Stark, Rodney. 1963. "On the Incompatibility of Religion and Science: A Survey of American Graduate Students." *Journal for the Scientific Study of Religion* 3(1):3–20.

Steensland, Brian, Lynn D. Robinson, W. Bradford Wilcox, Jerry Z. Park, Mark D. Regnerus, and Robert D. Woodberry. 2000. "The Measure of American Religion: Toward Improving the State of the Art." *Social Forces* 79(1):291–318.

Stein, Benjamin, Logan Craft, Walt Ruloff, John Sullivan, and Kevin Miller. 2008. *Expelled: No Intelligence Allowed*. DVD. Directed by Nathan Frankowski. Los Angeles: Premise Media Corporation.

Stock, Gregory, and John H. Campbell. 2000. *Engineering the Human Germline*. New York: Oxford University Press.

Strauss, Anselm, and Juliet M. Corbin. 1990. *Basics of Qualitative Research: Grounded Theory Procedures and Techniques*. Thousand Oaks, CA: Sage.

Sullins, D. Paul. 1993. "Switching Close to Home: Volatility or Coherence in Protestant Affiliation Patterns?" *Social Forces* 72(2):399–419.

Susumu, Shimazono. 2011. "The Ethical Issues of Biotechnology: Religious Culture and the Value of Life." *Current Sociology* 59(2):160–172.

Taylor, Bron. 2009. *Dark Green Religion: Nature, Spirituality, and the Planetary Future.* Berkeley: University of California Press.

Thomas, Jeremy N. 2013. "Outsourcing Moral Authority: The Internal Secularization of Evangelicals' Anti-Pornography Narratives." *Journal for the Scientific Study of Religion* 52(3):457–475.

Troster, Lawrence. 2008. "Tikkun Olam and Environmental Restoration: A Jewish Eco-Theology of Redemption." *Jewish Educational News* 28(2):1–6.

Truelove, Heather Barnes, and Jeff Joireman. 2009. "Understanding the Relationship Between Christian Orthodoxy and Environmentalism: The Mediating Role of Perceived Environmental Consequences." *Environment and Behavior* 41(6):806–820.

Tyson, Neil deGrasse. 2012. *Space Chronicles: Facing the Ultimate Frontier.* New York: W. W. Norton.

Unitarian Universalist Association of Churches. 2011. "Pass the Stem Cell Research Enhancement Act." Retrieved July 22, 2014. http://www.uua.org/statements/statements/8064.shtml.

US Bureau of Labor Statistics. Retrieved October 3, 2014. http://www.bls.gov/.

US Census Bureau. Current Population Survey, 2013. Annual Social and Economic Supplement. Retrieved August 7, 2014. http://www.census.gov/prod/techdoc/cps/cpsmar13.pdf.

Vaidyanathan, Brandon, David Johnson, Pamela Prickett, and Elaine Howard Ecklund. "Rejecting the Conflict Narrative: American Jewish and Muslim Views on Science and Religion." *Social Compass* 63(4):478–496.

Vaidyanathan, Brandon, Simranjit Khalsa, and Elaine Howard Ecklund. N.d. "Naturally Ambivalent: Religion's Role in Shaping Environmental Action." Unpublished manuscript.

Vaisey, Stephen. 2009. "Motivation and Justification: A Dual-Process Model of Culture in Action." *American Journal of Sociology* 114(6):1675–1715.

Vaisey, Stephen. 2014. "Is Interviewing Compatible with the Dual-Process Model of Culture?" *American Journal of Cultural Sociology* 2:150–158.

Van Biema, David. 2006. "God vs. Science." *Time,* November 5. Retrieved October 1, 2014. http://content.time.com/time/magazine/article/0,9171,1555132,00.html.

Veldman, Robin Globus, Andrew Szasz, and Randolph Haluza-Delay, eds. 2014. *How the World's Religions Are Responding to Climate Change.* London: Routledge.

Weasel, Lisa H., and Eric Jensen. 2005. "Language and Values in the Human Cloning Debate: A Web-Based Survey of Scientists and Christian Fundamentalist Pastors." *New Genetics and Society* 24(1):1–14.

Weber, Max. 2004. The Vocation Lectures: "Science as a Vocation." Edited by David Owen and Tracy B. Strong. Indianapolis, IN: Hackett.

West, Cornel. 2002 [1982]. *Prophesy Deliverance! An Afro-American Revolutionary Christianity.* Louisville, KY: Westminster John Knox Press.

White, Lynn. 1967. "The Historical Roots of Our Ecologic Crisis." *Science* 155(3767):1203–1207.

White, Robert S., ed. 2009. *Creation in Crisis: Christian Perspectives on Sustainability.* London: Society for Promoting Christian Knowledge.

Wikipedia. "Carbon Credit." Retrieved August 30, 2016. https://en.wikipedia.org/wiki/Carbon_credit.

Wikipedia. "Devil's Advocate." Retrieved July 1, 2015. https://en.wikipedia.org/wiki/Devil's_advocate.

Wikipedia. "Miracle." Retrieved October 1, 2014. http://en.wikipedia.org/w/index.php?title=Miracle&oldid=626889308.

Wikipedia. "Tower of Babel." Retrieved July 27, 2016. https://en.wikipedia.org/wiki/Tower_of_Babel.

Will, Jonathan F. 2013. "Beyond Abortion: Why the Personhood Movement Implicates Reproductive Choice." *American Journal of Law and Medicine* 39(4):573–616.

Withey, Stephen B. 1959. "Public Opinion About Science and Scientists." *Public Opinion Quarterly* 23(3):382–388.

Wray-Lake, Laura, Constance A. Flanagan, and D. Wayne Osgood. 2010. "Examining Trends in Adolescent Environmental Attitudes, Beliefs, and Behaviors Across Three Decades." *Environment and Behavior* 42:61–85.

Wynne, Edward A. 1995. "Transmitting Character in Schools—Some Common Questions and Answers." *Clearing House* 68(3):151–153.

Zacharias, David, Timothy Nelson, P. S. Mueller, and Christopher C. Hook. 2011. "The Science and Ethics of Induced Pluripotency: What Will Become of Embryonic Stem Cells?" *Mayo Clinic Proceedings* 86(7):634–640.

Zaimov, Stoyan. 2013. "Richard Dawkins Explains Why He Doesn't Debate Young Earth Creationists." *Christian Post*, October 22. Retrieved February 3, 2015. http://www.christianpost.com/news/richard-dawkins-explains-why-he-doesnt-debate-young-earth-creationists-107196/.

Zaleha, Bernar Daley, and Andrew Szaz. 2014. "Keep Christianity Brown! Climate Denial on the Christian Right in the United States." Pp. 209–224 in *How the World's Religions Are Responding to Climate Change*, edited by R. G. Veldman, A. Szaz, and R. Haluza-Delay. London: Routledge.

INDEX

Numbers in *italics* indicate tables.